MONOGRAPH 43

CERAMICS OF POSTCLASSIC CHOLULA, MEXICO

Typology and Seriation of Pottery from the UA-1 Domestic Compound

Geoffrey G. McCafferty

The Cotsen Institute of Archaeology
University of California, Los Angeles
2001

Edited by Rita Demsetz, Marilyn Gatto, Pat Hardwick, Brenda Johnson-Grau, and Kathy Talley-Jones
Designed by Brenda Johnson-Grau
Production by Erin Carter, Merlin Ramsey, and Alice Wang

Library of Congress Cataloging-in-Publication Data

    McCafferty, Geoffrey G.
      Ceramics of postclassic Cholula, Mexico typology and seriation of
    pottery from the UA-1 domestic compound / Geoffrey G. McCafferty.
          p. cm.
    Includes bibliographical references.
      ISBN 0-917956-97-4
      1. Indian pottery--Mexico--Cholula de Rivadabia--Themes, motives. 2.
    Indian pottery--Mexico--Cholula de Rivadabia--Classification. 3.
    Indians of Mexico--Mexico--Cholula de Rivadabia--Antiquities. 4.
    Excavations (Archaeology)--Mexico--Cholula de Rivadabia. 5. Cholula de
    Rivadabia (Mexico)--Antiquities. I. Title.
      F1219.1.C5 M38 2001
      972'.48--dc21
                        2002000676

Cover illustration: Ocotlan Red Rim subtype Cristina Matte. *Illustration by Sharisse McCafferty*

Illustrations credits: All drawings by Sharisse D. McCafferty, except 5.1, which was
drawn by Elena Eritta. All photographs by the author, except 1.5, 1.6, 1.7, and 5.2,
which were taken by Daniel Wolfman, and 3.5 a & b, 4.7a,b,c, 4.27, 4.34, 4.38, and
4.42, which were taken by Michael Lind.

Contents

Preface

One of the more glamorous aspects of archaeology is the promise of discovery, that the next pass with the trowel might expose some new tidbit of the past that will enhance our understanding or at least provide a nice illustration for the final report. In contrast, the long hours that turn into months of analysis are characterized by cramped and dusty lab work and tedium. Unfortunately, far more sites are excavated than analyzed; consequently, many important discoveries remain tucked away in cloth bags on forgotten shelves. A variety of factors conspire to prevent analysis: funding agencies tend to support glitzy research projects; research budgets get slashed in order to be competitive, often at the expense of analysis; the inevitable "big find" at the end of the field season forces additional excavation, again at the expense of lab time and/or funds; the students who were drafted to conduct analysis as thesis topics move on to other things; the field observations do not relate to the research questions of the principal investigator, who also moves on to other things; other projects become more pressing; or, simply, the grass is greener and the sites richer in the next valley over. Whatever the reasons, hundreds if not thousands of excavated contexts exist unanalyzed in museums, universities, and storage facilities throughout Mexico and the United States.

This monograph reports on the problems and potentials of analyzing a curated collection long after its initial excavation. The UA-1 excavation was conducted in 1968 as an archaeological field school on the University of the Americas campus at the eastern edge of Cholula, a major pre-Columbian religious center in the central highlands of Mexico. The class was taught by Daniel Wolfman, a doctoral candidate who eventually completed his dissertation on archaeomagnetic dating in Mesoamerica. Wolfman was assisted by two graduate students and eighteen undergraduate students from a number of US universities. After four weeks of excavation, an additional four weeks were devoted to washing, labeling, and preliminary sorting and quantification of the artifacts. Wolfman produced a preliminary report for the Departamento de Monumentos Prehispanicos in Mexico (Wolfman 1968) and requested additional funding from the Universidad de las Américas (UDLA) for continued analysis and some additional excavation. When this was not granted, Wolfman returned to his own dissertation work and the UA-1 analysis was eventually abandoned.

The UA-1 field school was exemplary for a number of reasons. The field methods were state-of-the-art for 1968: 1.5 x 1.5 m excavation units were separated by 50-cm balks that were maintained until the units were complete and then excavated as needed; units were excavated at arbitrary 25-cm levels unless stratigraphic changes were noted (this was particularly true for the balk excavations); and all matrix was screened through wire mesh. All sherds, even the tiniest fragments, were collected in sherd bags by unit and level, with a sherd bag card filled out with pertinent data. Objects (for example, lithics, figurines, spindle whorls, and bone) were often plotted in three dimensions and were each given object numbers and recorded on individual object cards (lithics and bone were treated collectively, so that each level within a unit had a lithic bag and bone bag that received an object number). Unit forms recorded general information on each excavation unit, such as soil conditions, level depths, sherd bags and objects from each level, features encountered, and initial observations and interpretations. Additional documentation recorded each feature, including floors, walls, burials, and so on.

Each student maintained a field notebook for observations about the day's progress. Unit plans and wall profiles were drawn, soil and charcoal samples were collected, and hundreds of photos were shot to record each level of each unit and many of the objects in situ. All in all, this excavation was outstanding, and the level of documentation preserved the archaeological context to such a degree that it could still be analyzed fifteen years later.

Nevertheless, fifteen years is a long time. During that period the UA-1 materials were transported to the Anthropology Department at the old Mexico City College campus and then back to Cholula when the University of the Americas was relocated in 1970. The collection was broken up, with the skeletal remains (and perhaps the faunal remains) taken to the Instituto Nacional de Antropología e Historia (INAH) physical anthropology lab for analysis. Some of the documentation was taken to the Frissell Museum in Mitla, Oaxaca, perhaps along with some of the objects (oral tradition [rumor] maintained that the complete vessels were stored there at one point). When the roof of the UDLA Archaeology Lab collapsed, the UA-1 materials were transported across campus and piled in another building during repairs to the lab and then moved back in wheelbarrows (my first exposure to the collection!) to be piled again on the floor. Throughout these changes, elements of the collection were dispersed and lost—some of the nicer objects may have even been stolen during a prolonged strike by students in the mid-1970s. Fortunately, the detailed object cards provide information on some missing materials, such as lithic objects (projectile points, for example) and reconstructable vessels. Other materials, such as the soil and charcoal samples and the plan and profile sketches, may still be hidden in some corner of the university; I was very fortunate when Zee Green (UDLA archaeology lab director at the time of my analysis) uncovered the original negatives and unit forms.

The prospect of undertaking an analysis of the UA-1 materials was daunting, and even now I shudder at the thought of the enormous pile of jumbled sherd bags, many still filled with unwashed potsherds, and the frustrations of piecing together an excavation using fragmentary data. Why bother with such a collection? Should existing data be analyzed before collecting more, since excavation is fundamentally the controlled destruction of the archaeological record? The answer is certainly yes, but from my lonely stool in the UDLA Archaeology Lab I was not driven by such lofty ideals.

No, it was the pottery that made me do it. While transporting the one thousand-odd bags of potsherds across campus in a crusted old wheelbarrow, I noticed that the polychrome sherds were distinctively different from the UA-79 excavation we were studying in Mickey Lind's ceramics seminar. UA-79 had sampled a variety of features relating to the Late Postclassic period, and Lind and his students were in the process of creating a revised typology that included Apolo, Aquiahuac, Coapan, and Torre polychromes (Caskey and Lind ND). The bags of UA-1 sherds were almost completely lacking in these decorated types. Two things were immediately obvious: the UA-1 materials represented a very different temporal context than UA-79—Early Postclassic if the other was Late Postclassic; and if this was so, then there was something very wrong with the accepted ceramic sequence for Postclassic Cholula in general and UA-1 in particular.

Florencia Müller's (1978) ceramic sequence placed all Cholula polychromes as contemporary, postdating 1325 CE; this did not jibe with such completely distinct assemblages as those of UA-79 and UA-1. Wolfman, basing his preliminary interpretation on Noguera's (1954) ceramic sequence, had placed the UA-1 compounds at the Terminal Postclassic/Early Colonial period because of the high frequency of *policroma firme* (Torre Polychrome) that Noguera had used as a diagnostic of his Cholulteca III and the presence of glazed-ware sherds above the floors. Yet, the UA-79 assemblages disputed the importance of *firme* in the Late Postclassic, and, as it turned out, Colonial artifacts were very rare beneath the plow zone at UA-1.

The more I learned about the UA-1 context, the more potential I saw. The importance of household archaeology is by now well established (Wilk and Rathje 1982; Wilk and Ashmore 1988; MacEachern, Archer, and Garvin 1989; Santley and Hirth 1993), but during the early 1980s the focus on domestic contexts was still novel in Mesoamerican studies (Winter 1976; Flannery and Winter 1976). UA-1 included the only two houses ever excavated in Cholula. Furthermore, the apparent depositional context of materials in the floor contact levels suggested that at least some objects represented de facto refuse, abandoned where they had been used (Schiffer 1987). The 133 spindle whorls represented one of the largest collections from a controlled context anywhere in Mesoamerica and became the portal to investigations of pre-Columbian gender relations and textile production (McCafferty and McCafferty 1991, 2000).

And still there was the pottery. I quickly discovered that the typology being created for the UA-79 assemblage was inadequate to account for the new variations from UA-1. Through the process of integrating the new with the old, however, I found it necessary to make structural modifications to the classificatory system developed by Caskey and Lind and that, in turn, has created additional complexity.

One of the practical pitfalls of the hypothetico-deductive method is the impossibility of maintaining a theory-neutral stance throughout the analytical process; the systems flowchart that calls for analysis followed by hypothesis testing does not account for the months of daydreaming/pattern recognition that takes place at the lab table. Countless ideas were formulated and then reformulated at the La Lunita bar across from the Great Pyramid.

In the end, I still think that the great contribution of the UA-1 project was the ceramic assemblage. Virtually every ceramic type from the twenty-five hundred years of Cholula's pre-Columbian history was present. In a recent discovery, Müller's extensive type collections were found in a tunnel within the Great Pyramid, where they had been lost in storage for the past twenty years; after inspecting hundreds of reconstructable polychrome vessels, I found no types or subtypes that were different from ones found at UA-1. The variety of depositional contexts found at UA-1 spans the Postclassic period, providing a basis for at least four phase divisions. This has radically changed the interpretation of Postclassic Cholula chronology, and while further refinements will certainly occur, I'm confident that the general framework is now in place.

A second contribution of this project, however, was the salvaging of information from UA-1 that was locked away in the unopened bags in the UDLA Archaeology Lab. This was, in a sense, the archaeology of the dig itself, with new discoveries each time a bag was dumped onto the lab table or a new entry read from a field notebook. The most surprising discovery, and a further example of the confused nature of the collection, was a bag that contained part of a type collection for Oaxaca that Caso, Bernal, and Acosta had used to illustrate their *La Ceramica de Monte Albán* book (1967); apparently several collections of Oaxacan ceramics had been re-bagged using bags with UA-1 labels. By recognizing the postexcavation history of a collection, a clearer perspective can be gained for the importance of complete and even redundant documentation. Struggling with the many half-answered questions has made me more careful in the field and especially more attentive in the lab. Analysis of a curated collection is a valuable learning experience as well as an important means of resurrecting previously excavated contexts.

ACKNOWLEDGMENTS

Many people helped with the project along the way. Mickey Lind and Dave Peterson directed my studies at the Universidad de las Américas when I began the UA-1 analysis, and the staff of the Archaeology Lab facilitated the study both while I was a student there and later when I returned to complete the analysis. Bill Isbell, Randy McGuire, Ann Stahl, and John Hoopes read the various drafts of my dissertation at the State University of New York, Binghamton and helped expand its theoretical frontiers. Sergio Suárez C. of the Puebla Regional Center of INAH has been a steady colleague and friend, and one of my strictest critics. Janet Anderson, Lon Bulgrin, Garry Cantley, Chuck Caskey, Marty Dudek, Tom Evans, Zee Green, Carolyn McKay, and Ashley Withers all served as sounding boards along the way, hearing more about Cholula ceramics than they ever cared to. More recently my students from Brown University—Josh Bell, Kerri Flanagan, Byron Hamann, Jen Kimpton, and Erik Stower—have helped field test the classification through further investigations in Cholula.

Two mentors deserve special mention. Dan Wolfman not only directed the UA-1 excavation but also provided information and moral support during my analysis. I'll never forget our first meeting when, immediately after presenting my preliminary results at the Society of American Archaeology meeting in 1986 and collapsing back into my seat, he loomed over me and said, "I'm Dan Wolfman and we have to talk! Outside!" Dan, who passed away in 1994, continues to be missed.

Mickey Lind first pointed me toward the UA-1 collection as a research topic and has stuck by me throughout the analysis and aftermath. Mickey has guided me through the ins and outs of Mesoamerican archaeology and played devil's advocate to most of my ideas about Cholula. Rereading the text of this study yet again, I realize how profoundly his teachings still resonate in my perspectives on Cholula and its pottery.

Finally, my wife Sharisse McCafferty deserves enormous credit for helping in all phases of this project: from washing sherds, to preparing polychrome illustrations, to sleeping on the couch when the bed was covered by drafts of my dissertation. Thanks, pardner.

— GEOFFREY G. McCAFFERTY

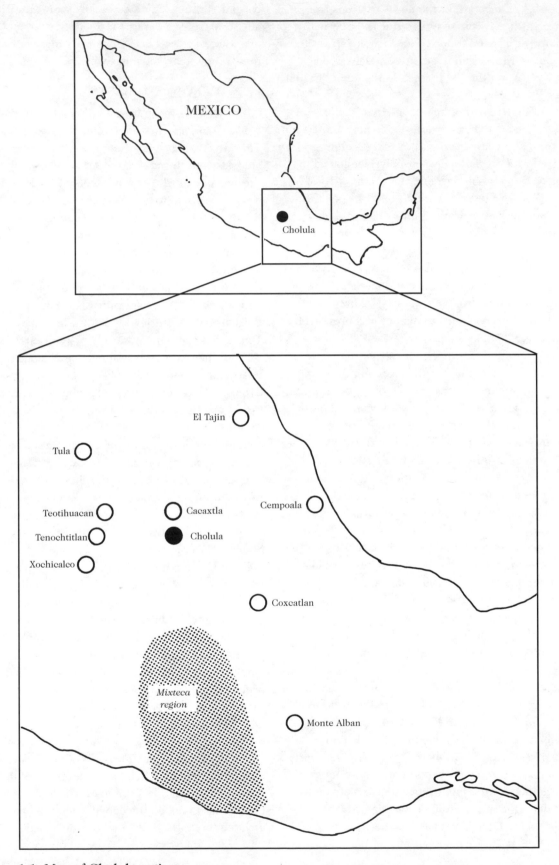

MEXICO

Cholula

El Tajin

Tula

Teotihuacan

Tenochtitlan

Xochicalco

Cacaxtla

Cempoala

Cholula

Coxcatlan

Mixteca
region

Monte Alban

1.1 Map of Cholula region

The pre-Columbian center of Cholula, Puebla, Mexico, is famous for the production of finely decorated, highly symbolic polychrome pottery during the Postclassic period, circa 900–1520 CE. Cholula polychrome was often traded and emulated, forming the basis for what is widely identified as the Mixteca-Puebla horizon (Vaillant 1938, 1941; Nicholson 1960, 1982; Nicholson and Quiñones Keber 1994; McCafferty 1994). Despite the renown of Cholula polychrome ceramics, contradictory interpretations of their production history have added to the general confusion surrounding this important yet enigmatic site. This monograph presents details of a recent ceramic analysis using excavated materials from two Postclassic household compounds on the outskirts of Cholula (McCafferty 1992a). It includes an alternative ceramic typology and a revised ceramic sequence based on a seriation of primary and secondary depositional contexts. In part because of the revised ceramic chronology, this research provides the basis for a reevaluation of Postclassic Cholula culture history, particularly in relation to its role in the development of the Mixteca-Puebla stylistic tradition (McCafferty 1994, 1996a).

CHOLULA IN ITS PHYSICAL AND HISTORICAL CONTEXTS

Modern Cholula is a city of about forty thousand inhabitants located on the outskirts of the state capital of Puebla, in the Puebla/Tlaxcala valley of central Mexico (figure 1.1). Beneath the modern town are the archaeological remains of the pre-Columbian city, continuously occupied since at least the Middle Formative period, circa 1000 BCE (McCafferty 1996a). As the result of long-term cultural processes such as construction and an extensive brick-making industry, the archaeological site has suffered considerable destruction, and cultural resources are in constant danger.

Postclassic Cholula was famous as a religious and economic center for central Mexico. It was the principal center for the cult of Quetzalcoatl (Carrasco 1982); nobles from throughout the region came to the temple for confirmation of their lineage titles (Rojas 1927 [1581]), while commoners came on pilgrimage for the elaborate religious festivals that celebrated fertility and ritual renewal (McCafferty and McCafferty 1995). In addition to his role as god of wind, of the planet Venus, and of sacred knowledge, Quetzalcoatl was also patron of the *pochteca* (merchants) who brought rare and valuable goods to the marketplace. Tied to its role as a marketplace, Cholula was a center of craft production, including elaborately decorated pottery, textiles, feather work, and jewelry (Durán 1971 [1576–1579]:278; Rojas 1927 [1581]; McCafferty and McCafferty 2000). This connection with exotic crafts was integrated into the religious aspect of the city, with the patron deities Quetzalcoatl and Xochiquetzal both worshiped by artisans. Xochiquetzal was patroness of "all those whose profession it was to imitate nature" (Durán 1971 [1576–1579]:239), including weavers, painters, embroiderers, silversmiths, and sculptors (Sullivan 1982:17).

The *tepetate* (subsoil) has historically been exploited by Cholula's ceramic industry and more recently for commercial brick production (Bonfil Batalla 1973:80–82). Decorated Cholula pottery was a valued serving ware in the Postclassic period. The Spanish conquistador Bernal

Díaz del Castillo (1963 [1580]:226) noted that the Aztec lord Moctezuma was served on "Cholula ware," and López de Gómara (1964 [1552]:131) described the "thousand different designs and colors" in the native pottery market. The Colonial *corregidor* (overseer) of the city, Gabriel de Rojas (in Bonfil Batalla 1973:74–75), discussed the importance of the ceramics industry in the early Colonial period. Pottery was still produced into the twentieth century (Bonfil Batalla 1973:80), although at a reduced scale. The *talavera* pottery industry of the nearby city of Puebla, on the other hand, has grown to great importance, drawing on the same source of raw material and, at least during the Colonial period, from the expertise of Cholula craftsmen (Kaplan 1980; Lister and Lister 1978, 1982).

The polychrome pottery of Postclassic Cholula is one of the most famous ceramic styles found in Mesoamerica not only for its high quality and aesthetic beauty (Noguera 1954:85–87) but also for the glyph-like representations that were often incorporated into the designs. Codex-style motifs became a cornerstone of the Mixteca-Puebla style as originally proposed by George Vaillant (1938, 1941), and "Cholula polychrome" and its imitations were identified throughout Mesoamerica as evidence of the diffusion of that style (Nicholson 1960, 1982; McCafferty 1994; but see Smith and Heath-Smith 1980).

As originally proposed, "Mixteca-Puebla" defined a cultural synthesis of the Mixteca region of Oaxaca with the Puebla/Tlaxcala valley (Vaillant 1938, 1941; Nicholson 1960, 1982). Cholula was identified as the center of the "culture complex," and Cholula-style polychrome pottery was considered a diagnostic of Mixteca-Puebla influence. However, because of problems in dating Cholula polychrome (for example, Müller 1970, 1978) and the recognition of distinct polychrome traditions in other regions, the significance of Cholula to the Mixteca-Puebla concept has sometimes been questioned (Smith and Heath-Smith 1980; but see McCafferty 1994).

Archaeological investigations at Cholula have been conducted since the eighteenth century and almost continuously since the 1930s (Merlo J. 1989; McCafferty 1992a:51–69, 1996a; Suárez C. and Martínez A. 1993). Two major projects have explored the Great Pyramid, both inside and out (Marquina 1951, 1970b, 1975; Noguera 1954; Messmacher 1967, ed.; McCafferty 1996b). Recent investigations have moved away from the pyramid to study other aspects of the site (Mountjoy and Peterson 1973; Suárez C. 1985, 1989; McCafferty 1996a).

The most notable archaeological feature of Cholula is the Great Pyramid, known ethnohistorically as Tlachihualtepetl, or "man-made mountain" (Durán 1971 [1576–1579]; Rojas 1927[1581]). The Great Pyramid has been the focus of archaeological investigations for more than one hundred years (Bandelier 1976[1884]; Marquina 1951, 1970, 1975; Peterson 1987; McCafferty 1996b). The pyramid was built in a series of four major construction stages over a period of 1700 years (circa 500 BCE to 1200 CE). Extensive excavations concentrated on exposing architectural remains of the Great Pyramid and the associated ceremonial precinct. Although the excavated and partially reconstructed pyramid façades create a popular tourist attraction, these investigations were largely unsuccessful at resolving many fundamental questions concerning Cholula's culture history. For example, the standard ceramic chronology used (Müller 1970, 1978) was highly problematic, especially for the Postclassic period. Consequently, interpretations of the settlement history are confused and even contradictory, with the accepted archaeological synthesis in conflict with ethnohistorical accounts (McCafferty 1996a). Thus while the ethnohistorical record indicates that Cholula was continuously occupied by a succession of ethnic groups from the Classic through the Postclassic period (Jiménez Moreno 1942, 1966; Olivera and Reyes 1969; Chadwick 1971b), archaeological evidence from the Great Pyramid has been interpreted as indicating a break in the sequence following the end of the Classic period (Dumond 1972; Dumond and Müller 1972; Mountjoy 1987; García Cook 1981; García Cook and Merino Carrión 1990; Suárez C. and Martínez A. 1993; but see McCafferty 1996a).

In 1930 and then in the mid-1960s, two research projects concentrated excavations in and around the Great Pyramid. Initial explorations sought to identify the different construction phases of the pyramid itself (Noguera 1937; Marquina 1951), with a secondary emphasis on describing the ceramic sequence for the site (Noguera 1954). During the second phase of investigations (Messmacher 1967; Marquina 1970), the Proyecto Cholula excavated on the south and west sides of the pyramid, where complex architectural remains were exposed. Additional ceramic analysis was directed by Florencia Müller (1970, 1978).

Preliminary indications suggested that the Great Pyramid was built in successive stages that completely covered previous construction. Because of the immense size

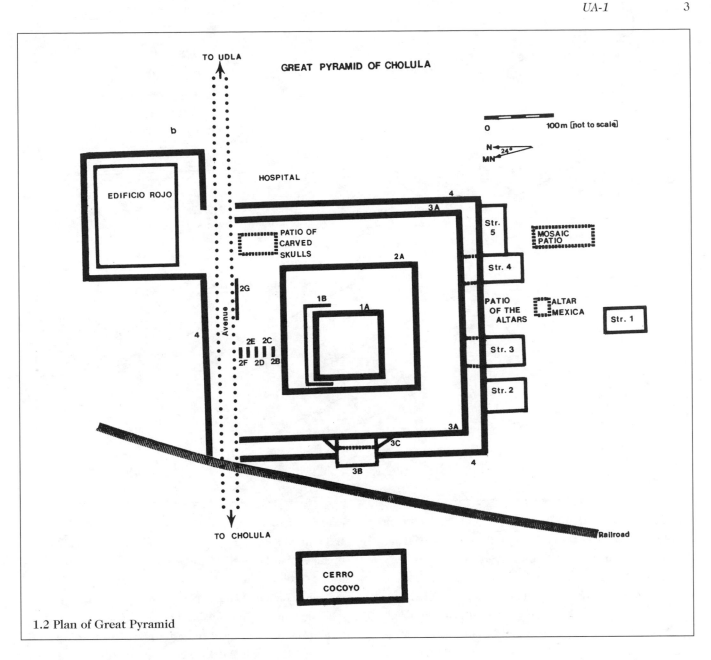

1.2 Plan of Great Pyramid

of the mound, explorations were conducted using a series of tunnels, ultimately totaling 8 km in length (Marquina 1970a:33). The earliest levels of the ceremonial precinct were built directly over the natural surface, sealing Formative-period ceramics beneath the construction fill (Noguera 1954:199–200). Four major construction stages plus at least nine minor modifications changed the form and symbolic significance of the Great Pyramid (figure 1.2; McCafferty 1996b, 2001). Based on stylistic attributes, ceramic frequencies, and especially the stratigraphic location of the Early Postclassic Altar Mexica beneath the Patio of the Altars (Acosta 1970:52), the final construction dated to the Early Postclassic period (Mc-

Cafferty 1996b). This is further supported by recent investigations at an Epiclassic palace associated with the Patio of the Carved Skulls on the northeast platform of the Great Pyramid (McCafferty 1996a, 2000; McCafferty and Suárez C. 1995).

Following the arrival of the Tolteca-Chichimeca ethnic group at the end of the Early Postclassic period, the Great Pyramid was abandoned and the ceremonial center was shifted to the present town *zócalo* (square) of San Pedro Cholula. While the Great Pyramid remained a shrine to the rain deity Chiconauquiahuitl, the religious center of the city became the Pyramid of Quetzalcoatl on the east side of the square (Durán 1971 [1576–1579];

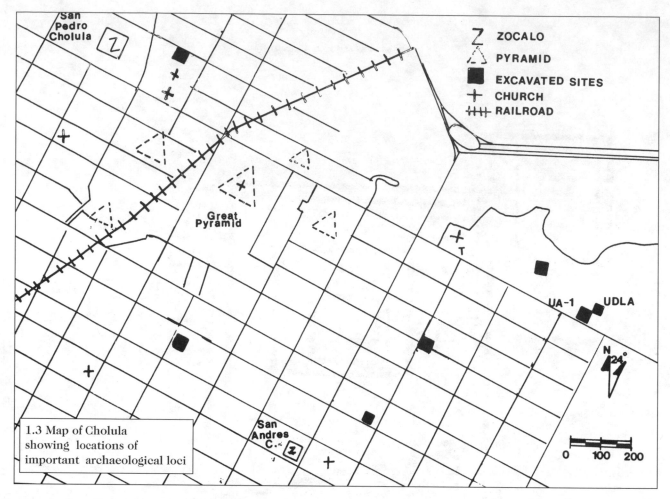

ZOCALO
PYRAMID
EXCAVATED SITES
CHURCH
RAILROAD

Great
Pyramid

San
Pedro
Cholula

San
Andres
C.

UA-1   UDLA

N
24°

0   100   200

1.3 Map of Cholula
showing locations of
important archaeological loci

Rojas 1927 [1581]). Late Postclassic Cholula was a multi-ethnic community divided into six barrios (Olivera and Reyes 1969; Carrasco 1970; Lind 1990) ruled by two priest/lords, the Aquiach and the Tlalchiach. Cholula remained an independent kingdom throughout the Postclassic period, a center of religious administration and international commerce. Although it participated in shifting political alliances with the Huexotzincas, Tlaxcaltecas, and, perhaps, the Mexica, Cholula was never incorporated into the tribute system of the Aztec Triple Alliance (Berdan 1985).

Relatively little is known archaeologically of the Postclassic period, primarily because of the dominant research focus on the Great Pyramid (but see Hernández Reyes 1970). Several domestic contexts have been studied from the campus of the Universidad de las Américas (UDLA)(Wolfman 1968; Mountjoy and Peterson 1973; Lind 1979; McCafferty 1992a). Burial patterns from Postclassic Cholula are relatively well known as a result of the analysis of more than four hundred skeletons from the Great Pyramid (López A., Lagunas R., and Serrano 1976) and a mass burial from San Andrés Cholula

(Suárez C. 1989). Another important burial context from the Capilla Real adjacent to the San Pedro Cholula zócalo included nearly seven hundred skeletons, possibly relating to the Cholula massacre of 1519 (Castro and Garcia Moll 1972; Peterson and Green 1987).

Following the intensive investigations at the Great Pyramid, archaeological research has continued on a more modest scale but with a broader focus (figure 1.3). Projects have been organized by the Centro Regional de Puebla of the Instituto Nacional de Antropología e Historia (INAH) and UDLA. Excavations by the Centro Regional have generally concentrated on small-scale *rescates*, or salvage excavations, prior to residential construction and have been conducted throughout the town. A few more extensive excavations have been conducted, for example, at the Hotel Villas Arqueológicas south of the Great Pyramid (Caskey 1988; also Suárez C. 1985, 1989) and at the Transito site (McCafferty, Suárez C., and Edelstein N.D.). Excavations by archaeologists from the UDLA have usually been conducted on the university campus located about 2 km east of the Great Pyramid and have included excavations of Formative, Classic, and

Postclassic period loci (Wolfman 1968; Baravalle and Wheaton 1974; Mountjoy and Peterson 1973; Lind 1979; McCafferty 1992a).

As part of the extensive archaeological investigations at Cholula, two major descriptive studies have been made of the ceramic complex. The first, by Eduardo Noguera (1954), was a lavishly illustrated volume that quickly became a standard of excellence for pottery description in Mesoamerica. A second study (Müller 1970, 1978) was based on excavated materials from the Proyecto Cholula. Unfortunately, problems with the archaeological contexts of the excavated samples, contradictions between these two studies, and ambiguities in the defined types have resulted in general confusion about the Postclassic ceramic complex.

One significant cause for confusion about the archaeological data has been the lack of attention to depositional contexts and formation processes at and around the Great Pyramid. As a "man-made mountain," the pyramid and its surroundings have undergone enormous episodes of earth-moving and tumultuous redeposition. The results are thick layers of construction fill, probably mined from the immediate vicinity. A more productive research strategy—at least for the purpose of obtaining contextually meaningful evidence—is to focus excavation away from the Great Pyramid. Excavations on the campus of the UDLA have produced a variety of archaeological features dating to all phases of occupation. One of the most intensive of these excavations, designated UA-1, recovered remains of two Postclassic domestic compounds and related features. Ceramic assemblages from these contexts provided an opportunity to create an alternative typology and construct an independent ceramic sequence through the seriation of assemblages.

UA-1 EXCAVATION

UA-1 was excavated in 1968 as an archaeological field school under the direction of Daniel Wolfman. Over a period of four weeks, Wolfman and his students excavated an area of 202 m^2, including portions of two "habitation compounds" dating to the Postclassic period and part of a low platform structure probably dating to the Terminal Formative/Early Classic period (figure 1.4). Preliminary analysis was conducted on a sample of the ceramic remains and on the other artifact classes during a four-week lab component of the class but analysis was discontinued when additional funding was not granted. Wolfman submitted a preliminary report on the excavation

and analysis to the Departamento de Monumentos Prehispánicos (Wolfman 1968).

The domestic compound designated structure 1 was the most completely exposed. It contained four rooms, an oval *temazcal* (sweat bath), associated porch areas, and a patio with an extensive midden deposit (figures 1.5, 1.6, 1.7). Artifacts found in situ on the stucco floor and the presence of ash and charcoal on the floor suggest that the structure may have been destroyed by fire, with at least some of the objects in the floor contact levels representing de facto refuse (Schiffer 1987:89–90). Room 3 featured a low platform altar and beside it was a small niche that contained remains of three anthropomorphic *braseros* (incense burners) similar to the *xantil braseros*, incense burners with anthropomorphic appliqué on exterior, discovered at Coxcatlán in association with household altars (Sisson 1992). Room 2 was interpreted as a storage area on the basis of the quantity and variety of objects found, including several manos and metates, a spinning kit, projectile points, and several reconstructable vessels.

The midden deposit located in the patio southeast of structure 1 contained numerous partially reconstructable vessels and an estimated forty thousand sherds as well as a wide range of other objects (such as spindle whorls and figurines). Based on contextual evidence, the midden is tentatively interpreted as contemporary with the final occupation of the house and may have been systemically linked to its abandonment.

Structure 2 was a second multiroom structure located to the east of structure 1 that was only partially excavated because of lack of time. Structure 3 was a solid platform located to the south of structure 1, which was later excavated as UA-69 and UA-70 (Mountjoy and Peterson 1973). Isolated features included three wells and several sherd concentrations, plus several burials representing a total of nineteen individuals.

Because of the traditional focus on the ceremonial architecture at Cholula, the UA-1 locus remains the most completely excavated domestic area from the pre-Columbian center and despite the problems inherent to the analysis of curated collections, it is considered a valuable window to Early Postclassic Cholula. My analysis of the UA-1 materials began in 1982 while I was a graduate student at UDLA and continued while I finished my Ph.D. at the State University of New York at Binghamton. My dissertation topic was the evaluation of the UA-1 material culture as it related to an ethnohistorical model for

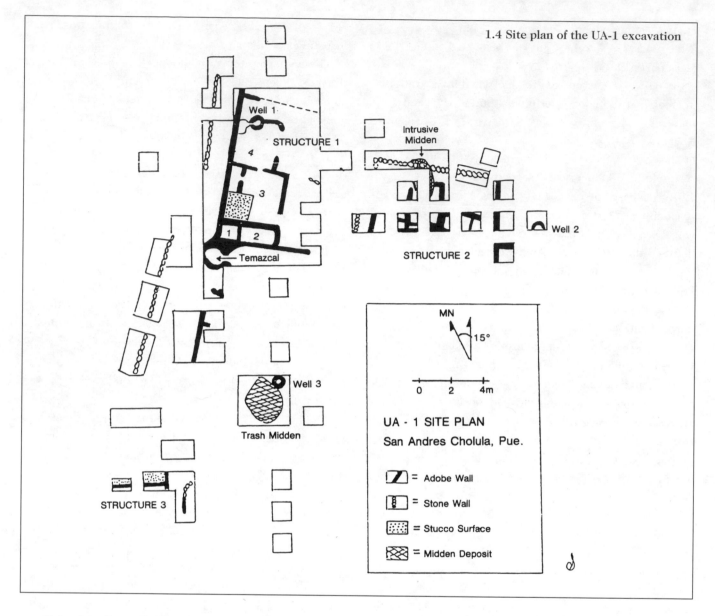

pre-Columbian household organization (McCafferty 1992a). Specifically, I argued that the combination of architectural features from structure 1 with the social composition of the residential group (including adult males and females and children) and the presence of such domestic activities as food preparation and consumption supported the interpretation that this was a household unit. Several analytical steps were prerequisites to the larger study, including

- development and description of a revised ceramic typology for Postclassic Cholula;
- construction of a revised ceramic chronology for the site using seriation analysis of discrete depositional contexts, and

- analysis of vessel forms to identify evidence for domestic foodways.

The typology presented in this study is based on a classification developed at the UDLA for the UA-79 Late Postclassic ceramics (Caskey and Lind N.D.). It is modified to include distinctive types found at UA-1 and to create a more dynamic system of classification. The typology emphasizes attributes of surface treatment and decoration to distinguish basic types, with variation identified through subtypes defined by additional decorative techniques. This system recognizes overarching similarities as well as lower level differences to provide a sensitive framework for distinguishing temporal as well as social variation in ceramic assemblages. Ceramic collections

Above left, 1.5 UA-1 Structure 1, rooms 1 to 3
Left, 1.6 UA-1 Structure 1, room 4
Above right, 1.7 UA-1 Structure 1, temazcal

from a variety of depositional contexts are analyzed using the revised ceramic typology. Thirteen of these assemblages are seriated for the Postclassic and early Colonial periods using Gelfand's system of arranging the Brainerd-Robinson Indices of Agreement (Gelfand 1971; Marquardt 1982[1978]:419–421). This ordering contrasts with previous ceramic chronologies for Cholula developed by Noguera and Müller and subdivides the Postclassic into five periods of relatively short duration.

The final research objective of the ceramic analysis is the detailed definition of vessel forms, with subsequent grouping of morphological forms into functional "vessel types" and more general "vessel classes." The purpose of this analysis is to identify and interpret functional differ-

ences based on the patterned deposition of vessel types. These differences may be related to variations in either spatial or temporal patterning. Since the cultural model for household activities indicates the importance of food preparation and consumption, the functional interpretation of vessel form provides one of the best criteria for inferring domestic behavior.

The ceramics of Postclassic Cholula have the legacy of being among the most beautiful ever made in Mesoamerica but also the daunting reputation of being incredibly complex. The reinterpretation presented here is an attempt to organize the ceramic classification in such a way that it will be more useful as a tool for reconstructing Postclassic society.

2 Historical Context and Research Objectives

In book 6, **"Rhetoric and Moral Philosophy,"** of the *Florentine Codex*, Bernardino de Sahagún characterized the Nahua conception of simple-mindedness in this way: *"yn aia qujmomachitia in tlalli, in tapalcatl cololoa"* (they are those who know nothing, those who pile up earth [and] potsherds) (1950-1982 [1547–1585], Book 6:2).e

In this chapter, I present the research objectives for the UA-1 ceramic analysis, as well as theoretical and background information to distinguish this study from an exercise in "piling up potsherds." I discuss the development of a revised typology for Postclassic Cholula, the basis for redefining the Postclassic ceramic sequence, and the relationship of vessel form to function and its significance for interpreting the UA-1 structural compounds.

TYPOLOGY OF POSTCLASSIC CHOLULA CERAMICS

Cholula ceramics have previously been the subject of numerous studies (Acosta 1975; Barrientos 1980; Caskey 1982a,b, 1988; Fajardo 1985; Joy N.D.; Lind 1994; López V. 1967; McCafferty 1992a, 1994, 1996a; Müller 1970, 1978, 1981; Noguera 1941, 1954; Peterson 1972; Suárez C. 1994, 1995). Yet, ambiguities and even contradictions in these studies have resulted in fundamental problems for the interpretation of Postclassic assemblages. These difficulties are caused in part by the tremendous diversity and complexity of the Cholula ceramic complex.

The first systematic study of Cholula ceramics was carried out by Eduardo Noguera (1941, 1954), who analyzed pottery recovered during the initial phase of explo-rations at the Great Pyramid. Samples came from strati-graphic pits, tunnel excavations, and block excavations at the Patio of the Carved Skulls. He published the final results in *La Cerámica Arqueológica de Cholula* (1954), which featured numerous illustrations including photographs and true-color plates. The book became a standard for ceramic description in Mesoamerica, and its wide impact undoubtedly increased the fame of Cholula polychrome pottery.

Noguera based his ceramic analysis on attributes of paste, surface treatment, decoration, and vessel form (1954:59). He recognized that the relative homogeneity of ceramic paste used at Cholula minimized its utility as a trait for distinguishing types. After an initial division into plain (*lisa*) and decorated wares, he defined types based on such attributes as color and decorative techniques. Five major polychrome types were defined (Noguera 1954:85–142):

- *policroma laca* (a polished, lacquer-like surface poorly bonded to a white base coat);
- *policroma mate* (a dull matte surface usually of white/light grey with black and orange painted decoration)
- *policroma firme* (polished surface with firmly bonded painted decoration);
- *decoración roja o negra sobre fondo anaranjado* (red and/or black painted decoration over streaky orange base); and
- *decoración sencilla* (simple decoration over streaky orange base).

Other Postclassic diagnostics included *decoración negra*

sobre el color natural del barro (black over the natural orange color of the clay), and an incised type, *esgrafiado*.

Although the types were clearly described and illustrated, ambiguities existed because of the great diversity of Cholula polychrome decoration, particularly since Noguera's system lumped together several potential distinctions. Contradictions were even present in Noguera's illustrations. For example, on page 127 sherds of *firme*, *mate*, and *laca* all appear in a single figure identified as *policroma firme*. But Noguera intended that *La Cerámica Arqueológica de Cholula* should simply lay the groundwork for further revision of the typology (Lind 1982), and to some extent this goal was realized (for example, Lind 1967). The preliminary analysis of the UA-1 ceramics employed Noguera's classification, and Wolfman (1968:5) intended to use the UA-1 artifacts to eventually refine the initial categories.

The second major ceramic study was directed by Florencia Müller (1970, 1978; Acosta 1975) as part of the Proyecto Cholula. The analysis was based on more than 2.5 million sherds from twenty-six stratigraphic pits, as well as from features such as burials, wells, and middens (Müller 1978:13). Müller's classification considered general classes of surface treatment, for example, *sin engobe* (without slip), or *pulido* (polished), followed by types defined on the basis of vessel form. These categories collapsed the polychrome types created by Noguera so that even fewer distinctions were available in the ceramic assemblage. The final results of this analysis were published in *La Alfarería de Cholula* (Müller 1978). Despite the problems that were created by Müller's typology, it has been the standard used on the majority of recent INAH projects in Cholula (a modification of this system was recently developed by Fajardo 1985).

Alternative ceramic classifications have been developed by archaeologists at the University of the Americas. David Peterson (1972) analyzed ceramics from a large midden deposit in the faculty housing complex and developed a typology in his Master's thesis. Results of ceramic analyses using the same system but with different type names were reported in *Man and Land in Prehispanic Cholula* (Mountjoy and Peterson 1973). In the late 1970s, Michael Joy (N.D.) employed yet another typology for Late Postclassic ceramics in an unfinished thesis based on excavations at the barrio of Jesús Tlatempa.

The most extensive revision of the Postclassic ceramic typology was developed by Michael Lind and his students using pottery from the UA-79 excavation. This classification synthesized the previous UDLA studies into a typology that recognized fifteen distinct polychrome types (Caskey and Lind N.D.). The classification emphasized the characteristics of surface treatment and decorative elements, including the use of specific colors. Vessel form was considered as an independent variable for decorated types, while it was given greater weight for undecorated utilitarian types. The most complete application of this typology was by Catalina Barrientos (1980) in an analysis of more than three thousand ceramic artifacts from a single midden deposit (feature f-10). The typology was further developed by Charles Caskey (1982a,b) in his analysis of a large ceramic collection from the Cholula Fonatur excavations at the Hotel Villas Arqueológicas.

Several problems exist with the UDLA classification as it was originally developed. Foremost, a concise, well-illustrated presentation was never published, so that only a few analysts had access to the system. Consequently, its interpretation became subjective, with individual interpretations of the type definitions. In addition, the UDLA classification was based purely on Late Postclassic ceramics, at least in its initial stages. As more components of the Cholula ceramic sequence were incorporated, inconsistent criteria were used to designate types.

In an attempt to alleviate the confusion about the UDLA classification, Lind (1994) has recently proposed an alternative set of type names, again based on ceramic data from excavations on the UDLA campus. This classification includes eight polychrome types representing the Postclassic sequence.

In this study, I have chosen to modify the original UA-79 classification rather than adopt Lind's new typology (table 2.1). This decision is based in part on a desire to maintain a degree of consistency, since I have previously presented segments of the UA-1 analysis using the modified UDLA classification (McCafferty 1986, 1992a, 1994, 1996a). Furthermore, because the laboratory analysis was based on that system, type collections in storage in Cholula are already labeled with these original type names.

The goal of my modified ceramic classification is to develop a typology that accommodates the diversity of the Cholula assemblage, while at the same time it recognizes similarities that may link meaningful clusters of attributes. The dual emphasis on differentiation and similarity is accomplished using a type/subtype system that recognizes types based on shared patterns of surface

Table 2.1 Correlation of Cholula polychrome ceramic typologies

NOGUERA (1954)	MCCAFFERTY (1992a)	LIND (1994)
Decoración negra sobre el color natural del barro	Cocoyotla Black on Natural, Sencillo subtype Cocoyotla Black on Natural, Banded subtype Cocoyotla Black on Natural, Chalco subtype	Xicotenco Black on Orange
Policroma mate	Cuaxiloa Matte Polychrome Cocoyotla Black on Natural, Elegante subtype Ocotlán Red Rim, Cristina Matte subtype	Cristina Polychrome
Policroma firme	Torre Red and Orange on White Polychrome Aquiahuac Burnt Orange Polychrome. Santa Catarina subtype Ocotlán Red Rim, Elegante subtype	Albina Polychrome Estela Polychrome
Policroma laca	Coapan Laca Polychrome San Pedro Polished Red, Elegante subtype Apolo Black and Red on Orange Polychrome, Elegante subtype	Catalina Polychrome
Decoración roja o negra sobre fondo anaranjado	Apolo Polychrome, Geométrico subtype Aquiahuac Polychrome, Zócalo subtype	Diana Polychrome
Decoración sencilla	Apolo Polychrome, Sencillo subtype Aquiahuac Polychrome, Sencillo subtype Ocotlán Red Rim, Sencillo subtype Ocotlán Red Rim, Banded subtype	Nila Polychrome Silvia Polychrome Marta Polychrome

treatment and subtypes defined primarily on the basis of elaboration of decorative techniques. An additional element for ceramic identification—vessel form—is treated as an important but independent variable.

The overarching objective of this classification is to identify both functional and stylistic characteristics in the pottery that permit interpretations of cultural variability that may relate to temporal and/or social factors. This approach emphasizes the role of ceramic consumption as a series of choices made in relation to a range of cultural variables (Spencer-Wood 1986), and it also incorporates what Lind (1987) has termed "consumer-oriented" criteria. Thus, ceramic consumption refers not only to the social context of pottery vessels—including their functions as storage containers, cooking pots, or serving bowls—but also to their potential for the transmission of symbolic information regarding status or ethnic affiliation. This approach is in contrast to the more traditional "producer-oriented" analysis characterized by the type/variety system of classification (Gifford 1960; Smith,

Willey, and Gifford 1960), which has tended to emphasize variables of how and where pottery was made. While this information is undeniably important, it is more appropriate to a different set of research questions, such as regional economic exchange.

In summary, my objective in modifying the UDLA classification is to create a more sensitive alternative to the existing typologies of Postclassic Cholula ceramics. By providing an expanded system for quantifying the variability of the ceramic complex, potential differences between ceramic assemblages can be detected that may relate to temporal and/or social variation.

CERAMIC SERIATION AND POSTCLASSIC CHRONOLOGY

In 1856, Edward B. Tylor visited Cholula and observed that "though there was plenty of coloured pottery to be found in the neighborhood of the [Great P]yramid, the pyramid itself had only fragments of uncoloured ware imbedded in its structure; which seems to prove that it was built before the art of colouring pottery was invented" (1970 [1861]:275).

Despite the numerous archaeological investigations that have since been conducted at the site, understanding of the Cholula ceramic sequence has progressed remarkably little since Tylor's visit. An important consequence of the creation of an alternative ceramic typology is the potential for critical evaluation of the existing ceramic chronologies for Postclassic Cholula. Conflicting sequences proposed by Noguera (1954) and Müller (1970, 1978) were based primarily on stratigraphic excavations into and around the Great Pyramid. Confusion about the Postclassic chronology has had wide-reaching impact on the culture history of Cholula and, as a consequence, for all of central Mexico (Nicholson 1982:243–244; Smith and Heath-Smith 1980:36-37; Sanders, Parsons, and Santley 1979:133; McCafferty 1996a). Seriation analysis of pottery from UA-1 provides the opportunity to revise and refine the Postclassic sequence.

In previous investigations at Cholula, deep test pits were the standard technique used for obtaining stratified ceramic samples. The pits were excavated into and around the Great Pyramid and its surrounding ceremonial precinct, largely consisting of platforms built of adobe and earthen fill. The depositional contexts of these units are distorted by the monumental construction activities. Examples of the degree of disturbance can be found in

the original reports; for example, Noguera (1954:46–49) described and illustrated a unit where the Classic and Postclassic deposits were inverted. The utility of stratigraphic test pits has been demonstrated in innumerable test cases, but problems may appear when pits are used without regard for site formation processes, particularly in situations where construction activities involve the extensive use of earthen fill (Schiffer 1987:137-139). Under such conditions artifacts relate to the deposits from which the fill was taken and only indirectly provide a temporal context for the structure.

Despite these problems, Noguera (1954) made a significant attempt to relate Postclassic ceramics to the Cholula cultural sequence, particularly in terms of the polychrome types. Polychromes were found in virtually all the stratigraphic units, especially in the upper levels, but often throughout the deposit. Polychromes were also found on the surface of the Great Pyramid, though rarely in tunnels into its interior (Noguera 1954:229–232).

On the basis of decorated ceramic types, Noguera divided the Postclassic into three phases, termed Cholulteca I, II, and III (1954:268–282, 296–297). These phases were loosely correlated with the Valley of Mexico sequence of Aztec I, II, and III, but no absolute dates were assigned to define the periods. Cholulteca I was identified by the presence of *policroma laca* and *decoración negra sobre el color natural del barro*. Cholulteca II was poorly represented, with *policroma mate* as its only diagnostic. Cholulteca III was defined by the presence of *policroma firme*, *decoración sencilla*, and *decoración roja o negra sobre fondo anaranjado*.

While these types were used to define the general ceramic sequence, this was intended to be a preliminary classification, and inconsistencies were also described. For example, Noguera (1954:106) noted one context where *policroma firme* was found in association with Aztec II ceramics.

More problematic was Noguera's observation (1954:271) that *policroma laca* remained in use throughout the Postclassic period. Problems with Noguera's own identification of *laca* undoubtedly added to this ambiguity. Consequently, the isolated presence of *laca* could not be used reliably as a diagnostic of the Cholulteca I phase, and stratigraphy alone cannot explain why it became so closely associated with the initial phase of the Postclassic period. Instead, Noguera inferred a close evolutionary relationship between this type and the Classic period "fresco ware" found at Teotihuacan :

> *[E]ste mismo procedimiento [laca] se observa en la cerámica de cultura teotihuacana denominada de cloisonné . . . todo lo cual induce a pensar que tal vez el antecessor de esa técnica tan peculiar al primer período cholulteca, bien puede encontrarse en el aludido período de la cultura teotihuacana.*
>
> This same technique [*laca*] is found in the ceramics of the Teotihuacan culture known as *cloisonné* [fresco ware] . . . all of which leads us to believe that perhaps the predecessor of this type so diagnostic of the Cholulteca I phase could well be found in the above-mentioned period of the Teotihuacan culture. (1954:142; my translation)

The evolutionary relationship between *laca* and Teotihuacan fresco ware fits with an ethnohistorically based notion that Cholula was the major culture center which continued after the collapse of Teotihuacan (Noguera 1954:302–303; Covarrubias 1957; Jimenez Moreno 1966; Weaver 1972; see Davies 1977:113–114). According to ethnohistoric accounts, different groups dispersed following the Classic period with some, such as the Pipiltin, traveling as far as Central America (Jiménez Moreno 1966; Fowler 1989). The most important of these groups were the Nonoalca, "par excellence the *Kulturvolk*, the bearers of the most prized arts and skills of Mesoamerica and the guardians of the ancient lore" (Davies 1977:167). The Nonoalca and especially the closely related Olmeca-Xicallanca were linked to Epiclassic Cholula, and this historical connection prejudiced Noguera's archaeological interpretation of the Postclassic ceramic sequence.

Noguera's investigations were important for identifying stylistic differences in the polychrome complex and suggesting a sequence for these types. His *La Cerámica Arqueológica de Cholula* (1954) set a high standard for ceramic description and illustration, while at the same time spreading the fame of Cholula polychromes. A critical evaluation of Noguera's inherent culture historical biases, however, reveals some of the inconsistencies in his scheme.

The enormous effort of the Proyecto Cholula revised the ceramic sequence for the Postclassic period (Müller 1970, 1978; Acosta 1975). Unfortunately, the new sequence retained Noguera's original phase names of Cholulteca I, II, and III, while adding IV. Furthermore, Müller collapsed Noguera's entire polychrome sequence into a single phase (Cholulteca III), thus introducing a major contradiction since Noguera had defined his different phases on the basis of specific polychrome types.

Müller assigned dates to the phases, but the criteria for the chronology were not made explicit; few absolute dates were available at the time and Müller was apparently unaware of those that did exist (Peterson 1972; Mountjoy and Peterson 1973). From Müller's discussion it is likely that her dates were adopted directly from historical events in the Valley of Mexico (see Smith 1987a). For example, Cholulteca II (900–1325 CE) began with the founding of Tula and lasted until the traditional date for the foundation of Tenochtitlan by the Aztecs (see Davies [1973:37] for discussion of this date). Cholulteca III (1325–1500 CE) was identified with the Mixteca-Puebla horizon. The final phase, Cholulteca IV, spanned the period of Contact and ended in 1600 CE.

The reliance on historical events rather than absolute chronology committed Müller to preconceptions that were then used to organize the archaeological data. For example, by identifying Cholulteca II with Toltec material culture (such as Coyotlatelco and Mazapan ceramics), bichrome ceramics could occur during this phase but not polychromes. Under Müller's sequence, polychrome pottery was not introduced until after 1325 CE. The methodology used by Müller is questionable because it assumes a direct correlation between regional stylistic similarities, ethnohistorical events, and cultural processes. In contrast, archaeological studies should use material remains to inform about the relationship between historical and cultural processes (see also M.E. Smith 1987a).

The Proyecto Cholula ceramic analysis radically changed the Postclassic ceramic sequence while retaining Noguera's original phase terminology. By lumping all polychrome pottery into the Late Postclassic and by virtually ignoring the type distinctions proposed by Noguera, the potential for refining the Postclassic sequence was lost. Furthermore, by considering all assemblages with polychrome as Late Postclassic, earlier Postclassic assemblages became relatively rare. As a consequence, Dumond and Müller (1972; Dumond 1972; also Mountjoy 1987; García Cook and Merino C. 1990) were led to conclude that Cholula was abandoned following the Classic period and only regained its status as an urban center toward the end of the Postclassic period. This interpretation has caused considerable confusion in the archaeological literature (Davies 1977; Weaver 1981, 1993; but see Sanders 1989; McCafferty 1996a), adding to the enigmatic status of Cholula in Mesoamerican culture history.

A second dilemma was that by lumping all polychromes

after 1325 CE, Cholula became one of the last areas in Mesoamerica to use "Cholula polychrome." This gap has caused difficulties in interpreting the development of the Mixteca-Puebla stylistic tradition (Nicholson 1960, 1982; Smith and Heath-Smith 1980; Nicholson and Quiñones Keber 1994; McCafferty 1994).

Even as Müller was developing her revised Postclassic ceramic chronology, UDLA archaeologists were acquiring information to challenge it. Excavations at the campus faculty housing complex produced a radiocarbon date of 1250 CE ± 95 (GX-1815) from a trash pit containing a high concentration (20% in the dated stratum) of polychrome pottery (Mountjoy and Peterson 1973:30). Although this lone date does overlap slightly with Müller's Cholulteca III phase at the 1-sigma range (1155–1345 CE), it also illustrates a diverse assemblage of polychrome types at this relatively early period. In other excavated contexts from the campus, differences in polychrome frequencies demonstrated a lack of contemporaneity between distinct types (Peterson 1972:200–201, Table 18; Mountjoy and Peterson 1973:81, Table 8), thus challenging Müller's assertion that all polychromes were in use at the same time.

The UDLA focus on primary contexts as units of analysis was continued with Lind's UA-79 excavation (Lind 1979). Analysis of the f-10 Late Postclassic midden (Barrientos 1980) indicated that in contrast to Noguera's predicted association of *policroma firme* (Torre Polychrome), *decoración sencilla* (Apolo Sencillo and Aquiahuac Sencillo), and *decoración roja o negra sobre anaranjado* (Apolo Geometrico), there was relatively little *firme* (Torre), while *policroma laca* (Coapan Laca and Apolo Elegante) was present in low to moderate frequencies.

The UA-79 analysis laid the groundwork for the present analysis of the UA-1 ceramics, because it raised important questions about Noguera's Postclassic sequence. Specifically, preliminary inspection of the UA-1 materials indicated that there were fairly high concentrations of ceramic types that were not well represented in the UA-79 collections, including *policroma firme* (Torre Polychrome), *policroma mate* (Cuaxiloa Matte Polychrome), and *decoración negra sobre color natural del barro* (Cocoyotla Black on Natural). In addition, Ocotlán Red Rim, which was not defined in the UA-79 assemblage, was identified as a major component of the UA-1 collection.

The UA-1 excavation produced numerous deposi-

tional contexts suitable for seriation analysis, including materials from two sealed floors, an extensive midden deposit, ceramic concentrations found in three wells, and several other sherd concentrations. These assemblages, especially when combined with the other analyzed features from the UDLA campus and other recent excavations, provide a sufficiently varied assortment of contexts with which to evaluate the proposed chronological sequence. Establishing these associations using the detailed typology developed in chapter 4 offers the potential for further refinement of the Postclassic sequence.

Several ceramic assemblages that have been analyzed since the UA-1 analysis supplement the UDLA assemblages and provide additional chronometric calibration for the sequence. A well from San Pedro Cholula contained Ocotlán Red Rim and Cocoyotla Black on Natural ceramics in association with charcoal samples that were radiocarbon dated (calibrated 1-sigma range) at 897 to 1018 CE (1065 ± 55 BP; INAH-1102) and 905 to 1220 CE (960 ± 140 BP; INAH-1103) (McCafferty 1996a, Suárez Cruz 1994). Another well from the UDLA campus contained an assemblage similar to that from UA-79 f-10, including Apolo Black and Red on Orange Polychrome, with a C14 date of 1333 to 1448 CE (500 ± 50 BP; I-14, 614) (Uruñuela and Alvarez-Méndez 1989:70; in Lind 1994:81, n.4). A Classic period house from San Pedro Cholula, designated R-106, produced four C14 dates ranging between 400 and 650 CE (McCafferty, Suárez C., and Edelstein N.D.; McCafferty 1996a); an intrusive Postclassic midden included Torre and Cuaxiloa polychromes. Finally, excavations on the northeast platform of the Great Pyramid exposed the construction sequence of the Patio of the Carved Skulls (where Noguera [1937] had previously excavated an elite altar/tomb), with a ceramic assemblage that featured Tepontla Burnished Grey/Brown and Cocoyotla Black on Natural (McCafferty and Suárez C. 1995; McCafferty 1996a). The framework for the Postclassic sequence has been constructed based on these dated assemblages (McCafferty 1992a, 1994, 1996a; but see Lind 1994):

Early Tlachihualtepetl	700–900 CE
Middle Tlachihualtepetl	900–1050 CE
Late Tlachihualtepetl	1050–1200 CE
Early Cholollan	1200–1400 CE
Late Cholollan	1400–1520 CE

CERAMIC FORM AND FUNCTION

The final component of this ceramic analysis involves the analysis of vessel form and the interpretation of vessel function. Within the "consumer-oriented" analysis suggested by Lind (1987), vessel form is considered an important variable in the decision-making process for ceramic consumption. Vessel-form analysis provides a means for interpreting functional attributes including cooking, storage, food consumption, and ceremonial activities. Ethnohistorical sources indicate that these activities all took place in domestic contexts. Consequently, the presence of specific functional types may be used as one line of evidence to interpret patterns of site utilization.

An additional research potential of vessel-form analysis relates to cultural foodways, combining food preparation, patterns of consumption, and aspects of food symbolism. Through the development of a model for archaeological foodways, comparisons between temporally or spatially distinct assemblages may be used to infer possible ethnic or status differences, thus providing potential insight into these aspects of social identity.

The use of vessel form to interpret vessel function is often implicit in ceramic analysis. These assumptions, however, can be criticized as incorporating the analyst's own ethnocentric biases regarding cultural foodways. In a study designed to identify the range of emic variability within a relatively homogeneous community in the Puebla/Tlaxcala area, Willett Kempton used cognitive theory to identify "folk classifications" of contemporary ceramic forms (1981). He concluded that "prototypical" form classes included a "fuzzy set" of morphological variations that diverged from the ideal (1981). The definition of each form category was culturally defined, however, with even minor societal subgroups (based on such factors as age, status, level of education, and gender) using distinctive systems of ceramic classification.

In an ethnoarchaeological analysis of pottery vessels from central India, Daniel Miller concluded that pots play a fundamental part in "framing" cultural behavior in addition to their functional roles as containers (1985). Ceramics help to create a variety of contexts recognizable to actors fluent in a "grammar" of cultural patterns. This communication does not necessarily occur on a conscious level but is created by patterned assemblages of different types of vessels. For example, a kitchen assemblage would evoke a certain set of cultural concepts, while a ritual assemblage would evoke others. Miller suggests that since these contexts are constructed using material culture, the patterns are potentially recoverable archaeologically as well as ethnographically.

In the absence of ethnographic data, emic categories for vessel function are less assured but not necessarily irretrievable. In a cross-cultural survey of vessel form and function, Henrickson and McDonald (1983) found a series of morphological regularities. For example, large globular vessels with constricted orifices are more often used to store liquids, while shallow vessels with open orifices are more often used for food consumption. Other studies (such as Robertson 1983; Halley 1986) have also looked at the relationship of ceramic form and function using ethnohistorical evidence for past foodways to interpret vessel function.

Pottery vessels are still produced and used in central Mexico, so that ethnographic analogies provide a potentially useful means of interpreting vessel function. Much of the explicit information on ceramics has focused on ceramic production (for example, Krotser 1974; Kaplan 1980; Lackey 1981), with information on function presented only incidentally. Other studies have considered vessel use life (Foster 1960), decoration (Friedrich 1970; Hardin 1984), and cognitive meanings (Kaplan and Levine 1981). Information on vessel function, perhaps because of the implicit, semi-conscious level at which pots operate within society (Miller 1985), is seldom given more than cursory attention. Vessels are depicted photographically, however, in contexts of use that provide information at least on primary functions.

Ethnohistorical data from Colonial and pre-Columbian Mexico also provide valuable information on past vessel functions. The *Florentine Codex* (Sahagún 1950–1982 [1547–1585]) provides detailed descriptions of daily activities in which ceramic vessels were depicted. It also illustrates aspects of ceramic use in food preparation and consumption (figure 2.1). Ceramics were also described in ceremonial contexts as special vessels for offerings or ritual feasting (figure 2.2).

Comparing ethnographic data with ethnohistoric information on vessel function indicates a high degree of consistency in the primary functions of different vessel forms. For example, wide, shallow vessels (*comales*) are now and were in the Contact period used for heating tortillas over a fire. Globular vessels with a constricted neck (*ollas*) are now and were used for cooking and for storing liquid foods. Large vessels with an unconstricted opening

2.1 Vessel function in pre-Columbian central Mexico: *a*, man drinking from biconical bowl and tripod serving bowl. *After Sahagún 1950-82, Book 2:Ill.43*; *b*, men eating from tripod bowls and hemispherical bowls. *After Sahagún 1950-82, Book 2:Ill. 26*

(*cazuelas*) are and were used for cooking stew-like foods. Liquids are still consumed from small, subhemispherical vessels with open orifices (*cajetes*) as they were depicted in pre-Columbian codices. These vessel types form the basis of the kitchen "tool kit," that is, those vessels that would typically be necessary for domestic food preparation and consumption. Using these and other analogous relations of form to function, archaeological ceramics can be used to reconstruct the composition of kitchen tool kits.

Kitchen tool kits in the archaeological record can be used to infer past foodways using ethnographic and ethnohistoric analogies to known methods of food preparation. Variations in cooking assemblages over time or across space could indicate differences in food use relating to technological or cultural differences. For example, the tremendous increase in the frequency of comales during the Early Postclassic period provides a dramatic example of change in the kitchen tool kit of central Mexico that must have had wide-reaching cultural impact. Blanton et al. (1981:71–72, 195) discuss the importance of comales in Preclassic Oaxaca, and the significance of their absence among the Classic Maya (also Feinman 1986; Isaac 1986). Comales were rare in Classic period contexts from Cholula (McCafferty, Suárez C., and Edelstein N.D.) and Teotihuacan (Sejourne 1966:98). Following

the changes precipitated by the collapse of the Classic Teotihuacan empire, however, comales appeared in abundance, suggesting a significant change in foodways.

The preparation of maize for making tortillas is a labor-intensive process that would have required a considerable reapportionment of domestic labor beginning in the Postclassic period (Isaac 1986; Brumfiel 1991). The causes for this radical change are unknown, but may relate to social transformations that occurred during the Classic/Postclassic transition. Detailed analyses of the strategic adoption of comales could yield insights into not only food technology and diet, but also ethnic migrations and changes in the gender-based division of labor.

Foodways encompass more than simply which foods are prepared and how. They can also include rituals of consumption, such as how meals are organized, and the ideological significance of particular foods. Recent anthropological studies of the symbolism of food practices have emphasized its role as a fundamental structuring principle for society (Douglas 1979; Johnsson 1986). For example, foodways are one of the most resilient attributes of ethnic identity, comprising a subjective sense of identity at the same time that they construct a set of contrasts for boundary maintenance (McCafferty 1989:85).

The investigation of archaeological foodways is a developing field involving both improved methods for recovering evidence (for example, chemical residues from inside cooking vessels) and more detailed analyses of subsistence remains (that is, faunal and botanical materials). Ceramic vessel-form analysis has the potential to complement this study through interpretation of the cultural dimension of food preparation and consumption.

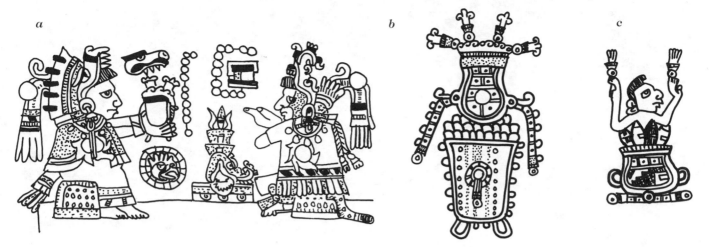

In addition to subsistence data, archaeological residues of food, especially faunal remains, have been used to interpret status under the assumption that higher-status households would have had greater access to food resources. A similar measure is available through variation in the quantity and quality of associated material remains, including ceramic vessels (Smith 1987b). An explicit method for quantifying relative value has been applied to Mesoamerican ceramics using the amount of invested labor as defined by the number of production steps (Feinman, Upham, and Lightfoot 1981; Blanton et al. 1981). This represents a particularly rigorous method for quantifying what is heuristically practiced with interpretations of "fine wares" versus "crud wares."

An alternative measure of status using ceramic assemblages involves ratios of different vessel forms. Drennan (1976) suggested the ratio of bowls to jars as a measure for comparing relative status. This assumes that higher-status households would tend to possess relatively more serving than utilitarian vessels in contrast to lower-status households. For the Postclassic Valley of Mexico, Brumfiel (1991) has used vessel-form ratios of jars to griddles as a means of comparing domestic

2.2 Ritual use of vessels from pre-Columbian central Mexico: *a*, woman offering chocolate in tripod *copa. After Codex Nuttall 1975:21-II*; *b*, olla of chocolate heating on tripod brasero filled with coal. *After Codex Borgia 1963:63*; c, ears of maize and human cooking in decorated olla. *After Codex Borgia1963:57*

strategies of food preparation involving wet versus dry foods, especially as they related to domestic decision-making processes.

The preceding discussion samples the range of interpretive information that is potentially available from vessel-form analyses involving archaeological ceramics. The purpose is not to critique these analytical strategies but simply to demonstrate that ceramic analysis has more to offer than "piles of earth and potsherds" on a lab table. Relating vessel forms to their functional context provides potential insights into a range of cultural interpretations, including specific activity areas, foodways, social organization, ethnic identity, status, and gender relations. In this respect, functional interpretations of ceramics are an important component of a consumer-oriented analysis (Lind 1987).

3 Methodology

This chapter describes the laboratory and analytical procedures used in the UA-1 pottery analysis. The first section describes the ceramic assemblage as it existed when the analysis began and the steps taken to organize the materials. Because of the large number of potsherds recovered, a sampling strategy was developed for selecting a representative subset that could provide the maximum amount of information. The attributes are then defined for the type descriptions and vessel-form analysis and the methodology is described for how these attributes were manipulated to interpret the assemblage. Finally, the specific depositional contexts used in the seriation analysis are identified, with discussion of stratigraphy and possible sources of contamination.

UA-1 CERAMIC ASSEMBLAGE

When the present analysis of the UA-1 ceramics began in 1982, the collection consisted of a large, unorganized mound of sherd bags that had been hastily removed from the UDLA Archaeology Lab when the roof collapsed. The majority of the bags contained unwashed artifacts exactly as they had come out of the field in 1968. The present project began with an inventory of the collection, and selected proveniences were identified for analysis. As the washing and labeling of the sherds progressed, the field school students' notes were reviewed for information on stratigraphy and excavation conditions. Other important documentation from the project included forms from the individual excavation units, inventory cards for the sherd bags and objects, and the original photos; all documentation is on file at the Archaeology Lab of the UDLA,

Cholula, Puebla. Some information was missing from the lab archives and could not be consulted: the field notes of Wolfman and his graduate assistants, sketches of unit plans and profiles, and the results of the preliminary artifact analysis. Furthermore, some artifact classes (for example, skeletal and faunal remains, lithic objects, and most of the complete vessels) were missing at the time of my analysis, although some data on these materials were available on the individual object cards.

The UA-1 excavations recovered approximately one thousand bags of potsherds from 671 proveniences defined by unit, level, and feature. On the basis of preliminary sorting, Wolfman (1968:5) estimated the total assemblage at more than one hundred thousand sherds, but subsequent analysis indicates that the total is at least double that amount. One of the first objectives in the analysis, therefore, was to devise a sampling strategy to organize the ceramic assemblage.

Collection units selected for study included primary and secondary contexts suitable for seriation. Thus, analysis focused on excavated levels associated with midden deposits, wells, burials, and floor contact of structures 1 and 2. Plow-zone and collapsed adobe-wall deposits were generally eliminated from the analysis.

A second sampling criterion was the selection of rim sherds for detailed analysis and quantification. Rims are particularly useful for identifying vessel form (Whallon 1968; M.F. Smith 1985). Information on form frequencies is important for interpretations of functional variation in ceramic assemblages. Body sherds can also provide information on form, but it is less detailed and more susceptible to bias based on vessel size. In the UA-1 analysis, body sherds were rebagged for possible reconstruction of whole pots or for future stylistic analysis; unfortunately, the sherds from UA-1 were later buried on the UDLA grounds to conserve lab space.

With only rims selected, it is estimated that the analysis retained approximately 15% of the pottery from the selected contexts, eliminating the 85% that were body sherds (also including bases, supports, and handles). This estimate is based on a sample of total counts made during the initial sorting of rims from body sherds and is consistent with sherd counts from the Valley of Mexico that were tabulated by Parsons and colleagues (Parsons et al. 1982:Tables 39–55).

Rim sherds were subjected to one final sampling step. During sorting, very small rim sherds were found to be difficult to classify as to form. Even for type designations it was suspected that decorated types, by virtue of having more identifiable characteristics, would be overrepresented in relation to undecorated types. To control for this potential bias, rim sherds that measured less than 2 cm on a side (roughly the size of a quarter) were set aside. These were counted as "Unidentifiable/too small" in the classification. Approximately 25 to 30% of the rim sherds analyzed fell into the "Unidentifiable/too small" category.

Quantification of the ceramics was based on sherd counts, but an additional measure was employed for rim sherds from the large trash midden located south of structure 1. The measurement of degrees of arc (see Plog 1985) provided an alternative value that was useful for determining the minimum number of individual vessels for each type and form and is therefore a more accurate means for estimating the kitchen tool kit. Comparisons between the sherd count and degree-of-arc values provide an opportunity to correct for overrepresentation of large rim forms as opposed to small rim forms (for example, *comales* [griddles] that break into many pieces in contrast to small-mouth *ollas* [jars] that produce only a few rim sherds from a large vessel).

Another potential of the degree-of-arc measurement is that it allows an estimate of average sherd size for vessels of similar rim diameter. Assuming that sherd size is affected by the amount of disturbance in a deposit (Bradley and Fulford 1980; Schiffer 1987:267–269), the degree-of-arc value can provide a means for interpreting the formation processes for particular deposits. Consequently, rim sherds from an area that has been exposed to exten-sive disturbance (through erosion, trampling, or construction) should have a smaller average degree-of-arc value than rims from a deposit that was covered quickly and with less disturbance.

A complementary means for measuring depositional disturbance is the percentage of Unidentifiable/too small sherds from each provenience, where relatively more small rims would be expected in more disturbed levels or in areas of traffic and regular sweeping. Midden deposits often contain a high frequency of large vessel fragments, while plow-zone levels have a higher frequency of small fragments. For example, the plow-zone deposit (level 1) of unit N3/W1 east balk contained 73% ($n = 83$) sherds in the Unidentifiable/too small category. Considering that very small sherds are often discarded during analysis (Schiffer 1987:269), this artifact category is put to a positive use as a measure of disturbance and/or site function.

A total of 16,396 rim sherds were analyzed from primary and secondary contexts, usually associated with the two Postclassic structures and related features. Assuming that rims make up about 15% of a typical assemblage, approximately 110,000 potsherds were processed. This total represents only a portion of the sherds from the UA-1 site, however, since the unanalyzed plow-zone layers usually contained large quantities of small sherds.

In addition, eighty-one complete or reconstructable vessels were recovered at UA-1 (McCafferty 1992a:489–493). Because most of these were missing from the UDLA Archaeology Lab at the time of the analysis, they were not included in ceramic tabulations. More than half of the complete or reconstructable vessels (N = 47) were found in the large trash midden associated with structure 1, and an additional thirteen vessels were discovered beneath the floor of room 3, structure 1, perhaps as ritual interments because they were placed near the raised platform altar. Several other complete vessels were found in association with burials.

Ceramic data were coded, entered into a computerized data base, and processed using the SAS statistical program. This information is used to produce frequency tables for the types and subtypes, and for vessel form (see chapter 5).

UA-1 CERAMIC TYPOLOGY

The definition of pottery types was based on surface treatment and decorative techniques, with vessel form treated as an independent variable that was considered separately. The diversity of polychrome styles from Post-classic Cholula provides an exceptional basis for defining types that are potentially sensitive to temporal as well as social variability. Surface treatment, decoration, and vessel form are meaningful criteria associated with consumer choice (Spencer-Wood 1986; Lind 1987).

Classification of the UA-1 ceramic assemblage identified thirteen major pottery types, with an additional twenty-three minor types that were either foreign imports or anachronistic, that is, from a time period other than the Postclassic (table 3.1). In the UA-1 analysis the definition of a "major" type was based on the arbitrary figure of 2% of the total assemblage, with types that appeared as less than 2% designated as "minor" types. In practice, this generalization worked quite well, with the exception of Coapan Laca Polychrome, a highly decorated type that is the prototypical "Cholula Polychrome" in most previous studies. The type was rare in the UA-1 assemblage, however, probably because of temporal and/or social factors. It is included among the major types because it is so well known.

Many of the types exhibited variation in decorative treatment that could be subdivided as distinct subtypes deriving from the basic type. For example, the type Ocotlán Red Rim is defined by its polished orange slip and a red painted band on the rim. When it occurs with only these decorative elements, it is classified as the subtype Sencillo (simple). This basic subtype, however, is often elaborated using such techniques as incising (usually in a horizontal panel that is painted brown/black) or different degrees of painted decoration (ranging from simple horizontal bands to complex polychrome motifs). Yet regardless of the degree of elaboration, the fundamental attributes of the type are maintained. Subtype variation can thereby be discriminated without losing the underlying consistency of the type identity.

Minor types are those that can be identified as imported or are most common at Cholula during other time periods. These were grouped by the time period for which they are diagnostic: Colonial/Historic period, Late Postclassic period, Early Postclassic period, Classic period, and Preclassic period.

Two categories were created for rim sherds that were classified as Unidentifiable, either because they were too eroded or burnt or because they were too small to give consistently accurate information. An additional nineteen categories of Unidentified types were created for unique sherds that could not be assigned to any established type. Unidentified types are assumed to be either spatially or temporally foreign to Postclassic Cholula, but they could not be identified securely as to where or when they were used.

The ceramic types and subtypes are defined in chapter 4. For the thirteen major types, each description includes five categories:

- Paste and firing effects
- Surface treatment
- Decoration
- Vessel forms
- Discussion

The first category, paste and firing effects, considers such attributes as paste color, temper, compactness, hardness, firing core, and firing clouds. Noguera (1954:60–64) identified minor differences in the fineness of the paste relating to utilitarian as opposed to decorated serving wares and also noted that the paste color tended to be slightly darker brown in the thicker utilitarian wares, probably as a result of firing technique.

The most detailed discussion of Cholula paste appears in Mountjoy and Peterson (1973:33–34), who report on a total of forty-six sherds (representing each of their type categories) that were subjected to thin-section analysis. Temper was uniform in all samples, with plagioclase feldspar and mica as the two most common materials. Minor differences did occur in paste color, packing of the paste, and the amount of temper, but these differences could not be correlated with specific types and were considered idiosyncratic variations in the production process. The general homogeneity of Postclassic paste was recently confirmed by an independent paste analysis conducted by INAH (Suárez C. 1994:50).

In a recent study designed to distinguish Cholula polychromes from other Mixteca-Puebla style laca polychromes (Neff et al. 1994), three compositional "fingerprints" were identified from the Puebla/Tlaxcala valley relating to Cholula, Huejotzingo, and Tlaxcala. The values used to define these different regional types were very similar with considerable overlap, however, suggesting a general similarity in raw materials used in ceramic production.

Discussion of surface treatment includes the quality of the surface appearance, considering such factors as

Table 3.1 Ceramic types and subtypes

MAJOR POSTCLASSIC DECORATED TYPES

APOLO BLACK AND RED ON ORANGE POLYCHROME
  Sencillo
  Geometrico
  Elegante
  Carmen Grey on Orange
AQUIAHUAC BURNT ORANGE POLYCHROME
  Sencillo
  Santa Catarina Black and Red on Orange
  Zocalo Black on Orange
COAPAN LACA POLYCHROME
COCOYOTLA BLACK ON NATURAL
  Sencillo
  Incised
  Banded
  Banded Elegante
  Chalco Black on Orange
CUAXILOA MATTE POLYCHROME
  Polished Cream
  Fugitive Paint
  Xicotenco Black and Red on Orange
OCOTLAN RED RIM
  Sencillo
  Incised
  Banded
  Elegante
  Banded Elegante
  Cristina Matte
SAN PEDRO POLISHED RED
  Sencillo
  Incised
  Black on Red Incised
  Graphite on Red
  Graphite on Red Incised
  Graphite on Red Banded
  Graphite on Red Elegante
  Shallow Grooved
  Modeled
TORRE RED AND ORANGE ON WHITE POLYCHROME
  Unburnished Matte
  Polished Cream

MAJOR POSTCLASSIC UNDECORATED TYPES

CERRO ZAPOTECAS SANDY PLAIN
MOMOXPAN METALLIC ORANGE
SAN ANDRES RED
  Dark Red
TEPONTLA BURNISHED ·
  Incised
  Red Rim
XICALLI PLAIN

MINOR TYPES–FOREIGN/ANACHRONISTIC

Colonial/Historic period
COLONIAL SALT GLAZE
POBLANO GLAZE WARE
  White Glaze
  Brown Glaze
  Green Glaze
  Yellow and Black on White Glaze
POBLANO WHITEWARE
  White Glaze
  Green and Black on White Glaze
  Blue and Black on White
PUEBLA BLUE ON WHITE MAYOLICA

Late Postclassic period
AZTEC III BLACK ON ORANGE
COXCATLAN GRAY
MIXTECA BAJA BLACK ON ORANGE
TECALI BLACK ON ORANGE

Early Postclassic period
ISLA DE SACRIFICIOS WHITE ON CREAM
IMITATION WHITE ON CREAM
GULF COAST FINE ORANGE
  Incised
IMITATION FINE ORANGE
  Sencillo
  Incised
COMAC BUFF
  Sencillo
  Incised
  Red Rim

Classic period
TEOTIHUACAN THIN ORANGE
IMITATION THIN ORANGE
  Thin Tan
  Micaceous Orange
TECOLA POLISHED
  Groove Incised
LOS TETELES GRAY/BROWN
  Pinched Exterior
MANZANILLA ORANGE
ACOZOC TAN/ORANGE

Preclassic period
CHOLULA CREAM
  Incised
TOTIMEHUACAN BROWN
  Incised
AMALUCAN POLISHED BLACK
COAPA ORANGE

streaking, pockmarks, and symmetry. It also describes the treatment; for example, wiped (defined by parallel ridges of clay left from the wiping implement) as opposed to burnished surfaces. Finally, an attribute that overlaps with decoration is the use of a slip, often with a thin undercoat. Subtypes were occasionally defined on the basis of variations in surface treatment; for example, Cuaxiloa Matte Polychrome is usually lightly burnished, but some examples were burnished to a high luster, and were tentatively classified as subtype Polished Cream.

The description of decoration includes a more detailed discussion of slip, as well as other decorative techniques. Painted decoration was the most common technique used in Postclassic Cholula, usually involving the colors orange, white, red, and black. Incising also occurred, but was most common in the Early Postclassic period. Since most of the subtypes were discriminated on the basis of decorative elaboration, this is the section where subtype definitions usually appear.

The section on vessel forms identifies and describes the most common forms found in each type and subtype. This usually applied to those forms that appeared as more than 10% of the total type assemblage. Ceremonial forms are also described when they occurred in significant quantities.

The discussion section summarizes details of each type and relates it to other pottery types found in Cholula and surrounding regions. Comparisons of type frequencies from related excavations with those from UA-1 provide an initial basis for interpreting the chronological placement of the types.

Each of the major type descriptions presented in chapter 4 includes a frequency table of subtypes and forms, relating to the four primary depositional contexts (that is, wells 1, 2, and 3, and the trash midden) and to the total assemblage. These indicate an initial range of variation for the different types and also provide a preliminary pattern of change that is further developed in the seriation analysis in chapter 5.

VESSEL-FORM ANALYSIS

The identification of the UA-1 vessel forms is based on ethnographic analogy with pottery in use in contemporary Mexico, and is consistent with ethnohistoric evidence for pottery in use at the time of the Conquest. Three functional classes of vessels are recognized: utilitarian wares, serving wares, and ceremonial wares (table

Table 3.2 Vessel Forms and Rim Forms

UTILITARIAN WARES
COMAL
 Comal
 Vertical rim *comal*
OLLA
 Long neck *olla*
  Everted L-lip
 Small mouth *olla*
 Large mouth *olla*
CAZUELA
 Hemispherical cazuela
  Flared rim
 Conical cazuela
  Flared rim
  Everted lip
  Bolstered lip
MACETA
 Conical maceta
 Cylindrical maceta
TECOMATE
 Tecomate
  Inverted rim
  Vertical rim

SERVING WARES
PLATO
 Plate/lid
 Outleaned wall dish
  Flared rim
 Subhemispherical dish
CAJETE
 Outleaned wall bowl
  Everted lip
 Subhemispherical bowl
  Everted L-lip
 Hemispherical bowl
  Flared rim
 Conical bowl
  Impressed rim
  Flared rim
  Everted lip
 Cylindrical bowl
  Flared rim
  Everted lip
 Superhemispherical bowl
COPA
 Biconical *copa*

CEREMONIAL WARES
BRASERO
TRIPOD CENSER
SAHUMADOR
LANTERN CENSER
MINIATURE VESSEL

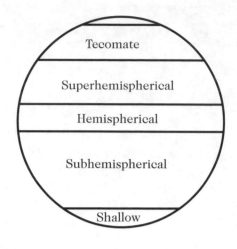

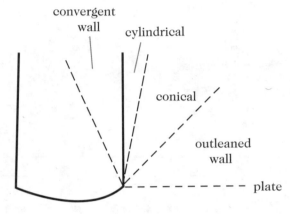

3.1 Schematized vessel-form classification

3.2). Within each of these classes there occur several functional types of vessels; for example, serving wares consist of *platos* (plates), *cajetes* (bowls), and *copas* (cups). Specific vessel forms relate to these functional types and are subdivided based on such attributes as standardized morphology, size, or rim dimension. Vessel forms are often described in relation to idealized geometric shapes (figure 3.1). A total of twenty-four separate vessel forms are distinguished, with nine possible variations in rim or lip form.

Utilitarian ware vessels were generally used in food preparation and storage. Five vessel types are recognized: *comales* (griddles), *ollas* (jars), *cazuelas* (cooking pots), *macetas* (basins), and *tecomates* (constricted-mouth jars) (figure 3.2).

Comales are wide, low vessels that were used to heat tortillas and other dry foods over a hearth fire. The inte-

rior surface is usually burnished, but the exterior surface is very coarse, probably intentionally roughened to enhance the transfer of heat and prevent slippage on the hearth stones. Rims are generally bolstered, sometimes with an exterior flange that looks like a base. Although there is considerable variation in rim forms, the only consistent pattern found was in vertical rims that project 1 to 3 cm above the body of the vessel. These rims are probably a temporal variant dating to the Epiclassic period. Other than the bolstered rims, vessel walls range from very thin to medium thickness depending on the ceramic type.

Ollas are large, globular vessels with a constricted orifice and flaring neck. They were used for storing and heating liquid foods. While the exterior is usually at least smoothed, the interior is unfinished or simply wiped. The exterior base is often blackened from exposure to heating fires, and interiors occasionally have sediments relating to the substances stored or processed in the containers. Bases are rounded, requiring a ring stand for support on the ground. Handles are often located on the vessel neck and/or shoulder, indicating that they may also have been suspended above the ground. Three vessel forms were identified on the basis of the orifice dimensions: long-neck ollas, small-mouth ollas, and wide-mouth ollas.

Cazuelas are large, open vessels that were used for cooking foods of stew-like consistency (such as *mole*). Surface treatment consists of smoothing on both the interior and exterior, with the interior usually more carefully finished. Examples have fairly thick vessel walls, and handles are found at the rim. No rim-to-base sherds were recovered at UA-1, but ethnographic examples and those illustrated in the codices have flat bottoms. Vessel forms include hemispherical cazuelas and conical cazuelas.

Macetas are large, thick-walled vessels that may have been used for storage. They are open vessels that can be distinguished from cazuelas by the thickness of the vessel walls and by the presence of a roughened bottom similar to that on comales. Vessel forms include conical macetas and cylindrical macetas.

Tecomates are large, superhemispherical vessels with a relatively small orifice. The exterior surface generally has a better finish than the interior, which is simply wiped. These are usually fairly tall vessels that tend not to have handles and were probably used for storage.

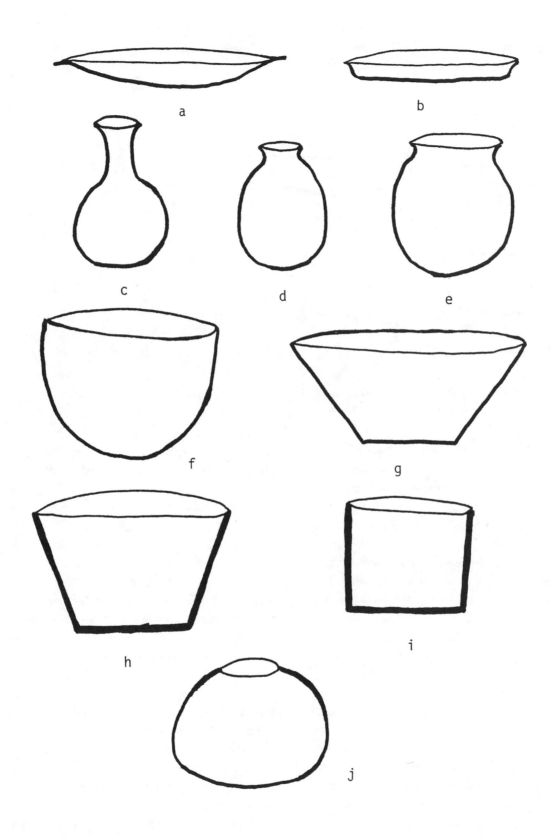

3.2 Utilitarian ware vessel types and forms: *a,b*, comales;
c–e, ollas; *f,g*, cazuelas; *h,i*, macetas; j, tecomate

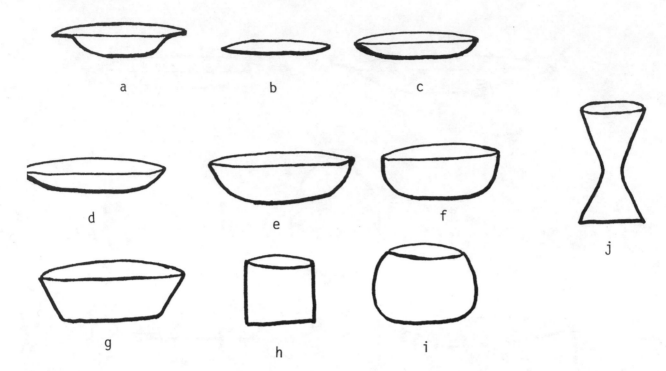

3.3 Vessel types and forms for serving ware: *a-c*, platos; *d-i*, cajetes; *j*, copa

Serving wares were generally used for food consumption, although some exceptions will be discussed. Three vessel types are recognized: platos, cajetes, and copas (figure 3.3).

Platos are defined as wide, low vessels that were probably used for the consumption of dry foods. They have either flat bases or slightly raised centers, and the most common vessel form (flared rim, outleaned wall dish) has a low wall that includes a wide, horizontal rim. Some examples include tripod supports, but this was rare in the UA-1 assemblage. They were often elaborately decorated and well-burnished on the interior surface, but with minimal decoration on the exterior. Other vessel forms include plates/lids and subhemispherical dishes.

Cajetes are relatively deep vessels that were probably used for the consumption of liquid foods. They usually have flat or flattened bases, and tripod supports are common. Very elaborate polychrome bowls occasionally have a tall ring base, giving the vessel an hourglass appearance. Cajetes are often decorated on the interior and/or exterior depending on the specific vessel form. This was the most abundant vessel type found at UA-1, and vessel forms include outleaned wall bowls, subhemispherical bowls, hemispherical bowls, conical bowls, cylindrical

bowls, and superhemispherical bowls.

In addition to their primary function in food consumption, several varieties of cajetes had alternative uses. *Molcajetes* (grinding bowls), for example, had a stamp-impressed interior base that created an abrasive surface used for grating chiles (McCafferty and Suárez C. 2001). Ethnohistoric evidence indicates that small bowls were used for supported spinning (see Smith and Hirth 1988), and bowls with heavily worn interior bases were found at UA-1 that might indicate such a function. A number of very small Momoxpan Metallic Orange bowls were found as grave goods in a mass burial in San Andrés Cholula (Suárez C. 1989), and their association with spindle whorls suggests the possibility that they may have functioned as spinning bowls (McCafferty 1992b). Finally, some of the superhemispherical bowls showed evidence of firing discoloration, suggesting that they may have been used over a fire, perhaps to heat food. Since evidence for alternative uses for cajetes usually requires a relatively complete vessel fragment, no attempt is made to separate these from the serving ware class. It should be noted, however, that there is some ambiguity in this category.

Copas are defined as tall vessels with a relatively small rim diameter. They were probably used for the consumption of beverages, possibly *pulque* (fermented maguey juice) or chocolate. The most common vessel form was

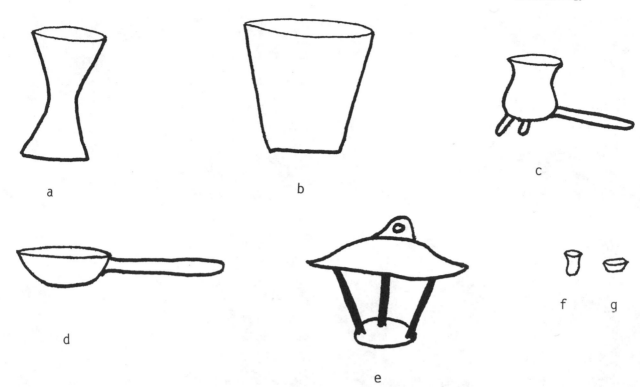

3.4 Ceremonial ware vessel types and forms: *a,b*, braseros; *c*, tripod censer; *d*, sahumador; *e*, lantern censer; *f,g*, miniature vessels

the biconical copa, with a tall ring base that gives the vessel an hourglass shape. Decoration appears on the exterior surface, which is usually well-burnished. The interior of the upper section is more carefully finished than the interior of the base, which is usually just smoothed.

Ceremonial wares were used for ritual practice, especially for burning incense. Ethnohistoric sources describe a range of contexts in which ceremonial wares might be used, including domestic rituals. Ceremonial wares included braseros, tripod censers, *sahumadores*, lantern censers, and miniature vessels (figure 3.4).

Braseros, including xantiles, are large vessels that were probably used for burning incense. They may have played a special role in domestic ritual associated with a household altar (Sisson 1991/92). They are usually thick-walled and were often coarsely constructed. Three nearly complete braseros recovered from the brasero niche in room 3 of structure 1 were biconical vessels, measuring about 30 cm in height (figure 3.5). Two had anthropomorphic figures appliquéd onto the exterior. Other braseros are decorated with stucco and then painted in colors that include blue and black. Some braseros have appliqué braiding on the exterior, and others have pinched cones that protrude from the exterior vessel walls.

Tripod censers are small globular vessels that resemble miniature ollas. They are supported on two short legs, with a third, longer support that probably also served as a handle. These censers are usually highly burnished on the exterior, but plain and fire-blackened on the interior. A common decorative form is a lattice-work pattern created by carving away sections of the vessel wall to allow the smoke to escape through the sides.

Sahumadores resemble frying pans in that they have a shallow dish that is connected at the rim to a long handle. They were used for burning incense, especially during processions. The exterior of the vessel and handle are usually well-burnished, but the interior of the bowl is plain and fire-blackened. The handles are hollow, and complete examples occasionally have zoomorphic figures attached at the end (Müller 1978:166–167, Pl. 22).

Lantern censers are constructed of a flat, circular base; a domed roof; and three cylindrical supports that attach the roof to the base. Fire-blackening on the interior surface of the roof indicates that incense was probably burned on the base, with the smoke rising to coat the inside of the roof. A loop handle on top of the roof provided a means for suspending the censer. These censers were generally undecorated other than occasional incised crosshatching on the outer surface of the roof, giving it the appearance of a thatched roof.

Another censer type that was not found in the UA-1

3.5 Cerro Zapotecas Sandy Plain xantiles from the brasero niche at UA-1 structure 1: (a) UA-1 object 10896, (b) UA-1 object 9327

assemblage but that occurred in the UA-79 Late Postclassic assemblage is a conical bowl with two solid handles projecting out from either side of the vessel. These handles are often pierced by a round hole that passes from top to bottom, providing a means to suspend the censer. These vessels are usually highly decorated with elaborate polychrome motifs on the exterior, but are plain and fire-blackened on the interior.

Miniature vessels are a final type of ceremonial ware found on rare occasions at Cholula. They are usually less than 10 cm in height and 5 cm in diameter and often resemble ollas. It is unclear how they were used within a domestic context, but they do appear in mortuary assemblages at the ceremonial center of Cholula (López A., Lagunas R., and Serrano S. 1976). Miniature vessels are relatively abundant in Postclassic contexts from the Mixteca Alta (Spores 1972; Lind 1987).

A comparative analysis of vessel-form frequencies in chapter 5 is used to identify potentially different activity areas and/or patterns of disposal. When factored into the diachronic sequence produced by the ceramic seriation, variations in vessel form may be used to interpret changes in cultural foodways. Finally, the ratios of vessel class and vessel type provide a basis for comparison with other assemblages.

DEPOSITIONAL CONTEXTS AND UNITS OF ANALYSIS

One of the most significant sampling steps in the UA-1 ceramic analysis was the selection of primary and secondary depositional contexts. In addition to limiting the scope of analysis, this step isolated units of analysis with a higher level of archaeological integrity that were suitable for seriation analysis. In this section, the different depositional contexts are defined, and each is discussed in terms of its particular research potentials.

Collection units were eliminated that contained deposits that had been mixed by plowing or that were related to "melted" adobe from collapsed walls. In general, level I (0 to 25 cm) was eliminated as plow-zone.

Level II (25 to 50 cm) usually included some plow-zone, but also included mixed deposits from collapsed adobe walls in those units associated with the structural remains. Level III (50 to 75 cm) also contained collapsed wall material, but included materials that may have been deposited above the floor following abandonment of the structures. The floor contact deposit was usually located at the bottom of level III and in most cases was collected separately.

Four primary depositional contexts are considered superior from the perspective of their archaeological integrity. These are the trash midden located south of structure 1 and the three wells. Midden deposits are valuable archaeologically because they generally contain material refuse from a fairly brief period of time and often from a limited and interrelated segment of population. Wells were often used as convenient trash disposal areas, presumably after they were abandoned, in much the same way that privies were used in historic periods. Since these were fairly distinctive features, they were generally collected as discrete units and were relatively unmixed at the time of excavation.

The trash midden was the largest concentration of material remains found at UA-1, consisting of abundant pottery fragments and other artifact classes, mixed with layers of ash and charcoal. The deposit encompassed most of units S7/E1, S7/W1, S8/E1, S8/W1, and their connecting balks. It was first recognized in level II (25 to 50 cm below surface) and continued to a depth of 125 cm. Unfortunately, the midden was not excavated as a feature, and unit levels were maintained at 25 cm intervals (some of the balks followed natural levels), so there is the possibility of some mixing. The most notable example is bag 8153 (S8/E1, level III), where a high concentration of Classic period pottery indicates that another feature was intersected by the excavation unit (see chapter 5).

Well 1 was located on the north side of room 4, structure 1. In Wolfman's preliminary excavation report (1968:11), the well was interpreted as part of the compound and was used to tentatively infer a kitchen function for the room. The excavators described a low wall that surrounded the well, extending about 55 cm above the floor level. As described in chapter 5, ceramics from well 1 included a high concentration of the Late Cholollan Apolo Polychrome and were dis-

tinctively different from those of structure 1. A more plausible interpretation, therefore, is that the well relates to an occupation level above the floor that postdated structure 1, the low wall being the well structure itself.

Well 2 was located to the east of structure 2, in unit S2/E9 on the opposite side of the possible compound wall. The top of the well was only 30 cm below the ground surface. The walls of the well were constructed of cement and brick, at least in the uppermost section. Wolfman (1968:13–14) and his students interpreted this as a Colonial well on the basis of its elevation, construction technique, and materials found within it (including glazed-ware ceramics and faunal remains of European domesticates).

Well 3 was discovered at the bottom of the trash midden south of structure 1, although the original site map suggests that it may not have been covered by the deposit. At a depth of 125 cm below the surface, an oval stain (85 x 70 cm in area) was recognized in unit S7/E1 (Wolfman 1968:7–8). It extended to a total depth of 277 cm below the surface. Narrow ramps were identified leading into the well, and shallow "borrow" pits were located around the mouth of the well.

Other contexts that were analyzed do not have the same degree of integrity, either because of the excavation strategy employed (that is, arbitrary levels that mixed depositional contexts) or because of ambiguities in the recorded information. With caution, however, I feel that these also provide valuable information that can be used to interpret the spatial patterning of activities and supplement the seriation analysis. Additional depositional contexts relate to the two structural compounds, with materials not only from floor contact but also from below and immediately above the floor surface. Based on recent findings from pre-Columbian structures preserved by volcanic ash fall at Cerén, El Salvador (Sheets 1991), numerous artifact classes were stored in elevated contexts that would probably become part of the above floor assemblage if the structure were burned.

Proveniences from structure 1 included floor contact of interior rooms (rooms 1–4) and exterior porch areas (areas A–C), deposits sealed beneath the floor and porch, materials from within the oval temazcal structure, and mixed deposits from immediately above the floor but beneath the collapsed adobe walls.

Other analytical units include floor contact from structure 2 and mixed deposits from immediately above the floor; an intrusive midden that passed through the floor of structure 2 but was sealed beneath the stone wall to the north of the compound; two sherd concentrations located between structures 1 and 2; three separate burials; and two stratigraphic units where there was little construction disturbance.

The analysis of the depositional contexts employs both the ceramic typology and vessel form categories developed in the next chapter. The objectives of the analysis are twofold. First, seriation of type frequencies is used to define the sequence of Postclassic occupation at UA-1 so that further functional interpretations can be based on contemporaneous deposits. Second, since pottery vessels are important indicators of domestic production, analysis of the spatial distribution of vessel-form frequencies in the different depositional contexts provides useful information for initial functional interpretations.

4   Pottery Types

The following type descriptions define the characteristic traits of each type, including subtypes and vessel forms. The chapter is divided into three sections. "Major Undecorated Types" include Cerro Zapotecas Sandy Plain, Momoxpan Metallic Orange, San Andrés Red, Tepontla Burnished Gray/Brown, and Xicalli Plain. "Major Decorated Types" include Apolo Black and Red on Orange Polychrome, Aquiahuac Burnt Orange Polychrome, Coapan Laca Polychrome, Cocoyotla Black on Natural, Cuaxiloa Matte Polychrome, Ocotlán Red Rim, San Pedro Polished Red, and Torre Red and Orange on White Polychrome. Finally, "Minor Types" include imported or anachronistic types grouped by periods: Colonial/Historic types, Late Postclassic types, Early Postclassic types, Classic types, and Preclassic types. Also included is a listing of "Unidentified Types."

Type descriptions include the attributes discussed in the previous chapter: paste and firing effects, surface treatment, decoration, vessel form, and discussion. Tables present frequencies of subtypes and vessel forms by provenience for the four primary depositional contexts (the trash midden and wells 1, 2, and 3), and for the total assemblage. The total assemblage refers to all those rim sherds that were classified in this analysis ($n=16,396$) minus the unidentifiable sherds ($n=4,994$), equaling a total of 11,402. When frequencies are described in the text, "very high" means greater than 30%, "high" means 20 to 29%, "moderate" means 10 to 19%, "low" means 5 to 9%, and "very low" means 2 to 4%. When type frequencies were less than 2% they were considered a "trace" and therefore only a minor presence.

MAJOR UNDECORATED TYPES

These are Cerro Zapotecas Sandy Plain, Momoxpan Metallic Orange, San Andrés Red, Tepontla Burnished Gray/Brown, and Xicalli Plain.

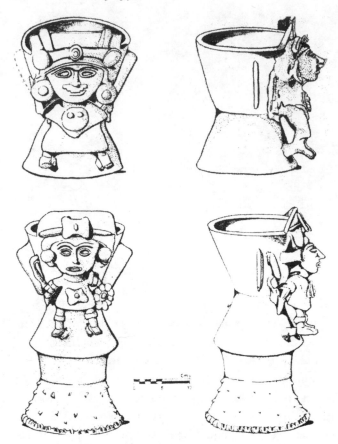

4.1 Cerro Zapotecas Sandy Plain braseros *After Müller 1978:204, Fig. 45*

4.2 Cerro Zapotecas Sandy Plain rim forms

✦ CERRO ZAPOTECAS SANDY PLAIN

Cerro Zapotecas Sandy Plain occurs as undecorated utilitarian and ceremonial wares with the diagnostic feature of a relatively sandy or gritty texture.

Paste and firing techniques. The paste is of local tepetate, but is coarse with a higher than normal proportion of sand temper inclusions. The paste color is usually tan to light brown. Vessel fragments occasionally exhibit a gray firing core and fire clouds.

Surface treatment. Vessel walls range from rough to lightly burnished, occasionally with streaks or pock marks from having been wiped while the clay was still wet. Braseros were probably intentionally roughened so that the stucco covering would bond to the vessel walls. The surface is generally unslipped (other than braseros), although some examples retain a fugitive wash in the same tan color as the paste.

Decoration. Cerro Zapotecas Sandy Plain is usually undecorated. The major exception is the brasero form, which often has a white stucco coating occasionally painted blue, green, and/or black. Some braseros are decorated with clay appliques and then covered with stucco. One common motif was a decorative pinched rim, others were studded with appliqué cones (figure 4.1).

Vessel forms. This type generally occurs as large utilitarian vessels (table 4.1), especially outleaned-wall and conical cazuelas, but other common forms include conical bowls and braseros (figure 4.2). Cazuelas have thick walls and rim diameters ranging from about 30 to 50 cm. Conical cazuelas occur in several rim forms, including everted and flared rims. Outleaned-wall cazuelas are distinguished by having low sloping vessel walls and relatively greater rim diameters than conical cazuelas. Conical bowls have medium wall thickness and the rim diameter is usually about 20 cm. Conical bowls also occur with everted lips and flared rims. Braseros have thick vessel walls and the rim diameter is about 25 cm. Rim forms are often vertical but may also include an acute rim flange and a decorative appliqué.

Discussion. Cerro Zapotecas Sandy Plain is similar to the predominant utilitarian ware found at the type site of Cerro Zapotecas, a volcanic outcrop located just west of Cholula (Mountjoy and Peterson 1973; Mountjoy 1987). Although a detailed ceramic analysis has not been published for the site, examples of this type are illustrated by Mountjoy (1987:142, Fig. 4a,b). Similar pottery has been observed on the surface at the site of Cacaxtla,

Table 4.1 Cerro Zapotecas Sandy Plain vessel-form frequencies

Vessel form	Well 1 *n* (%)	Well 2 *n* (%)	Midden *n* (%)	Well 3 *n* (%)	Totals *n* (%)
Plate/lid	...	...	5 (5)	1 (25)	7 (1.9)
Outleaned-wall bowl	...	...	...	...	3 (0.8)
Hemispherical bowl	...	...	...	...	1 (0.3)
Conical bowl	...	3 (21)	28 (29)	...	52 (14)
Superhemispherical bowl	...	...	2 (2)	...	2 (0.5)
Small-mouth olla	...	...	...	...	9 (2)
Wide-mouth olla	...	1 (7)	...	...	3 (0.8)
Outleaned-wall casuela	1 (33)	6 (43)	...	...	54 (15)
Hemispherical casuela	...	...	...	...	1 (0.3)
Conical casuela	1 (33)	4 (29)	28 (29)	2 (50)	111 (30)
Conical maceta	...	...	...	...	6 (1.6)
Brasero	1 (33)	...	34 (35)	1 (25)	106 (29)
Tecomate	...	...	...	...	10 (3)
TOTALS	3 (100) (0.8% of well 1)	14 (100) (4% of well 2)	97 (100) (3% of midden)	4 (100) (1.6% of well 3)	365 (100) (3.2% of total assemblage)

Tlaxcala. Both of these sites date to the Epiclassic period (600–900 CE). The pottery was, however, found as only a trace (<2%) in recent excavations at the Patio of the Carved Skulls (McCafferty and Suárez C. 1995; McCafferty 1996a).

Müller (1978:79, 87, 97, 109) described this type at Cholula for the Epiclassic and Postclassic, particularly the stucco-covered braseros. Noguera (1954:117–120) also provided detailed descriptions of the decorative elements of braseros.

A comparable type from the Tehuacán Valley, Coxcatlán Coarse occurs as braseros and utilitarian vessels (Mac-Neish, Peterson, and Flannery 1970:212–217).

Cerro Zapotecas Sandy Plain was identified as "San Pedro Plain" in the UA-79 ceramic analysis (Caskey and Lind N.D.), where it appeared in utilitarian wares. The type was found in the deepest levels of stratigraphic pits at UA-79, beneath the Late Postclassic component.

This type was found in very low frequencies (3.2% of the total assemblage, *n*=365) at UA-1. It appeared in very low but significant amounts in both well 2 and the trash midden, and as a trace in the other contexts. No clear pattern is apparent for diachronic differences in its use. Based on the UA-1 ceramics and other contextual information, it is likely that the type was most popular during the Epiclassic period (Early Tlachihualtepetl phase), although its relative scarcity at the Patio of the Carved Skulls is curious. It seems to have continued into the Early Postclassic period (Late Tlachihualtepetl phase) with certain ceremonial vessel forms used into the Colonial period.

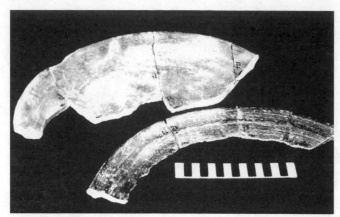

4.3 Momoxpan Metallic Orange comales

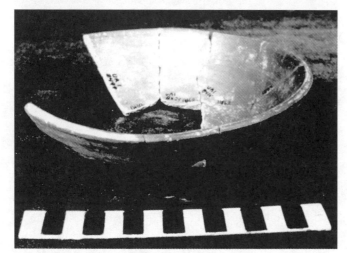

4.4 Momoxpan Metallic Orange cajete

✦ MOMOXPAN METALLIC ORANGE

Momoxpan Metallic Orange is characterized by a semilustrous surface finish that, through burnishing and firing technique, occasionally acquires a "metallic" luster. It is primarily a utilitarian ware, usually occurring as comales, but serving wware bowls are also present.

Paste and firing effects. This type has a fine to medium grain paste. Vessels are well-fired to a moderate to brittle hardness. The paste is tan to light reddish brown in color, with occasional dark gray firing cores. Fire clouding is common, giving the exterior surface its characteristic metallic luster.

Surface treatment. Vessels are usually burnished and slipped, with a light reddish-orange color. Comales are burnished on the interior, but the exterior is characteristically very rough except around the edge, which is wiped. Cajetes are burnished on both the interior and exterior. The surface is often irregular, with lumps and scratches in the finish.

Decoration. Other than the slip and characteristic fire clouds, this type is undecorated. Some comales have a distinctive checkerboard burnishing pattern on the interior surface, but this is probably a result of the burnishing technique, perhaps from the use of a corncob.

Vessel forms. Although the type is found in both utilitarian and serving wares, the most numerous form is the comal, at 87% of the type total (table 4.2). Comales range in diameter from 37 to 41 cm with a vessel height between 1.5 to 4.5 cm (figure 4.3). Vessel wall thickness varies based on distance from the rim, with the interior base often very thin (3 to 5 mm). Rim forms vary, but can generally be described as bolstered, often with a flange on the exterior. An interior ridge about 1 cm below the rim is also common. Analysis of the UA-1 materials did not identify a consistent pattern in rim form, and large vessel fragments can display variation in rim form on the same piece.

Other vessel forms that occur in low frequencies include subhemispherical and conical bowls. Subhemispherical bowls measure 14 to 17 cm in diameter and 3 to 4 cm in height. Conical bowls range from 14 to 24 cm in diameter and2 about 5 to 10 cm in height (figure 4.4). Conical bowls may have either a direct or slightly flaring rim.

Miniature bowls were a minor form in the UA-1 assemblage. They measure about 10 cm in diameter and 3 to 4 cm in height. These may have been used as spinning bowls during supported spinning; Suárez C. (1989) reports numerous miniature Momoxpan Orange bowls from a mass burial in San Andrés Cholula that was possibly associated with a Late Postclassic weaving compound (McCafferty 1992b).

Discussion. Momoxpan Metallic Orange is one of the most important components of the Postclassic Cholula ceramic complex, and one which shows remarkably little variation throughout the Postclassic period. Its principal vessel type, the comal, is indicative of heating tortillas, an activity that is known ethnohistorically to have occurred within the household compound. The presence of comal fragments can therefore be used to infer domestic activities.

This type has been identified in previous studies of Cholula pottery. Noguera (1954:73–74) and Müller (1978:111) describe the comal form, both pointing out the metallic appearance. Peterson termed this "Tecpanecatl Orange" in his Master's thesis (1972), and Mountjoy and Peterson (1973) identified it as "Román Orange." It

Table 4.2 Momoxpan Metallic Orange vessel-form frequencies

Vessel form	Well 1 n (%)	Well 2 n (%)	Midden n (%)	Well 3 n (%)	Totals n (%)
Plate/lid	...	...	...	...	3 (0.1)
Comal	74 (88)	71 (95)	488 (83)	38 (97)	1953 (87)
Subhemispherical bowl	4 (5)	1 (1.3)	25 (4)	...	105 (5)
Hemispherical bowl	...	...	...	...	1 (0.04)
Conical bowl	3 (4)	3 (4)	66 (11)	1 (3)	163 (7)
Long-necked jarra	...	...	7 (1.2)	...	7 (0.3)
Miniature bowl	3 (4)	...	...	...	9 (0.4)
Ladle	...	...	1 (0.2)	...	1 (0.04)
TOTALS	84 (100)	75 (100)	587 (100)	39 (100)	2242 (100)
	(24% of well 1)	(20% of well 2)	(20% of midden)	(16% of well 3)	(19.7% of total assemblage)

was present in moderate to high frequencies in Postclassic assemblages from the UDLA campus (Mountjoy and Peterson 1973:81, Table 8).

In the typology developed by Lind and his students (Caskey and Lind N.D.), the term "Momoxpan Orange" was used to identify the cajetes, while "Román Orange" identified comales. In the Late Postclassic F-10 trash midden at UA-79 (Barrientos 1980), "Román Orange" comales made up 13% (*n*=518) of the assemblage, while "Momoxpan Orange" cajetes accounted for another 6% (*n*=255), for a total of 19% of the total midden assemblage.

In the UA-1 typology, I have grouped both of these vessel forms into the Momoxpan Metallic Orange type based on the shared attributes of burnished orange slip and frequent metallic fire clouds. Momoxpan Orange made up 19.7% of the total assemblage and was present in moderate to high frequencies in all four of the primary contexts. In the assemblage as a whole, comales made up about 87% of the type total. This frequency is relatively

consistent for different depositional contexts. Cajetes, especially conical bowls, were most numerous in the trash midden, but even there they were much less abundant than in the UA-79 midden deposit.

Momoxpan Orange was present as only a trace in the R-106 subfloor deposits, suggesting that it was not a significant component of the Classic period ceramic complex (McCafferty 1996a). At the Patio of the Carved Skulls, Momoxpan Orange was present in low frequency, and exclusively as comales. Since comales were relatively rare in this Early Tlachihualtepetl assemblage, the low amount of Momoxpan Orange could be the result of the specialized context of this elite residential complex. I suspect, however, that it was also because it was an early stage in the development of the Postclassic ceramic complex. Thus the Patio of the Carved Skulls assemblage represents a transitional point between the Classic and Postclassic patterns, and the use of comales as a method for preparing tortillas was a relatively new innovation.

✦ SAN ANDRES RED

San Andrés Red is a versatile type that occurs in several important vessel types, including comales, ollas, and cazuelas. It is predominantly a utilitarian ware, characterized by relatively thick vessel walls and a reddish slip.

Paste and firing effects. The paste has a medium to coarse texture with a high proportion of medium to large inclusions as temper, giving eroded surfaces a sandy texture similar to Cerro Zapotecas Sandy Plain. The paste is tan to light reddish-brown, but often has a dark gray firing core, particularly in thicker pieces. Fire clouds are fairly common, but are often obscured by fire-blackening from use over a fire.

Surface treatment. Vessel walls are smoothed to slightly burnished, and the surface often has scratches and irregular lumps in the finish. The diagnostic trait of the type is a thin reddish-orange slip that often appears crackled. The interiors of globular ollas are usually unfinished. Cazuelas are finished on both the interior and exterior, although the exterior is usually more irregular. The upper, interior surface of comales is usually smoothed, while the exterior has the coarse texture typical of comal bases.

Decoration. San Andrés Red is undecorated other than the slip that ranges in color from reddish-orange to reddish-brown. A possible subtype, Dark Red, was identified that has a dark red slip on thin-wall, well-fired comales that resemble Momoxpan Metallic Orange comales in form.

Vessel forms. San Andrés Red is found in a variety of utilitarian ware vessel forms associated with food preparation and storage (table 4.3). The most common vessel types include comales, ollas, cazuelas, and macetas.

Comales measure about 35 to 50 cm in diameter with thick rims and relatively thick vessel walls. The interior upper surface is lightly burnished and has the characteristic reddish slip, while the exterior lower surface is unslipped and very rough. San Andrés Red comales are relatively thick in comparison to Momoxpan Orange comales, but are quite similar in form to Xicalli Plain comales. The Dark Red subtype was only identified in comales, and these were distinctive in their relatively thin rims and vessel walls, resembling Momoxpan Metallic Orange in general morphology.

Three main forms of olla are recognized on the basis of orifice size and shape, and each occurs in various spe-

Table 4.3 San Andrés Red vessel-form frequencies

Vessel form	Well 1 n (%)	Well 2 n (%)	Midden n (%)	Well 3 n (%)	Totals n (%)
Plate/lid	...	...	...	...	13 (1)
Comal	11 (22)	8 (7)	1 (0.5)	1 (4)	119 (9)
Outleaned-wall dish	...	1 (0.9)	...	...	12 (0.9)
Subhemispherical bowl	...	7 (6)	...	1 (4)	19 (1.4)
Hemispherical bowl	...	...	...	...	1 (0.08)
Conical bowl	...	...	11 (5)	...	27 (2)
Long-neck olla	17 (34)	12 (11)	45 (21)	5 (20)	184 (14)
Small-mouth olla	2 (4)	8 (7)	42 (19)	1 (4)	172 (13)
Wide-mouth olla	12 (24)	12 (11)	37 (17)	4 (16)	277 (21)
Hemispherical casuela	4 (8)	12 (11)	23 (11)	6 (24)	185 (14)
Conical casuela	...	13 (12)	24 (11)	2 (8)	147 (11)
Conical maceta	...	1 (0.9)	26 (12)	2 (8)	49 (4)
Cylindrical maceta	1 (2)	10 (9)	...	1 (4)	61 (5)
Superhemispherical maceta	...	3 (3)	...	...	6 (0.5)
Tecomate	...	...	7 (3)	1 (4)	19 (1.4)
SUBTOTALS	47 (94)	87 (81)	216 (100)	24 (96)	1291 (97)
Dark Red subtype					
Comal	3 (6)	21 (19)	...	1/4	38/3
SUBTOTALS	3 (6)	21 (19)	0	1/4	38/3
TOTALS	50 (100) (14% of well 1)	108 (100) (29% of well 2)	216 (100) (8% of midden)	25/100 (10% of well 3)	1329/100 (11.7% of total assemblage)

4.5 San Andrés Red long-neck olla

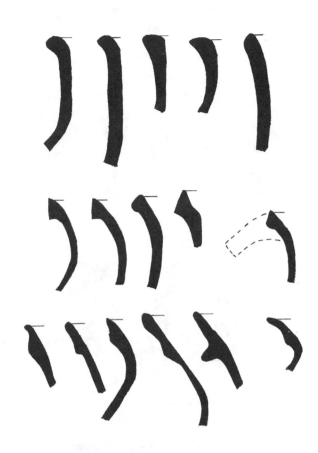

4.6 San Andrés Red long-neck olla rim profiles

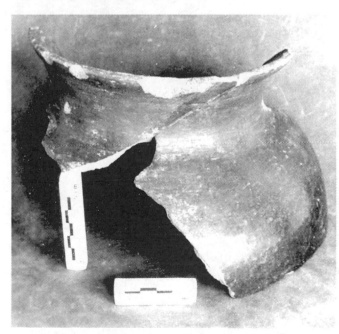

4.7 San Andrés Red small-mouth olla

4.8 San Andrés Red wide-mouth olla

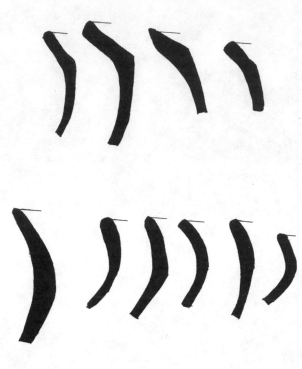

4.9 San Andrés Red small-mouth olla rim profiles

4.10 San Andrés Red wide-mouth olla rim profiles

cific rim forms. Long-neck ollas (also known as *cantaros*) have constricted orifices measuring between about 10 to 15 cm in diameter with relatively long necks ranging from 2 to 6 cm in height (figures 4.5–4.6). Flattened spouts have been found suggesting that at least some of these may have functioned as pitchers. A common attribute of long-neck ollas is a flange, or ridge, around the neck 1 to 2 cm below the lip that may have been used to secure a cover on the vessel. Small-mouth ollas also have constricted orifices measuring 10 to 17 cm in diameter, but the neck is generally low, only about 1 to 3 cm in height (figures 4.7, 4.9). Wide-mouth ollas have an orifice of about 22 to 26 cm and a rim height of 2 to 5 cm (figures 4.8, 4.10). Handles are associated with all of these olla forms.

Cazuelas occur in two major forms: hemispherical cazuelas and conical cazuelas (figure 4.11). Both are large vessels measuring about 25 to 35 cm in diameter, with a vessel height estimated at between 15 to 40 cm. Hemispherical cazuelas can be distinguished by their curving wall form, although they often have a composite silhouette with a 1 to 2 cm vertical rim before the curve begins.

Conical cazuelas have a steeply sloping direct wall, often with a flattened rim. Small nub handles occur on cazuelas.

Macetas occurred in low frequencies in the total assemblage, but were more common in the trash midden deposit (figure 4.12). These are often similar in form to cazuelas, but are even larger and heavier. They usually occur in either vertical wall or conical forms. Macetas have particularly thick vessel walls, and in some rim-to-base sherds, the exterior base has a roughened surface similar to a comal.

Discussion. San Andrés Red is one of the most important and diverse utilitarian wares of the Postclassic Cholula ceramic complex, although variations in vessel-form frequencies indicate that specific forms may have changed through time.

Noguera (1954:72) classified this as *cerámica cafe claro* (light brown ceramic) on the basis of paste color, but more often identified it as simply *sin decoracion* (undecorated). Müller (1978:98–99, 111–112) identified red-slipped ollas, comales, cantaros, and cazuelas from the Postclassic period. These appear in her Sin Engobe (without slip) class, despite the detailed description of

4.11 San Andrés Red cazuela rim profiles

4.12 San Andrés Red maceta rim profiles

their slip color.

The type was identified in early ceramic analyses from the UDLA as "Huitzil Corrugado" (Peterson 1972) and "Fierro Monochrome modeled" (Mountjoy and Peterson 1973). These were relatively minor types in the assemblages, however, and consisted of only 0.5% (n=21) of the Faculty Housing midden deposit (Peterson 1972:200, Table 18).

In the UA-79 trash deposit (F-10), San Andrés Red made up 7.6% (n=311) of the assemblage, with "flanged jars" (long-neck ollas), comales, and "basins" (cazuelas) as the most abundant vessel forms (Barrientos 1980).

At UA-1, San Andrés Red was present as 11.7% (n=1329) of the total assemblage. This frequency was fairly consistent between deposits, with the exception of well 2 where San Andrés Red appeared as 29% (n=108) of the assemblage. This relatively high figure is due in part to the presence of the Dark Red subtype comales, which may have replaced Momoxpan Metallic Orange to some extent in the Colonial period. San Andrés Red comales in general were more numerous in wells 1 and 2 than in the midden and well 3 assemblages. Other vessel-form frequencies remained fairly consistent. San Andrés Red was not found in the R-106 subfloor deposits and was present only as a trace at the Patio of the Carved Skulls (McCafferty 1996a). It is a useful diagnostic for the Postclassic complex, although it also continued into the Colonial period.

✦ TEPONTLA BURNISHED
GRAY/BROWN

Tepontla Burnished Gray/Brown usually appears in serving wares, especially conical bowls. It was most common in the Classic period, but continued into the Early Postclassic in very low frequencies. It is characterized by its burnished surface finish and monochrome color, usually gray to brown.

Paste and firing effects. The paste is light to medium brown in color. It is fine to medium grain, with few inclusions. Sherds are compact and exhibit medium hardness. Firing cores are rare, but surface color appears to be re-

4.13 Tepontla Burnished Gray/Brown conical bowl

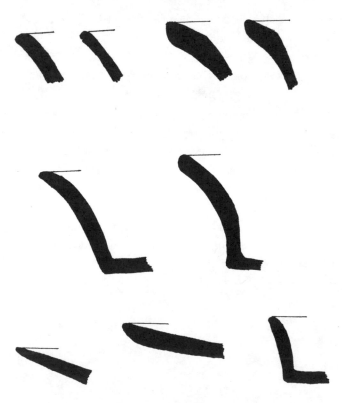

4.14 Tepontla Burnished Gray/Brown rim profiles

lated to firing technique, with frequent firing clouds and variations in color that were possibly dependent on how a vessel was placed in relation to the fire.

Surface treatment. This type is characterized by numerous burnishing marks over the slipped exterior and/or interior surface. The interior finish is usually medium-burnished, while the exterior tends to be wiped to medium-burnished with relatively more rough spots, scratches, and streaks. Burnishing marks are diagnostic of this type, which contrasts with the better-quality finish of Tecola Polished.

Decoration. Tepontla Burnished is generally undecorated apart from the monochrome slip that covers the entire vessel. The most common colors are gray to brown, but it also occurs in reddish brown, light tan, and reddish orange. Two minor subtypes were identified at UA-1: Incised and Red Rim (table 4.4). The Incised subtype has shallow geometric and curvilinear incising on the exterior of hemispherical bowls. The Red Rim subtype has a narrow band of reddish paint on the interior and/or exterior rim of serving vessels.

A subtype that was identified in the R-106 assemblage featured pattern-burnishing on the exterior wall of conical bowls; the pattern was usually a panel of Xs (figure 4.13). Since the R-106 sequence spanned the Middle Classic period, the Pattern Burnished subtype may become a useful temporal diagnostic (McCafferty 1996a; McCafferty, Suárez C., and Edelstein N.D.).

Vessel forms. Tepontla Burnished generally occurs in serving ware vessels, including outleaned-wall bowls, subhemispherical bowls, and conical bowls, but small-mouth ollas also occur in low frequency. The conical bowl is by far the most common form (53% of the type total), with medium thick walls, a rim diameter measuring 20 to 25 cm, and vessel height of 5 to 10 cm (figure 4.14). A characteristic of this vessel form is its flat base and a pronounced angle formed where the vessel wall joins the base. Nubbin supports were a fairly common feature among examples from the R-106 assemblage. Conical bowls often have a slightly flared rim and interior tapering of the lip.

Discussion. Tepontla Burnished is the predominant diagnostic of the Classic period in Cholula. Noguera (1954:188–189) described it in reference to Teotihuacan-style ceramics and this formed the basis for his relative chronology and further cultural reconstructions. Müller (1978) described the type under her Pulido class for the

Table 4.4 Teplontla Burnished vessel-form frequencies

Vessel form	Well 1 n (%)	Well 2 n (%)	Midden n (%)	Well 3 n (%)	Totals n (%)
Plate/lid	...	...	4 (5)	...	5 (1.6)
Comal	...	...	5 (7)	...	6 (1.9)
Outleaned-wall dish	...	...	...	...	2 (0.6)
Outleaned-wall bowl	...	...	8 (11)	1 (33)	32 (10)
Subhemispherical bowl	...	1 (50)	16 (21)	...	65 (21)
Conical bowl	3 (100)	1 (50)	32 (43)	2 (67)	164 (53)
Cylindrical bowl	...	...	2 (3)	...	5 (1.6)
Small-mouth olla	...	...	...	...	21 (7)
Large-mouth olla	...	...	2 (3)	...	2 (0.6)
Conical cazuela	...	...	2 (3)	...	2 (0.6)
Biconical vase	...	...	...	...	1 (0.3)
SUBTOTALS	3 (100)	2 (100)	71 (95)	3 (100)	305 (98)
Incised subtype					
hemispherical bowl	...	...	...	...	2 (0.6)
SUBTOTALS	0	0	0	0	2 (0.6)
Red Rim subtype					
Outleaned wall bowl	...	...	1 (1)	...	1 (0.3)
Subhemispherical bowl	...	...	1 (1)	...	1 (0.3)
Hemispherical bowl	...	...	2 (3)	...	2 (0.6)
SUBTOTALS	0	0	4 (5)	0	4 (1.3)
TOTALS	3 (100) (0.8% of well 1)	2 (100) (0.5% of well 2)	75 (100) (3% of midden)	3 (100) (1.2% of well 3)	311 (100) (2.7% of total assemblage)

Classic and Epiclassic periods. Tepontla Burnished made up 53% of the R-106 subfloor assemblage (McCafferty, Suárez C., and Edelstein N.D.; McCafferty 1996a). Although the type is most common in Classic period contexts, such as the construction fill from the Great Pyramid, it is also prominent at the Epiclassic site of Cerro Zapotecas and at the Patio of the Carved Skulls, where it made up about 30% of the assemblage (McCafferty 1996a).

Regionally, similar pottery is known from the Tlaxcala area and also from the Valley of Mexico. In both areas it is regarded as diagnostic of the Classic period. This type was not classified with Postclassic pottery from previous UDLA excavations, perhaps because when present, it was interpreted as mixed Classic-period material.

At UA-1, the relative frequency of the type in the trash midden context (3%) indicates that Tepontla Burnished was still in use as a small but significant element of the assemblage. Its frequency, however, was greatly reduced in wells 1 and 2. A single collection unit from the trash midden, bag 8153 produced an unusually high frequency of Tepontla Burnished (15%) along with anachronistic types such as Teotihuacan Thin Orange, indicating that this collection unit intersected a Classic period feature (see discussion in chapter 5).

Recognizing that Tepontla Burnished continued in use into the Early Postclassic is important for reinterpreting the culture historical sequence of the Classic/Postclassic transition. For example, the simultaneous occurrence of Tepontla Burnished and Cocoyotla Black on Natural at the Patio of the Carved Skulls contradicts the traditional interpretation that a significant cultural break occurred following the Classic period (Dumond and Müller 1972). Furthermore, it opens the door for revising the Epiclassic chronology, because areas that were previously interpreted as Late Classic based on the presence of this Teotihuacan-influenced ceramic may actually have been occupied into the Early Postclassic, depending on what other types were present in the assemblage.

4.15 Xicalli Plain subhemispherical bowl with stamp-bottom motifs

4.16 Xicalli Plain bowls with stamp-bottom motifs. *After Müller 1978:208–209, Fig. 49a*

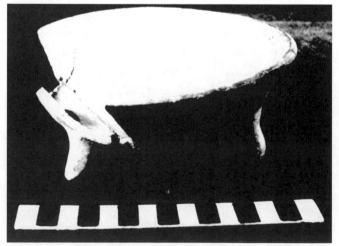

4.17 Xicalli Plain conical bowl with tripod supports

✦ XICALLI PLAIN

Xicalli Plain is characterized by an undecorated tan to light reddish-brown surface color and, in several vessel forms, by a coarse surface finish that may appear rough and cracked. It usually appears in serving wares, but is also found in utilitarian and ceremonial wares.

Paste and firing effects. The paste is medium grain with occasional inclusions. It exhibits medium hardness and often breaks irregularly (that is, with jagged edges). Paste color is usually tan to light reddish-brown that can occasionally be a light orange similar to the orange color of Cocoyotla Black on Natural. Dark gray firing cores and fire clouds occasionally occur.

Surface treatment. Surface treatment varies from rough to medium-burnished. Some vessel forms (for example, outleaned-wall dishes) have a coarse interior surface that is rough and cracked as if allowed to dry without any finishing treatment. Other forms, such as comales (exterior bases) and the interior of lantern censer lids have even coarser surfaces. The most common vessel form, subhemispherical bowls, is usually lightly burnished and can resemble Tepontla Burnished in color and in the presence of burnishing marks.

Decoration. Xicalli Plain is generally undecorated, even lacking a slip. Traces of a white wash and black paint are rarely found on outleaned-wall dishes. More common is mold-impressed decoration (*fondo sellado*) on the interior base of subhemispherical bowls (figure 4.15), with the stamped ridges therefore creating an abrasive surface probably used for grinding chiles. Common motifs on stamped bottoms are concentric geometric panels, but floral and zoomorphic motifs are also found (figure 4.16).

Vessel forms. The most common Xicalli Plain vessel forms include subhemispherical bowls, outleaned-wall dishes, and comales.

Subhemispherical bowls measure 16 to 20 cm in diameter and from 3 to 5 cm in height. Direct rims are characteristically thick and blunt. In addition to frequently having a stamped bottom, subhemispherical bowls often have stubby tripod supports (figure 4.17). The distinction between subhemispherical bowls and conical bowls was often difficult to identify and was not made in the analysis of the UA-1 trash midden.

Outleaned-wall dishes measure 12 to 16 cm in diameter and only 1.5 to 3 cm in height. Two rim forms occur:

a horizontally flared rim, and a direct rim with a flat or angled lip that appears to have been trimmed, perhaps with a blade, and never smoothed (figure 4.18). The interior surface of both varieties of outleaned-wall dishes is rough and cracked, although the flared rim itself is wiped down to about 1 cm from the rim. Short tripod supports are common with this vessel form.

Comales have thick walls and rims, with a rim diameter of between 35 to 60 cm. The interior base is wiped smooth, leaving ridged streaks. The exterior is very rough, characteristic of comales, but the rim is wiped smooth. In general, the form is similar to San Andrés Red comales, lacking only the red slip.

One minor vessel form deserves further discussion. Lantern censers consist of a domed lid supported by three ceramic supports (measuring about 10 cm in length) above a smaller ceramic disk (around 15 cm diameter). On top of the censer lid is a loop handle that was probably used to suspend the censer. A complete censer is illustrated in Müller (1978:129, Fig. 2), and another was recovered at UA-79 (figure 4.19). A nearly complete censer lid with reconstructable supports (UA-1 10761) was found in the UA-1 trash midden (figure 4.20). Censer lids resemble comales in form, with similar surface treatment on both the interior and exterior surfaces. Lantern censers are smaller, however, measuring 25 to 34 cm in diameter, and instead of a flat base, they are domed in the center. Some examples are decorated with incised cross-hatching on the exterior rim. Another distinction is that the underside of lantern censer lids are usually blackened, possibly from burning incense.

Discussion Xicalli Plain is an important undecorated serving ware, particularly for the Middle and Late Tlachihualtepetl periods. Despite its relative significance in the UA-1 assemblage, the type has not been well-defined in previous studies.

A type corresponding to Xicalli Plain that included subhemispherical bowls and outleaned-wall dishes was identified by Noguera (1954:78) simply as *ceramica lisa* (plain ceramic). Vessels with stamped-bottom decoration, however, were classified separately (Noguera 1954:116–117), even though these commonly occur in Xicalli Plain (McCafferty and Suárez C. 2001). Müller (1978:113) identified stamp-bottom molcajetes, and also identified the lantern censer as a "brasero lid" (Müller 1978:93). She illustrated one inside of a stucco-covered brasero (Müller 1978:128–129, Figs. 4,1,2), but it is unclear

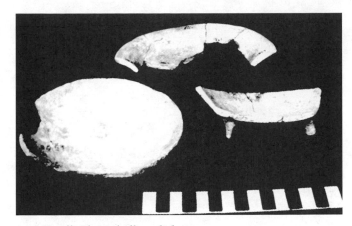

4.18 Xicalli Plain shallow dishes

4.19 Xicalli Plain lantern censer lid from UA-79

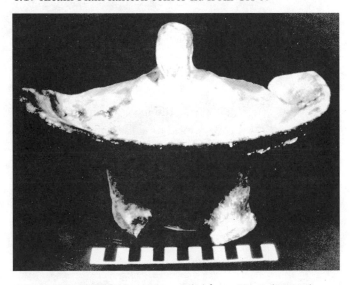

4.20 Xicalli Plain lantern censer lid from UA-1 (10761)

Table 4.5 Xicalli Plain vessel-form frequencies

Vessel form	Well 1 n (%)	Well 2 n (%)	Midden n (%)	Well 3 n (%)	Totals n (%)
Plate/lid	...	...	1 (0.1)	...	25 (1)
Comal	1 (7)	4 (19)	91 (11)	16 (36)	317 (12)
Outleaned-wall dish	5 (33)	5 (24)	295 (35)	11 (25)	563 (22)
Shallow bowl	4 (27)	2 (10)	6 (0.7)	3 (7)	81 (3)
Subhemispherical bowl	2 (13)	8 (38)	430 (51)	9 (20)	1422 (55)
Conical bowl	1 (6)	...	*	4 (9)	113 (4)
Cylindrical bowl	...	...	...	...	1 (0.04)
Superhemispherical bowl	1 (7)	...	...	...	2 (0.08)
Miniature bowl	...	...	...	...	7 (0.3)
Brasero	...	...	2 (0.2)	...	2 (0.08)
Lantern censer	1 (7)	2 (10)	16 (1.9)	1 (2)	56 (2)
TOTALS	15 (100)	21 (100)	841 (100)	44 (100)	2589 (100)
	(4% of well 1)	(6% of well 2)	(29% of midden)	(18% of well 3)	(22.7% of total assemblage)

* Conical bowls were not distinguished from subhemispherical bowls in the midden analysis.

if the two objects were originally found together or were simply assembled as a unit after excavation. Since the loop handle on top of the lantern censer suggests that it was suspended, Müller's reconstruction seems unlikely.

In previous UDLA ceramic analyses, Xicalli Plain ("Perez Plain" in Mountjoy and Peterson 1973) was distinguished from Fondo Sellado bases (Peterson 1972), implying that a rim and the associated stamp-impressed base could belong to different types. Combining these two categories, Xicalli Plain would have constituted about 9% (n=340) of the Faculty Housing midden deposit (Peterson 1972: 200–201, Table 18).

Xicalli Plain plates and cajetes were recognized in the UA-79 ceramic assemblage, where they made up about 6% (n=241) of the F-10 midden deposit (Barrientos 1980). Utilitarian forms, however, were classified as San Pedro Plain, while lantern censers were included among San Andrés Red.

At UA-1, Xicalli Plain was the most abundant type found, making up 22.7% of the total assemblage (table 4.5). It was particularly plentiful in the trash midden and well 3 assemblages, constituting 29% and 18%, respectively. It was present in low frequencies in wells 1 and 2, suggesting that it could be a useful temporal diagnostic.

Xicalli Plain was present as only a trace in the Classic period R-106 assemblage (McCafferty 1996a). It was more common at the Patio of the Carved Skulls where it accounted for 6% of the Early Tlachihualtepetl assemblage.

Characteristics of surface treatment and paste color, and the morphology of the subhemispherical and conical bowls, are quite similar between Xicalli Plain and Cocoyotla Black on Natural. At times the only way to distinguish the two types was on the basis of the diagnostic black painted decoration associated with Cocoyotla. This similarity suggests a close association between the two types. On the basis of the burnished surface treatment, this type can also resemble Tepontla Burnished, although the vessel forms are distinctive. Xicalli Plain is a diagnostic type of the Middle and Late Tlachihualtepetl phases, although it continued into the Late Postclassic in low frequency in particular vessel forms, especially braseros.

MAJOR DECORATED TYPES

These are Apolo Red and Black on Orange Polychrome, Aquiahuac Burnt Orange Polychrome, Coapan Laca Polychrome, Cocoyotla Black on Natural, Cuaxiloa Matte Polychrome, Ocotlán Red Rim, San Pedro Polished Red, and Torre Red and Orange on White Polychrome.

✦ APOLO RED AND BLACK ON ORANGE POLYCHROME

Apolo Polychrome is characterized by a swirled, semi-transparent orange slip over a white base coat. Decoration appears in the form of red and black painted motifs, exhibiting a range of elaboration that is subdivided into four different subtypes.

Paste and firing effects. The paste is light brown to light reddish-brown, typical of the Cholula clay source. It is medium grain with few inclusions. Apolo Polychrome is well-fired and usually hard to brittle. Firing cores and clouding occasionally occur, and discoloration of the painted decoration and orange slip (sometimes to a light green) is probably caused by firing conditions.

Surface treatment. Apolo Polychrome features a white base coat that is covered with an orange slip. The slip was apparently applied with a feather brush, because swirled, streaky brush strokes are a characteristic of the type. The resultant surface is variegated between darker areas where brush strokes overlapped, to sections where the orange slip is semi-transparent. The surface is generally medium- to well-burnished, with the Elegante subtype polished to a brilliant luster. Where the slip was not applied, usually on the exterior base and lower portions of exterior vessel walls, the surface is a natural light brown to light reddish-brown color and is smooth to lightly burnished.

Decoration. Painted decoration in red and occasionally black is applied over the orange slip. In addition to the basic style, called the Sencillo subtype, three other subtypes are recognized, depending on variations in the degree and configuration of decorative elaboration.

In the Sencillo subtype, the typical decoration is a panel on the exterior rim that consists of simple geometric designs, usually horizontal or diagonal interlocked S motifs (figure 4.21a,b). The interior is usually undecorated other than the swirled orange slip that is often quite pronounced, but zoomorphic designs [including stylized turkeys or *izquintle* (hairless dogs)] occasionally occur on the interior base.

In the Geométrico subtype, painted decoration in red and/or black occurs on the interior and occasionally the exterior vessel walls. Designs consist of simple geometric motifs, with one of the more typical patterns consisting of steps of painted blocks (figure 4.21c–f).

The Elegante subtype is the most elaborate subtype, with complex geometric motifs that occasionally include codex-style elements. A characteristic of this subtype is a polished red band on the interior rim of hemispherical bowls, with the painted decoration usually occurring on the exterior surface (figure 4.21g).

A relatively rare subtype is Carmen Gray on Orange, where the black painted decoration appears to have faded into light gray, perhaps as the result of a distinctive firing technique. The decorative patterns are similar to those of the Geométrico subtype.

Vessel forms. Apolo Polychrome appears in serving ware vessels, especially conical bowls and outleaned-wall dishes. Conical bowls are abundant forms in both the Sencillo and Geométrico subtypes and are relatively common in the Elegante subtype. They usually measure about 12 to 18 cm in diameter and 5 to 7 cm in height. Outleaned-wall dishes with rims flared to a horizontal plane occur in moderate frequency in the Geométrico subtype. Vessel diameter measures about 16 to 24 cm, while vessel height is only 2 to 3 cm.

Discussion Apolo Polychrome comprises much of what Noguera (1954:87–99) described as *decoración sencilla* and *decoración negra y roja sobre anaranjado* and which he identified as diagnostic of his Cholulteca III period. It is impossible to identify this type in Müller's typology, although much of it would probably fall into her "geometric" style of decorative elements dating to the Late Postclassic period (1978:224).

In ceramic studies conducted at the UDLA, this type was identified as "Apolo Multichrome," "Toxqui Orange" (Peterson 1972), and Cholula Polychrome A (Mountjoy and Peterson 1973). At the Faculty Housing midden deposit it constituted about 18% (*n*=696) of the assemblage, and it also appeared in moderate frequency in the UA-69 and UA-70 midden deposits (Peterson 1972:200–201, Table 18).

In the UA-79 excavation, Apolo Polychrome (including subtypes Sencillo and Elegante) was the most abundant type found. In the F-10 midden, for example, it accounted for 33% (*n*=1337) of the total assemblage (Barrientos 1980).

For the UA-1 typology, the subtype Geométrico was added to eliminate ambiguity between the relatively simple decoration that typifies Apolo Sencillo and more complex geometric decoration that was included with Apolo Elegante. The Carmen Gray on Orange subtype was formerly a separate type, but is included under Apolo because of its similar surface treatment, vessel forms, and design elements.

At UA-1, Apolo Polychrome appeared in very high

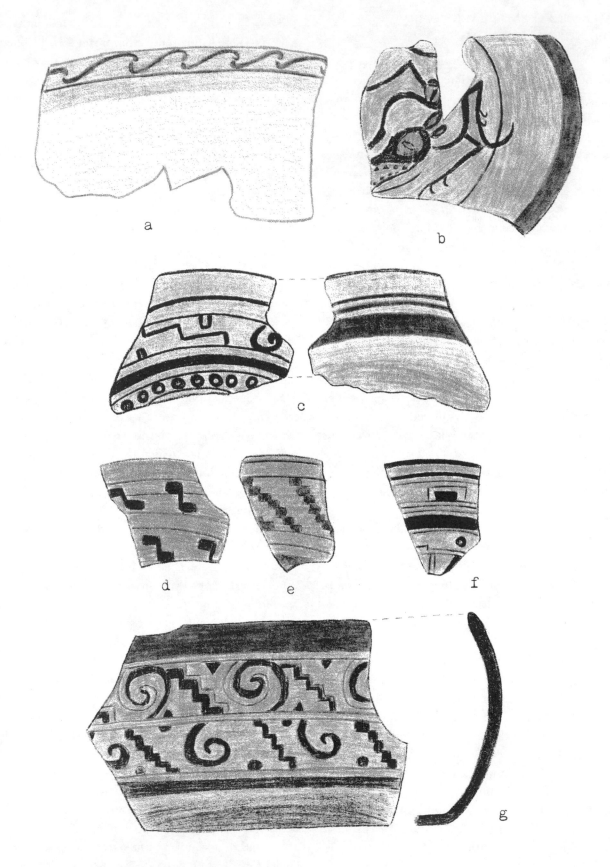

4.21 Apolo Red and Black on Orange Polychrome:
a, *b*, Sencillo; *c-f*, Geométrico; *g*, Elegante

Table 4.6 Apolo Red and Black on Orange Polychrome vessel-form frequencies

Vessel form	Well 1 n (%)	Well 2 n (%)	Midden n (%)	Well 3 n (%)	Totals n (%)
Sencillo subtype					
Plate	2 (1)	...	...	...	8 (1.2)
Outleaned wall dish	2 (1)	1 (4)	3 (25)	...	9 (1.3)
Subhemispherical bowl	4 (2)	1 (4)	3 (25)	...	26 (4)
Hemispherical bowl	7 (4)	...	...	...	29 (4)
Conical bowl	58 (36)	9 (38)	4 (33)	...	275 (40)
Miniature bowl	...	...	...	...	2 (0.3)
SUBTOTALS	73 (45)	11 (46)	10 (83)	0	349 (50)
Geométrico subtype					
Plate	4 (2)	...	...	...	11 (1.6)
Outleaned wall dish	40 (25)	3 (12)	2 (17)	...	118 (17)
Subhemispherical bowl	5 (3)	...	...	...	9 (1.3)
Conical bowl	25 (15)	6 (25)	...	...	103 (15)
Miniature bowl	1 (0.6)	...	...	...	2 (0.3)
SUBTOTALS	75 (46)	9 (38)	2 (17)	0	243 (35)
Elegante subtype					
Outleaned wall dish	...	...	...	...	6 (0.9)
Hemispherical bowl	5 (3)	...	...	...	35 (5)
Conical bowl	10 (6)	1 (4)	...	...	51 (7)
Superhemispherical bowl	...	2 (8)	...	...	9 (1.3)
SUBTOTALS	15 (9)	3 (12)	0	0	101 (15)
Carmen Gray on Orange subtype					
Conical bowl	...	1 (4)	...	...	2 (0.3)
SUBTOTALS	0	1 (4)	0	0	2 (0.3)
TOTALS	163 (100) (46% of well 1)	24 (100) (6% of well 2)	12 (100) (0.4% of midden)	0	695 (100) (6.1% of total assemblage)

frequency (46% of the assemblage) in the well 1 context (table 4.6), low frequency in well 2, and only a trace was found in the midden deposit, and then only in the uppermost stratum. It was completely absent in the well 3 assemblage.

Apolo Polychrome is an important temporal diagnostic for the Chollollan period, where it appears in very high frequencies, especially in Late Chollollan.

Since it is almost completely absent from the UA-1 trash midden and well 3 deposits, it is likely that these assemblages relate to a distinct phase of the Postclassic period. At the same time, however, design characteristics such as the orange slip over a white base suggest continuity of the stylistic tradition also represented by Aquiahuac Polychrome and Ocotlán Red Rim.

✦ AQUIAHUAC BURNT ORANGE POLYCHROME

Aquiahuac Polychrome is characterized by a medium to dark orange surface color that has a streaky brown or "burnt" appearance. Painted decoration is usually in red and black but can include white and other shades of orange.

Paste and firing effects. The paste is light brown to light reddish-brown in color. Vessels are well-fired to a medium to hard hardness. Firing anomalies such as cores and clouds are relatively rare, although the burnt appearance is possibly a result of firing technique. In some examples, the black painted decoration appears as a light gray color, possibly as the result of firing process, similar to the Carmen subtype of Apolo Polychrome.

Surface treatment. Aquiahuac Polychrome has a well-burnished medium to dark orange slip applied over a white base coat. While some brushstrokes are visible, the surface coat is more uniform than on Apolo Polychrome. Where the surface lacks both slip and base coat, it is a light brown to light reddish-brown and is light- to medium-burnished.

Decoration. Aquiahuac Polychrome combines painted decoration using black, red, and occasionally white and orange over the orange slip. A diagnostic decorative element found on the exterior rim is a panel of alternating groups of diagonally hatched lines of red and orange color, sometimes over the orange slip and sometimes over the white base coat. The same exterior decoration is also found on Torre Polychrome. Aquiahuac Polychrome occurs in four subtypes depending on the degree and configuration of decorative elements.

The Sencillo subtype has a black painted band around the lip, and a red band on the interior at the intersection of the base and the wall (figure 4.22). Painted decoration is occasionally added to the vessel walls in the form of thin black lines used to outline geometric or zoomorphic figures. The interior base often features an elaborate design that incorporates codex-style motifs.

The Santa Catarina subtype is an elaboration on the basic Sencillo subtype. Geometric patterns are filled in with two-tone orange color (figure 4.23a,b). Complex patterns on the interior base and exterior rim also occur.

Table 4.7 Aquiahuac Burnt Orange Polychrome vessel-form frequencies

Vessel form	Well 1 n (%)	Well 2 n (%)	Midden n (%)	Well 3 n (%)	Totals n (%)
Sencillo subtype					
Outleaned-wall dish	2 (14)	1 (6)	2 (29)	...	69 (19)
Subhemispherical bowl	1 (7)	2 (12)	...	...	13 (4)
Hemispherical bowl	...	...	...	...	1 (0.3)
Conical bowl	2 (14)	2 (12)	...	...	68 (19)
SUBTOTALS	5 (36)	5 (31)	2 (29)	0	151 (42)
Santa Catarina subtype					
Outleaned-wall dish	...	...	...	...	7 (1.9)
Conical bowl	1 (7)	...	1 (14)	...	8 (2)
Superhemispherical bowl	1 (7)	1 (6)	1 (14)	...	4 (1.1)
SUBTOTALS	2 (14)	1 (6)	2 (29)	0	19 (5)
Zocalo subtype					
Outleaned-wall dish	3 (21)	...	2 (29)	...	62 (17)
Conical bowl	1 (7)	1 (6)	...	...	41 (11)
Cylindrical bowl	...	...	...	...	4 (1.1)
Superhemispherical bowl	3 (21)	9 (56)	1 (14)	...	83 (23)
SUBTOTALS	7 (50)	10 (62)	3 (43)	0	190 (53)
TOTALS	14 (100) (4% of well 1)	16 (100) (4% of well 2)	7 (100) (0.2% of midden)	0	360 (100) (3.2% of total assemblage)

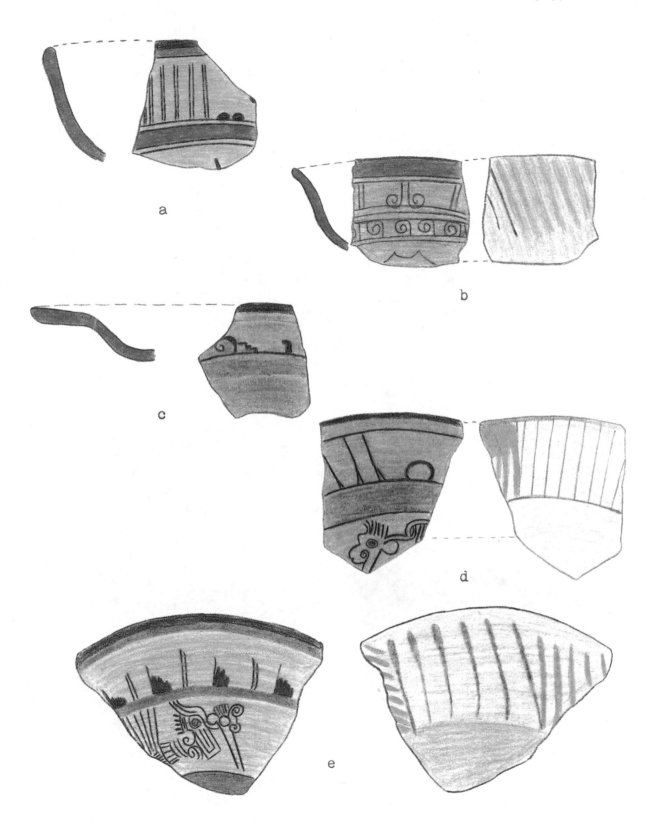

4.22 *a–e*, Aquiahuac Burnt Orange Polychrome
subtype Sencillo

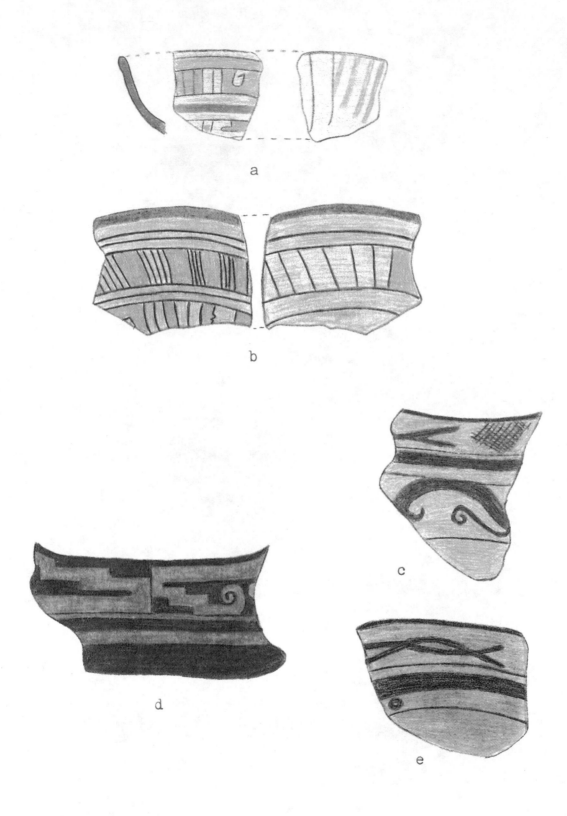

4.23 Aquiahuac Burnt Orange Polychrome subtypes: *a,b,*
Santa Catarina; *c–e,* Zócalo

The Zócalo subtype is distinguished by its predominant use of black paint to create often intricate geometric patterns (figure 4.23c–e). Both fine lines and solids are used to make up the designs, some of which are among the finest found on Cholula polychrome pottery. Other examples are less detailed, however, especially those found on superhemispherical bowls at UA-1, which may represent an early stage in the development of the subtype.

The Barracuda subtype is tentatively defined by its use of negative painting, appearing as a light gray, perhaps as the result of a distinctive firing technique. The decorative patterns are often similar to those of the Zócalo subtype. This subtype is defined on the basis of its presence in the UA-69 midden deposit and its association with the C14 date from that context (Peterson 1972). It was not identified in the UA-1 collections.

Vessel forms. Aquiahuac Polychrome occurs in serving wares, including outleaned-wall dishes, conical bowls, and superhemispherical bowls. Outleaned-wall dishes have horizontally flaring rims with the vessel height measuring about 2 to 3 cm, while the rim diameter is about 20 to 30 cm. They occur in moderate frequency in both the Sencillo and Zócalo subtypes. Conical bowls have a rim diameter of 16 to 24 cm and a vessel height of about 8 to 12 cm. They occur in moderate frequency in the Sencillo and Zócalo subtypes. Superhemispherical bowls occur in high frequency in the Zócalo subtype, where the painted decoration appears on the exterior vessel wall. These measure about 15 to 20 cm in diameter, with a vessel height of about 6 to 10 cm.

Discussion. Noguera (1954:87–99) lumped Aquiahuac with Apolo Polychrome in his types *decoración sencilla* and *decoración negra y roja sobre anaranjado*. It is impossible to distinguish the type in the classification developed by Müller (1978).

Examples of Aquiahuac, particularly the subtype Barracuda, were identified by Peterson at the Faculty Housing excavation from which he obtained the C14 date of 1250±95 CE (Mountjoy and Peterson 1973:30). Unfortunately, Peterson's type definition is somewhat ambiguous, so that it has been difficult to identify Barracuda with confidence. Examples of Aquiahuac Polychrome were found in moderate frequencies in one feature (F-16) at UA-79 and also at the UA-8b excavation (Lind et al. N.D.: Table 2).

At UA-1, Aquiahuac Polychrome occurred in very low frequencies in both wells 1 and 2 and only a trace was found in the upper levels of the trash midden (table 4.7). Greater concentrations of the type were recovered in association with structure 2 and in related sherd concentrations. These contexts will be discussed in chapter 5 in reference to the seriation analysis.

In summary, Aquiahuac Polychrome is a potentially important type for the construction of the Postclassic Cholula ceramic sequence. It is associated with one of the few chronometric dates from the Postclassic period. It also appears to have a greater popularity before the Late Cholollan period (as indicated by its low frequency in UA-79 F-10 and UA-1 well 1), but probably postdates the UA-1 trash midden and well 3, as well as the structure 1 assemblage. Similarities in the general decorative techniques of red and black paint over an orange slip suggest a relationship to Apolo Polychrome, while the distinctive exterior decoration of a panel of diagonal lines is a trait shared with Torre Polychrome.

✦ COAPAN LACA POLYCHROME

Coapan Laca Polychrome is characterized by its lacquer-like finish over a white base coat, and especially by the elaborate use of multiple colors in intricate codex-style motifs. Noguera (1954:138) described this as the most beautiful ceramic of Cholula and possibly of all of pre-Hispanic Mexico.

Paste and firing effects. The paste is light brown to light reddish-brown in color, typical of Cholula decorated wares. The paste is fine to medium grain with few inclusions. Recent trace-element analysis of polícroma laca (Neff et al. 1994) identified a distinctive compositional fingerprint for the Puebla area, with subregional variation from Cholula, Huejotzingo, and Tlaxcala. Coapan Laca is well-fired to a moderate to hard hardness. Firing anomalies were rare in the small sample from UA-1.

Surface treatment. The surface is covered with a thick white base coat over which is applied an orange slip with additional painted decoration. One of the characteristics of the type is the generally poor bond between the undercoat and the exterior paint, such that it tends to flake off (Noguera 1954:139). For this reason many archaeological examples of Coapan Laca are nearly unrecognizable because of the degree of deterioration of the outer surface. The painted surface was well-burnished, often to a high luster.

Decoration. Coapan Laca has painted decoration in complex geometric and naturalistic designs, often including codex-style glyphic symbols (figure 4.24). Colors include red, black, white, yellow, brown, and gray, in addition to the orange of the slip.

The tremendous variety in decorative themes and the elaboration with which they are created makes it difficult to characterize the painted motifs found on Coapan

Laca. Lind (1994) presents a detailed comparison of Coapan Laca ("Catalina Polychrome") and Pilitas Polychrome from the Mixteca Alta using complete or reconstructed vessels from excavated contexts and museum collections.

Approximately fifty distinct design motifs were identified for the Cholula polychrome, with the most common being *xicalcoliuhquis* (stepped fret motif), feathers, bone awls, and maguey thorns (probably representing autosacrifice), plumed serpents, sacrificial knives, and *xonecuillis* (horizontal "S" motifs associated with a kind of worm). On average, about three different motifs occurred on each vessel. The high frequency of symbolism relating to ritual sacrifice suggests a ceremonial function for this type (Lind 1994).

Vessel forms. Coapan Laca occurs in forms associated with serving wares, but because of the possible ritual uses for some of these forms, it probably has a ceremonial significance as well. The most common vessel forms recovered at UA-1 included conical bowls, flared-rim outleaned-wall dishes, and superhemispherical bowls. Based on his larger sample, Lind (1994) includes tripod cajetes, goblets, and hemispherical bowls. About half of the Laca vessels had vessel supports, usually in the form of a conical ring, but also with tripod supports. Decorated tripod supports included zoomorphic representations and the modeled face of the "Old Man" god Huehueteotl. Another significant type that occurs is a flared-rim cylindrical censer with decoration on the exterior while the interior is charred gray, probably from burning incense. This vessel form features two horizontal handles for carrying or suspending the vessel during use.

Discussion. Coapan Laca Polychrome is the most famous of the Cholula polychrome ceramics because of its

Table 4.8 Coapan Laca Polychrome vessel-form frequencies

Vessel form	Well 1	Well 2	Midden	Well 3	Totals
	n (%)	n (%)	n (%)	n (%)	n (%)
Outleaned wall dish	...	...	...	...	12 (30)
Conical bowl	...	...	...	...	20 (50)
Superhemispherical bowl	...	...	...	...	6 (15)
Hemispherical cazuela	...	...	...	...	1 (2)
Sahumador	1 (100)	...	...	...	1 (2)
TOTALS	1 (100) (0.3% of well 1)	0	0	0	40 (100) (0.4 of total assemblage)

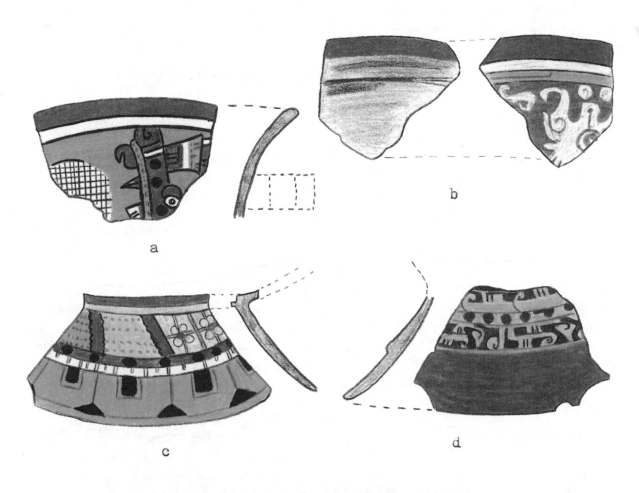

4.24 *a-e,* Coapan Laca Polychrome

high quality and codex-style motifs. Because of its fame, it is included among the Major Decorated types even though it comprised less than 2% of the total UA-1 assemblage.

Noguera (1954:296) concluded that polícroma laca was diagnostic of the Early Postclassic period, inferring an evolutionary relationship linking it to Classic period fresco ware from Teotihuacan (Noguera 1954:142). Similarities between this type and polychrome from the Mixteca Alta were fundamental in postulating a Mixteca-Puebla stylistic horizon (Noguera 1954:142; Nicholson 1960, 1982; Lind 1994).

As discussed in chapter 2, the type described by Noguera (1954:138–142) as polícroma laca combined varieties of several polychrome types, although Coapan Laca is probably the prototype. While numerous vessels were illustrated, Noguera (1954:140) noted that one of the characteristics of laca is its individuality, with each piece unique.

In previous ceramic analyses from the UDLA, Mountjoy and Peterson (1973:31, Table 1) divided laca into three types: Cholula Polychrome A, Cholula Polychrome B, and Cholula Polychrome D. These types also included additional polychrome types defined by Noguera.

At UA-79, feature F-10, Barrientos (1980) classified 3% (*n*=132) as "Coapa Polychrome." Lind (1994) renamed this type as "Catalina Polychrome" (a type combining Coapan Laca and Apolo Elegante), which occurred in up to 5% of the different UA-79 assemblages. Although these frequencies are still very low in terms of the total assemblage, they represent the highest concentration of the type from known excavated contexts. This suggests a Late Postclassic date for Coapan Laca, an interpretation in conflict with Noguera's original ceramic sequence. Additional evidence from an excavated burial from San Andrés Cholula (Suárez C. 1989, 1994) also supports a Late Postclassic date for Coapan Laca Polychrome.

Coapan Laca was a minor type at UA-1, accounting for only 0.4% of the total assemblage (table 4.8). The only primary depositional context at UA-1 in which this type was found was well 1, where it appeared as only a single sherd (0.3% of the well 1 assemblage). Consequently, it is difficult to assess the significance of Coapan Laca on the basis of the UA-1 data. On the other hand, its relative absence is negative evidence useful for posing questions about the cultural significance of the type. Was this a type with a relatively brief popularity not represented at the UA-1 excavation? Or was its use restricted to more elite or ceremonial contexts in which the inhabitants of the UA-1 structures did not participate? Based on the limited evidence available, I suspect that both temporal and social factors inhibited the consumption of this type at UA-1.

✦ COCOYOTLA BLACK ON NATURAL

Cocoyotla Black on Natural is characterized by black painted decoration over the natural orange color of the paste. Some subtypes include painted decoration over a matte white background.

Paste and firing effects. The paste is light brown to light reddish-brown in color. It has fine to medium consistency and is fired to a medium hardness that often results in irregularly jagged breaks. Dark gray firing cores occasionally occur.

Surface treatment. The surface is usually unslipped, but is light- to medium-burnished. The surface color is usually light brown to light reddish-brown. In the Banded subtypes an orange slip very close to the natural color of the paste was applied over a thin white base coat. Although this diverges from the concept of a "natural" surface finish, similarities in color, decorative themes, and vessel forms are the rationale for interpreting subtype variation.

Decoration. Decoration in the basic Sencillo subtype is black painted lines forming simple to complex patterns (figure 4.25a,b). A distinctive characteristic is the blurred appearance of the painted lines, as if the paint was smeared while still wet. The most common patterns are a series of concentric horizontal or wavy lines around the interior rim. More complex patterns include geometric and naturalistic floral and zoomorphic figures on the interior base (figure 4.26).

In addition to the basic Sencillo subtype, four other subtypes were recognized at UA-1: Incised, Banded, Banded Elegante, and Chalco Black on Orange.

The Incised subtype has a black painted panel on the exterior extending down 1 to 3 cm below the lip, with thinly incised decoration within the panel (figure 4.25c,d). Decorative motifs include curvilinear and geometric patterns, some of which are codex-style designs.

The Banded subtype is identified by two to four horizontal bands painted below the interior rim on an orange slip similar in color to the natural color of the paste (figures 4.25e,f, 4.27). A characteristic of this subtype is a matte white panel on the exterior rim extending 2 to 4 cm down from the lip, sometimes with additional horizontal bands painted in black. Matte white paint can also appear on the interior base, decorated with two to four concentric circles. Careful inspection indicates that the matte white is a base coat, over which the orange slip was applied.

The Banded Elegante subtype is similar to the previ-

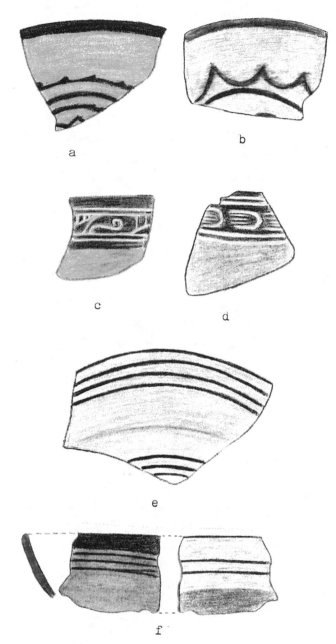

4.25 Cocoyotla Black on Natural subtypes: *a,b,* Sencillo; *c,d,* Incised; *e,f,* Banded

ous subtype, particularly in reference to the use of natural-colored orange slip over a white base and horizontal bands on the interior rim. Banded Elegante, however, has more elaborate painted decoration on the matte white panel of the exterior rim, with motifs including earth monster and other glyphic themes (figure 4.28a–e). In some examples patterns outlined with black lines are filled with orange color identical to the slip color.

Chalco Black on Orange subtype is similar to the basic Sencillo subtype in its use of black paint over

Table 4.9 Cocoyotla Black on Natural vessel-form frequencies

Vessel form	Well 1 n (%)	Well 2 n (%)	Midden n (%)	Well 3 n (%)	Totals n (%)
Sencillo subtype					
Subhemispherical bowl	...	6 (67)	62 (30)	...	240 (44)
Conical bowl	...	1 (11)	3 (1.5)	...	11 (2)
Superhemispherical bowl	...	...	...	...	1 (0.2)
SUBTOTALS	0	7 (78)	65 (32)	0	252 (46)
Incised subtype					
Hemispherical bowl	...	...	...	...	2 (0.4)
Conical bowl	...	...	...	...	13 (2)
Superhemispherical bowl	...	...	5 (2)	...	8 (1.5)
SUBTOTALS	0	0	5 (2)	0	23 (4)
Banded subtype					
Plate	...	...	...	...	1 (0.2)
Outleaned wall dish	...	...	1 (0.5)	...	1 (0.2)
Subhemispherical bowl	...	...	72 (35)	13 (65)	104 (19)
Hemispherical bowl	...	...	2 (1.0)	...	2 (0.4)
Conical bowl	...	1 (11)	35 (17)	4 (20)	54 (10)
SUBTOTALS	0	1 (11)	110 (54)	17 (85)	162 (30)
Banded Elegante subtype					
Outleaned-wall dish	...	...	...	2 (10)	16 (3)
Subhemispherical bowl	...	1 (11)	...	...	6 (1.1)
Conical bowl	...	...	...	1 (5)	34 (6)
SUBTOTALS	0	1 (11)	0	3 (15)	56 (10)
Chalco Black on Orange subtype					
Plate	...	...	...	...	1 (0.2)
Outleaned-wall dish	...	...	...	...	1 (0.2)
Subhemispherical bowl	...	...	8 (4)	...	9 (1.6)
Hemispherical bowl	...	...	...	...	11 (2)
Conical bowl	...	...	16 (8)	...	32 (6)
SUBTOTALS	0	0	24 (12)	0	54 (10)
TOTALS	0	9 (100) (2% of well 2)	204 (100) (7% of midden)	20 (100) (8% of well 3)	547 (100) (4.8% of total assemblage)

the natural surface, but is distinctive in terms of design configuration and surface treatment. The painted decoration is a horizontal panel delineated by straight and/or wavy lines usually around the interior rim (figure 4.28f–h). The panel is filled with geometric patterns often in the same style of blurry lines as in the basic Sencillo subtype. The surface is medium-burnished to a dull luster. The most common vessel form is a conical bowl, but with a slightly everted lip.

Additional subtypes identified at the Patio of the Carved Skulls included Cocoyotla Natural (lacking any black paint), Black Rim, and White on Natural. Since these were not identified at UA-1 they are not included in the tabulations.

Vessel forms. Cocoyotla Black on Natural appears as serving vessels, with the two most common forms being subhemispherical bowls and conical bowls. Subhemispherical bowls occur in nearly all subtypes (except Incised). Subtype Sencillo subhemispherical bowls measure 15 to 17 cm in diameter and about 3 to 4 cm in vessel height. Subtype Banded subhemispherical bowls are generally larger, measuring 14 to 24 cm in diameter and 4 to 6 cm in vessel height. Conical bowls occur in every subtype, but are most common in the Banded subtype, where they measure about 16 to 20 cm in diameter.

Discussion. Cocoyotla Black on Natural has previous-

4.26 Cocoyotla Black on Natural: examples of design motifs found on interior of subhemispherical bowls. *After Noguera 1954:105–107*

4.27 Cocoyotla Black on Natural subtype Banded, interior and exterior (UA-1 9549)

ly been identified by Noguera (1954:99–110) as *decoración negra sobre el fondo color natural del barro*. It has been compared to Early Aztec (Group I or Aztec I) Black on Orange pottery from the Valley of Mexico (Noguera 1954:282). Another source of comparison is with the Gulf Coast, where the type is similar in decoration, surface finish, and vessel form to X-Fine Orange (R. Smith 1958).

Noguera recovered this type in the earliest Postclassic levels, and it was the predominant decorated type found at the Altar of the Carved Skulls (Noguera 1937, 1954:100–101, 225–226, 282–283). For this reason Noguera considered it a valuable diagnostic for identifying the Cholulteca I pe-

riod. Müller (1978:101–105) identified several types of black on natural based on vessel form and used them as diagnostics for her Cholulteca II phase.

Mountjoy and Peterson (1973:31, Table 1) classified this as "Minutti Black on Orange." It appeared as only a trace (.7%, *n*=32) in the dated midden excavated at the Faculty Housing Complex (Mountjoy and Peterson 1973:33). At the UA-79 excavations, Cocoyotla Black on Orange was again found as only a trace (.3%, *n*=11) in the F-10 midden (Barrientos 1980). Cocoyotla Black on Natural pottery from a well in San Pedro Cholula occurred in association with other Early Postclassic types such as Ocotlán Red Rim (McCafferty 1996a).

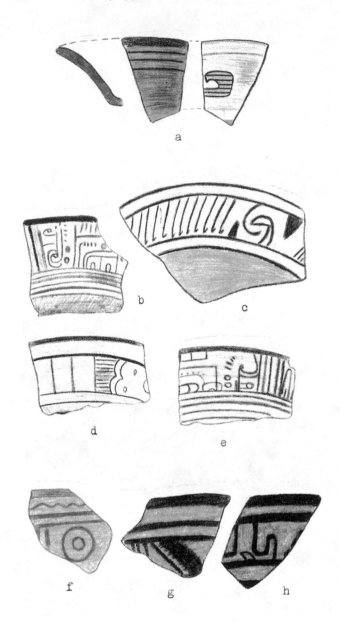

4.28 Cocoyotla Black on Natural subtypes: *a-e*, Banded Elegante; *f–h*, Chalco Black on Orange

In the UA-1 assemblages, Cocoyotla Black on Natural appeared in low frequencies in the trash midden and well 3 assemblages, 7% and 8% respectively (table 4.9). It should be noted that the most common subtype was Cocoyotla Banded, which is probably a later variation of the Cocoyotla type. From the floor contact deposits of structure 1, Cocoyotla made up 12% of the assemblage, with a higher proportion of the Sencillo subtype, while at structure 2 it appeared as 4% of the floor contact deposit. A complete Cocoyotla subtype Sencillo bowl (UA-1 10147) was found in association with individual 4 in an intrusive burial pit through the floor of structure 1.

When additional testing was conducted at the Patio of the Carved Skulls (McCafferty and Suárez C. 1995), Cocoyotla made up about 30% of the assemblage (McCafferty 1996a). Previously unrecognized subtypes such as Cocoyotla Natural and Black Rim were significant elements of the assemblage, while the Banded, Banded Elegante, and Chalco subtypes were not present. Since this is interpreted as an Early Tlachihualtepetl context, it reinforces the suggestion that Cocoyotla Black on Natural subtypes can be used to identify temporal change in Epiclassic and Early Postclassic Cholula.

The Chalco Black on Orange subtype holds additional potential for building a relative chronology linking Cholula with the Valley of Mexico. The attributes of vessel form, design configuration, and especially the slightly everted lip are similar to examples found at Operation B of Ch-Az-195 of "Early Aztec Black on Orange" described by Parsons and Parsons (1982). Four C14 samples from this excavation resulted in a consistent cluster of dates between about 650–850 CE (Whalen and Parsons 1982:19, Table 5). A recent series of dates from Xaltocan support an early date (700–1000 CE) for Early Aztec period Black on Orange pottery (Brumfiel 1992, Parsons, Brumfield, and Hodge 1996). Further reevaluation of the role of Black on Orange ceramics in Epiclassic and Early Postclassic sequence is ongoing (c.f. Parsons, Brumfiel, and Hodge 1996).

Spatial analysis of Black on Orange pottery from the southern Valley of Mexico has resulted in a refinement of type distinctions (Hodge and Minc 1990, 1991). Based on this classification, Chalco Black on Natural from UA-1 corresponds closely with the Mixquic variety of Early Aztec Black on Orange.

Although a detailed ceramic classification is not available from Cerro Zapotecas, "thin-line red design" ceramics appear to have similar attributes of design and possibly lip form (Mountjoy 1987:142, Fig. 4i–j). The site is dated between 600 and 800 CE (Mountjoy 1987; Wolfman 1990), consistent with the C14 dates collected by Parsons and Brumfiel.

In summary, Cocoyotla Black on Natural is an important type for correlating the Cholula ceramic sequence with the Valley of Mexico. It provides a basis for interpreting cultural contacts linking Epiclassic and Early Postclassic Cholula with the Valley of Mexico and the Gulf Coast. In addition, possible diachronic variation between the different subtypes of Cocoyotla may provide a means for further refinement of the ceramic sequence.

✦ CUAXILOA MATTE POLYCHROME

Cuaxiloa Matte Polychrome occurs in serving wares and is characterized by black and orange painted decoration over a matte white to light gray slip.

Paste and firing effects. The paste is light brown to light reddish-brown in color, often with an orangish tone similar to Cocoyotla Black on Natural. The paste is compact and fired to a medium hardness. Firing cores and clouds are rare. Fire clouds occur most often on superhemispherical bowls, possibly a result of cooking rather than firing techniques.

Surface treatment. The surface is wiped to medium-burnished, depending on vessel form. The interior surface of superhemispherical bowls tends to be the roughest, with frequent streaks and irregularities. Decorated surfaces are generally burnished. A dull whitish slip is applied on either (or both) the interior or exterior surface, giving the ceramic a powdery, matte texture; the subtypes Polished Cream and Fugitive Paint (discussed below) represent qualitative differences in surface treatment.

Decoration. Decoration is in the form of painted motifs, usually panels of geometric designs, especially xicalcoliuhquis. The most common colors used are black and orange, but tan and red also occur. One characteristic motif is a series of vertical black lines in a panel over the white slip, interspersed with a cluster of vertical lines filled with orange paint (figure 4.29). Another typical motif is a hatched geometric figure, often a triangle, filled with orange. More elaborate design motifs, including codex-style figures, appear on the interior bases of vessels.

Three subtypes have been tentatively identified in addition to the basic type: Polished Cream, Fugitive Paint, and Xicotenco Black and Red on Orange. Only subtype Polished Cream has appeared in quantity, and it is possible that these subtypes represent regional variations or production anomalies.

The Polished Cream subtype differs from the basic type in its well-burnished surface finished to a luster similar to polícroma laca. Design motifs and vessel forms are identical to the basic type, although the quality of workmanship is superior (figure 4.30a–d).

The Fugitive Paint subtype varies from the basic type in that the painted decoration is poorly bonded to the vessel surface, so that only traces remain. This may represent an unfinished stage in the production process or could simply be a regional variation.

Xicotenco Black and Red on Orange subtype is similar to the basic type in decorative motifs and vessel forms, but is distinctive in its orange slip in place of the characteristic matte white (figure 4.30e). This may be a developmental innovation with chronological significance, but was too rare in the UA-1 excavated contexts for conclusive interpretation.

Vessel forms. This type generally occurs in serving ware vessels, although the frequent presence of fire clouds on the exterior of superhemispherical bowls indicates that at least this vessel form may have been used for food preparation. Superhemispherical bowls are the most common vessel form, representing more than half of the examples. Other significant vessel forms include outleaned-wall dishes and conical bowls.

Superhemispherical bowls measure 8 to 21 cm in diameter with vessel height at about 7 to 9 cm (figures 4.31, 4.32). This form occurs in very high frequency in the basic type, but is less common in the Polished Cream subtype. Outleaned-wall dishes have a horizontally flared rim and vessel height of 2 to 3 cm. They appear in moderate frequency in the basic type and low frequency in the Polished Cream subtype. Conical bowls range in diameter from about 18 to 23 cm and measure about 5 to 6 cm in vessel height (figure 4.33). They appear in moderate frequency in the basic subtype and low frequency in the Polished Cream subtype.

Discussion. Cuaxiloa Matte Polychrome is an enigmatic type in the Cholula ceramic complex. Noguera (1954:136–138) identified polícroma mate as a separate type and tentatively suggested that it was diagnostic of the intermediary Cholulteca II phase in the Postclassic sequence. Very little of it was recovered, however, and Noguera was hesitant to base interpretations on this poorly defined type (1954:271).

Peterson recovered a trace (1.5%, n=43) of mate polychrome at the Faculty Housing excavation (1972; Mountjoy and Peterson 1973:33). It was not recovered from the UA-79 excavations.

Similar ceramics are illustrated as diagnostic of Isla de Sacrificios II-III from the Gulf Coast (García Payón 1971:535–537), where they are related to the Historic period associated with the Toltec and Chichimec invasions. Unfortunately, type frequencies are not recorded for the Gulf Coast contexts so it is impossible to deduce the extent to which it was a significant component of the ceramic complex. The major difference between Cuaxiloa Matte and Gulf Coast varieties is in the distinctive Cholula paste composition in contrast to the exceptionally fine paste typical of Gulf Coast pottery. Stylistic similarities also exist

4.29 *a-h*, Cuaxiloa Matte Polychrome

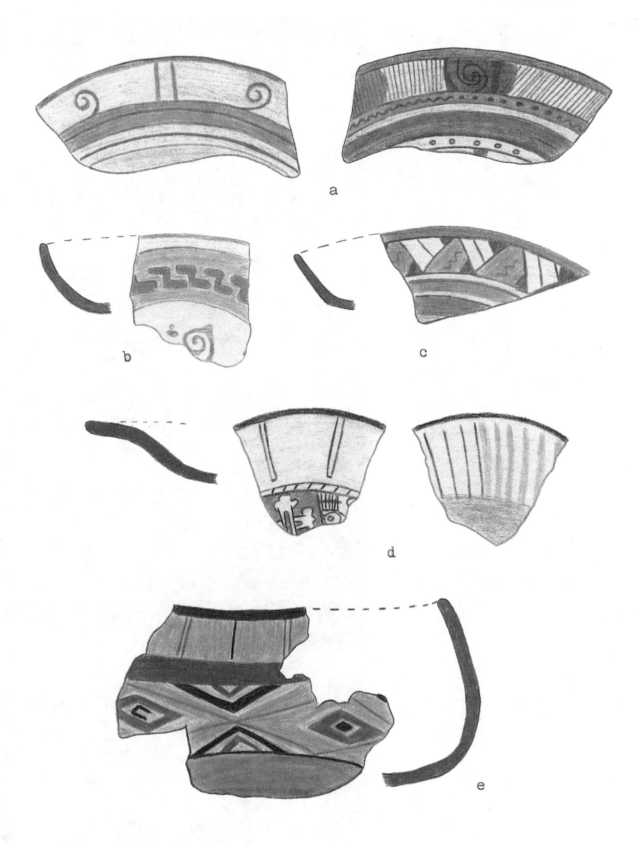

4.30 Cuaxiloa Matte Polychrome subtypes: *a–d*, Polished
Cream; *e*, Xicotenco Black on Orange

**4.31 Cuaxiloa Matte Polychrome
superhemispherical bowl (UA-1 11854)**

**4.32 Cuaxiloa Matte Polychrome
superhemispherical bowls**

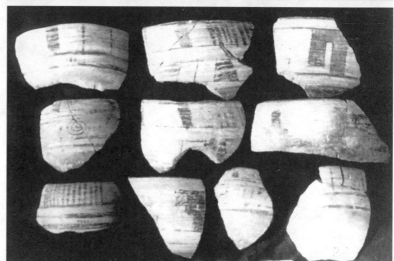

4.33 Cuaxiloa Matte Polychrome conical bowls

Table 4.10 Cuaxiloa Matte Polychrome vessel-form frequencies

Vessel form	Well 1 (n/%)	Well 2 (n/%)	Midden (n/%)	Well 3 (n/%)	Totals (n/%)
Outleaned-wall dish	1/17	1/14	31/13	...	51/10
Subhemispherical bowl	...	2/29	15/6	5/8	40/8
Hemispherical bowl	1/17	...	...	9/15	24/5
Conical bowl	...	1/14	40/17	2/3	59/12
Superhemispherical bowl	...	2/29	112/47	23/37	208/41
Miniature bowl	...	...	1/0.4	...	2/0.4
SUBTOTALS	2/33	6/86	199/84	39/63	384/76
Polished Cream subtype					
Outleaned-wall dish	1/17	...	14/6	1/1.6	19/4
Subhemispherical bowl	...	...	...	5/8	6/1.2
Hemispherical bowl	...	...	4/1.7	...	4/0.8
Conical bowl	...	...	7/3	6/10	17/3
Superhemispherical bowl	...	...	6/3	6/10	23/5
Biconical <u>copa</u>	1/17	1/14	...	2/3	18/4
SUBTOTALS	2/33	1/14	31/13	20/32	87/17
Fugitive Paint subtype					
Superhemispherical bowl	...	...	7/3	2/3	9/1.8
SUBTOTALS	0	0	7/3	2/3	9/1.8
Xicotenco Black and Red on Orange subtype					
Outleaned-wall dish	...	...	...	...	1/0.2
Cylindrical jar	...	...	...	...	1/0.2
Superhemispherical bowl	2/33	...	...	1/1.6	25/5
SUBTOTALS	2/33	0	0	1/1.6	27/5
TOTALS	6/100 (1.7% of well 1)	7/100 (1.9% of well 2)	237/100 (8% of midden)	62/100 (25% of well 3)	507/100 (4.4% of total assemblage)

with Vallejo Polychrome from Central America, particularly in the use of the motif of vertical lines (often filled with orange) in a panel over the white slip (Stone 1982; Hoopes and McCafferty 1989).

Similar pottery is also illustrated from the southern Valley of Mexico by Séjourné (1983: Figs. 171–174), where it is identified as "cerámica Chalco," dating to the Aztec I period and related to the arrival of Toltecs in the area (Séjourné 1983:264). Illustrations of this general type, however, include a wide range of polychrome styles that can be related to other Cholula types—Apolo Black and Red on Orange, Aquiahuac Burnt Orange, San Pedro Polished Red, and Torre Red and Orange on White Polychrome—and thus the temporal affiliation is questionable.

At UA-1, Cuaxiloa Matte was found as only a trace in wells 1 and 2, but comprised 8% of the trash midden and 25% of well 3 (table 4.10). The high proportion of polícroma mate in well 3 was noted by Wolfman (1968:8), who therefore interpreted the feature as predating the Postclassic structures. A relatively high amount of Cuaxiloa Matte was also found in a midden deposit from the Transito site (R-106) in San Pedro Cholula (McCafferty, Suárez C., and Edelstein N.D.).

In summary, Cuaxiloa Matte Polychrome is a potentially important pottery type as a temporal diagnostic and as a means of interpreting regional interaction. Unfortunately, it is still rare in excavated contexts from Cholula, perhaps because it had a relatively short period of use, perhaps because of restricted social functions relating to ethnic factors, or perhaps as an indicator of Gulf Coast affiliation.

4.34 Ocotlán Red Rim subtype Sencillo conical bowl
(UA-1 9591)

✦ OCOTLÁN RED RIM

Ocotlán Red Rim is characterized by a well-burnished, light orange slip and a red painted band on the
rim. It occurs in a basic Sencillo subtype, but is often
elaborated in subtypes defined by incised or painted
decoration.

Paste and firing effects. The paste is a light brown
to light reddish-brown color. It has a fine to medium
grain size, with a light density of small to very small inclusions. The paste is compact and ranges from medium
hard to hard. Small to medium firing cores are occasionally found, as are firing clouds. The interiors of superhemispherical bowls are occasionally a streaky white col-
or instead of the usual orange, probably as the result of
firing anomalies.

Surface treatment. Ocotlán Red Rim pottery is medi-
um- to well-burnished, often to a luster. The surface is
covered with a light orangish slip that is relatively uniform over a white base coat. The surface color is generally lighter than that of either Apolo Polychrome or Aquiahuac Polychrome, and it has somewhat fewer pronounced brush strokes than Apolo Polychrome.

Decoration. The diagnostic decorative element of this
type is a red painted band extending about 0.5 to 1.0 cm
down from the interior and/or exterior rim. While this
trait is nearly always present, on more elaborately decorated subtypes it may be incorporated into other aspects
of the decoration. In addition to basic Sencillo, five other
subtypes have been identified: Incised, Banded, Banded

Elegante, Elegante, and Cristina Matte.

The Sencillo subtype is defined simply by the burnished orange surface with the red painted band on the
rim (figures 4.34, 4.35a–e). This was the most common
subtype of Ocotlán Red Rim found at UA-1, comprising
76% of the type total (table 4.11). It usually occurs as
conical bowls, including both direct and flared-rim
forms, and superhemispherical bowls.

The Incised subtype has a dark brown/black painted
panel on the exterior that is decorated with fine line incising (figure 4.35f–h). Motifs include simple to complex
geometric designs and hatched circles. This subtype is
very similar to the Cocoyotla subtype Incised in terms of
the design configurations, but can be distinguished on
the basis of the characteristic surface treatment and red
band of the Ocotlán type. This subtype was rare at UA-1,
occurring as only 1.8% of the type total. It usually occurred on conical bowls.

The Banded subtype is characterized by a series of
two to four black painted lines placed horizontally on the
interior vessel wall just below the rim (figure 4.36a). As
with other subtypes of Ocotlán, a red painted band appears on the rim itself. This subtype is similar to the Cocoyotla subtype Banded in terms of the painted bands,
but can be distinguished based on the well-burnished
surface and the red painted band on the rim. This subtype only occurred as 1.1% of the type total, with conical
bowls as the most common vessel form.

The Banded Elegante subtype is similar to the Banded
subtype in terms of the black painted lines below the interior rim, but this subtype also features polychrome
decoration on the burnished exterior (figures 4.36b–c,
4.37). Colors include red, orange, and black over an off-
white background, with decoration occurring in a horizontal panel below the rim. Motifs include complex geometric designs and codex-style representations, notably the earth monster. This subtype occurs in very
low frequencies (3%) of the type total, with conical
bowls in both direct and flared rims as the most common vessel form.

The Elegante subtype features elaborate polychrome
decoration on the interior and/or exterior vessel walls
(figures 4.36d, 4.38, 4.39, 4.40). Colors and motifs are
similar to those on the exterior of the Banded Elegante
subtype. The Elegante subtype occurred in low frequency (8% of the type total), with conical bowls and flared-

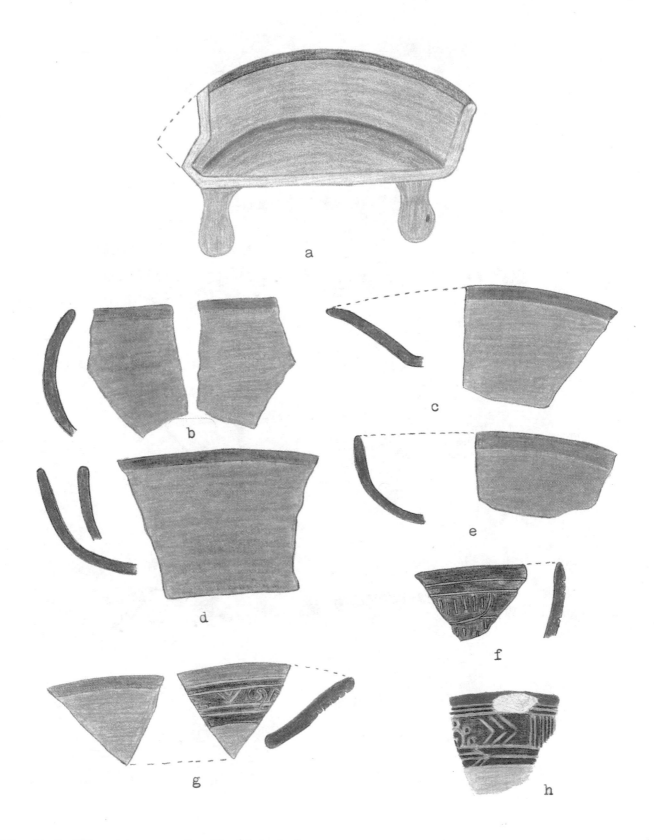

4.35 Ocotlán Red Rim subtypes: *a–e*, Sencillo; *f–h*, Incised

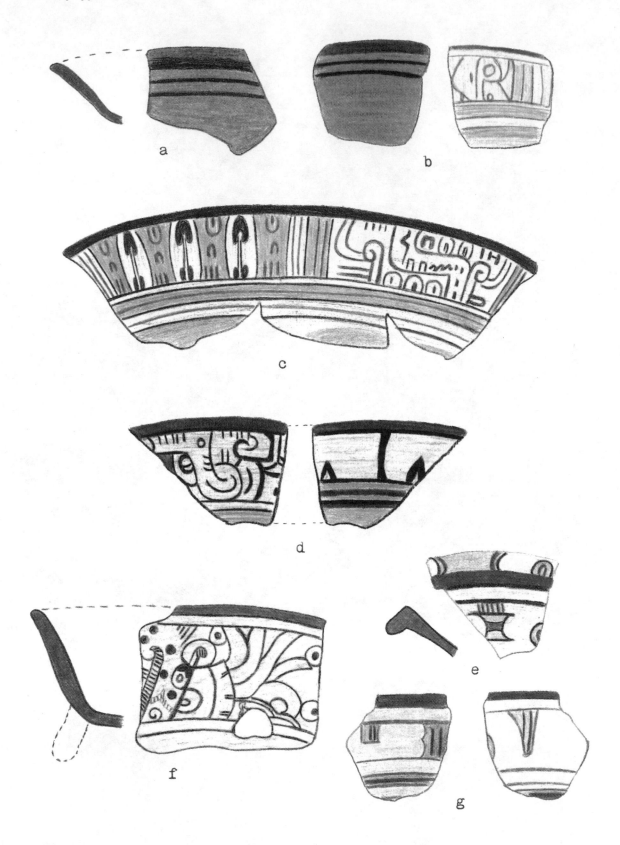

4.36 Ocotlán Red Rim subtypes: *a*, Banded; *b*, Banded
Elegante; *c-d*, Elegante; *e–g*, Cristina Matte

Table 4.11 Ocotlán Red Rim vessel-form frequencies

Vessel form	Well 1 n (%)	Well 2 n (%)	Midden n (%)	Well 3 n (%)	Totals n (%)
Sencillo subtype					
Subhemispherical bowl	...	...	18 (5)	...	75 (5)
Hemispherical bowl	...	...	12 (4)	1 (5)	69 (5)
Conical bowl	...	4 (67)	145 (44)	11 (52)	756 (49)
Superhemispherical bowl	...	...	71 (21)	4 (19)	259 (17)
SUBTOTALS	0	4 (67)	246 (74)	16 (76)	1159 (76)
Incised subtype					
Hemispherical bowl	...	...	2 (0.6)	...	2 (0.1)
Conical bowl	...	...	4 (1.2)	...	24 (1.6)
Superhemispherical bowl	...	...	...	1 (5)	2 (0.1)
SUBTOTALS	0	0	6 (1.8)	1 (5)	28 (1.8)
Banded subtype					
Subhemispherical bowl	...	...	...	...	5 (0.3)
Conical bowl	...	...	5 (1.5)	...	12 (0.8)
SUBTOTALS	0	0	5 (1.5)	0	17 (1.1)
Banded Elegante subtype					
Subhemispherical bowl	...	...	...	1 (5)	1 (0.07)
Conical bowl	...	...	19 (6)	...	52 (3)
SUBTOTALS	0	0	19 (6)	1 (5)	53 (3)
Elegante subtype					
Outleaned-wall dish	...	...	...	...	22 (1.4)
Subhemispherical bowl	...	...	...	...	6 (0.4)
Conical bowl	1 (100)	...	...	1 (5)	83 (5)
Biconical bowl	...	1 (17)	...	1 (5)	5 (0.3)
SUBTOTALS	1 (100)	1 (17)	0	2 (10)	116 (8)
Cristina Matte subtype					
Outleaned-wall dish	...	...	...	...	1 (0.07)
Subhemispherical bowl	...	...	1 (0.3)	...	6 (0.4)
Hemispherical bowl	...	...	1 (0.3)	...	2 (0.1)
Conical bowl	...	...	20 (6)	1 (5)	52 (3)
Superhemispherical bowl	...	1 (17)	34 (10)	...	96 (6)
Biconical copa	...	...	...	...	1 (0.07)
SUBTOTALS	0	1 (17)	56 (17)	1 (5)	158 (10)
TOTALS	1 (100) (0.3% of well 1)	6 (100) (1.6% of well 2)	332 (100) (11% of midden)	21 (100) (8% of well 3)	1531 (100) (13.4% of total assemblage)

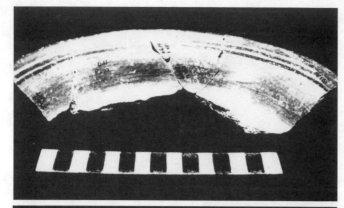

4.37 Ocotlán Red Rim subtype Elegante (UA-1 bag 8199; exterior and interior)

4.38 Ocotlán Red Rim subtype Elegante conical bowl (UA-1 bag 8602)

rim, outleaned-wall bowls as the most common vessel forms.

The Cristina Matte subtype is distinctive for its white background and motifs painted in red and black. Motifs include curvilinear designs, especially volutes, that often form codex-style representations (figures 4.36e–g, 4.41, 4.42). This subtype can resemble examples from Isla de Sacrificios on the Gulf Coast (García Payón 1971), but despite the elaborate painted decoration it retains the features of the basic Ocotlán type, that is, the burnished orange slip and the red band at the rim. The Cristina subtype occurred in moderate frequency (10%) in the type total, with superhemispherical bowls and conical bowls as the most common vessel forms.

Vessel forms. This type usually appears as serving vessels, although the unusual firing effects on Sencillo superhemispherical bowls may indicate a cooking function for this particular vessel form. The two major vessel forms were conical bowls and superhemispherical bowls.

Conical bowls occur with either direct or flared rims and are common to all subtypes. In the basic Sencillo subtype this form ranges in rim diameter from 15 to 30 cm. Direct rim conical bowls are deeper, averaging about 7 cm in vessel height, while flared-rim conical bowls average about 4 cm in height. This form often has bulbous, hollow supports, and will occasionally have a stamp-impressed grater bottom.

Superhemispherical bowls are common in the Sencillo and Cristina Matte subtypes. Sencillo subtype superhemispherical bowls have a rim diameter of about 15 to 20 cm and measure 8 to 10 cm in vessel height. An unusual characteristic of these vessels was a streaky, light gray color on some examples, probably as a result of firing technique or from cooking. Cristina Matte subtype vessels were slightly larger with rim diameters of 19 to 22 cm, but no examples were sufficiently complete to measure the vessel height.

Discussion. Ocotlán Red Rim is a distinctive type that has not been recognized previously (but see Suárez Cruz 1995). Noguera (1954:92) grouped the Sencillo subtype with his "decoración sencilla," which he attributed to the Late Postclassic period. Other subtypes were distributed among his "esgrafiada," "polícroma firme," "polícroma laca," and "blanca y roja sobre crema" types.

Mountjoy and Peterson (1973:31, 84) classified Ocotlán Red Rim in their "Sanchez" cluster of types, which also included Apolo and Aquiahuac Polychromes.

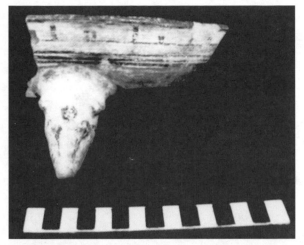

4.39 Ocotlán Red Rim subtype Elegante biconical copa

4.40 Ocotlán Red Rim subtype Elegante conical bowl (UA-1 bag 8127, interior and exterior)

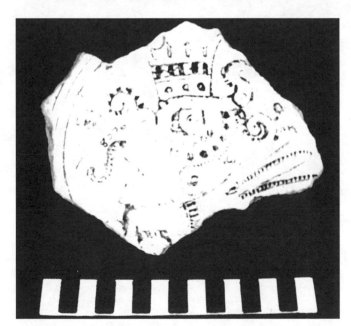

4.41 Ocotlán Red Rim subtype Cristina Matte plate bottom (UA-1 bag 8076)

4.42 Ocotlán Red Rim subtype Cristina Matte (UA-1 10927)

Ocotlán Red Rim was not found in the UA-79 excavations, but it has been identified at UA-9 (Turner N.D.) and at the Cholula Fonatur excavations (Caskey 1982a, 1982b). In Lind's (1994) ceramic classification, Ocotlán is divided into three types: "Marta Polychrome" includes the Sencillo and Banded subtypes, "Estela Polychrome" includes the Banded Elegante and Elegante subtypes, and "Cristina Polychrome" includes the Cristina subtype. These types are diagnostic of Lind's Aquiahuac Phase, corresponding to approximately 1000–1200 CE. Ocotlán Red Rim was the major polychrome type found in the San Pedro well deposit dated to the Middle Tlachihualtepetl phase (McCafferty 1996a).

Ocotlán Red Rim was the most abundant decorated type found at UA-1, making up 13.4% of the total assemblage (table 4.11). It appeared as only a trace in wells 1 and 2, but was prominent in both the trash midden (11%) and well 3 (8%). It was also found in high frequencies in structure 1 floor contact deposits (23%). In terms of the frequency distributions of the Ocotlán subtypes, the most significant difference is the relatively high frequency of the Cristina subtype in the midden deposit as compared to well 3, suggesting that this subtype may be useful for further refinement of the ceramic sequence.

The importance of Ocotlán Red Rim in structure 1, the trash midden, and well 3, in contrast to other features found at UA-1 and elsewhere in Cholula, indicates its potential value as a temporal diagnostic for the Middle and Late Tlachihualtepetl phases of the Early Postclassic. The fact that the Sencillo subtype has previously been lumped with types associated with Apolo Polychrome is one likely source for confusion over the Cholula Postclassic sequence, since in many contexts at UA-1 these two types do not co-occur.

The surface treatment of an orange slip over a white base coat is characteristic of Ocotlán as well as Apolo and Aquiahuac Polychromes and possibly indicates an evolving decorative tradition. Other decorative techniques, such as the Incised and Banded subtypes, are very similar to the corresponding subtypes of Cocoyotla Black on Natural, which may have been the precursor to the polychrome tradition. The decorative techniques found on the Elegante subtype are similar to Torre Polychrome. Finally, the Cristina subtype is similar to Cuaxiloa Matte Polychrome and is very similar to Isla de Sacrificios II White on Cream from the Gulf Coast (García Payón 1971). Ocotlán Red Rim was probably the earliest polychrome type at Cholula, and the stylistic diversity exhibited through its various subtypes related it to many of the other types from the Postclassic complex.

◆ SAN PEDRO POLISHED RED

San Pedro Polished Red is characterized by a well-burnished red slip that covers most if not all of the vessel. It may occur without additional decoration, but is usually either painted or incised, and sometimes both decorative techniques are used simultaneously.

Paste and firing effects. The paste is light brown to light reddish-brown. It is compact, and usually has a medium hardness. Dark firing clouds occasionally occur, particularly with the censer forms. Painted decoration (especially graphite paint) tends to have a negative appearance giving it a grayish color, probably as the result of firing either during production or through use as an incense burner.

Surface treatment. The surface is usually well-burnished to a lustrous finish. Most examples have a bright red (*guinda*) slip on the interior and/or exterior. The slip is occasionally applied only on the upper portions of the exterior vessel wall with the lower section retaining the natural brownish color. Censers, including sahumadores, are unfinished on the interior, and are usually a gray to dark gray/black color from repeated burning of incense.

Decoration. In addition to the highly burnished red slip, decorative techniques used include painted designs, fine-line incising, shallow grooves made before the slip was applied, modeling of the vessel walls, and carving through the vessel walls to form a lattice effect. Painted motifs are frequently outlined with incising. The quality of decoration is usually high and may include codex-style designs. This type occurs in a variety of decorative styles, resulting in at least nine subtypes: Sencillo, Incised, Graphite on Red, Incised Graphite on Red, Banded Graphite on Red, Graphite on Red Elegante, Incised Black on Red, Shallow Grooved, and Modeled.

The Sencillo subtype is undecorated other than the characteristic polished red slip (figure 4.43a). It appears most often as subhemispherical bowls and conical bowls.

The Incised subtype is identified by fine-line incising through the well-burnished red slip (figure 4.43b,c). Designs are in the form of curvilinear and rectilinear geometric motifs, but can also include codex-style representations. Incised decoration usually appears in panels around the exterior rim. Conical bowls are the most common vessel form.

The Graphite on Red subtype has painted decoration using a black graphite paint that produces a metallic

sheen. Painted decoration usually occurs on the rim. The most common vessel form was the tripod censer, often with carved lattice vessel walls. Similar censers have been found in the Mixteca Alta and at Tula, and they appear to have been a widespread ceremonial form.

The Incised Graphite on Red subtype is characterized by graphite painted decoration as well as incising, which is often used to outline the painted motifs (figure 4.43d,e). The predominant vessel form is the sahumador, a shallow, outleaned-wall bowl with a long handle. The exterior of the censer bowl is often decorated with alternating vertical panels of graphite paint and red slip, usually with the panels outlined with incising.

The subtype Graphite on Red Banded was represented by only a single example, making this a tentative assignment. It had graphite paint on the rim and also in horizontal bands below the rim in a style similar to the Banded subtypes of Cocoyotla Black on Natural and Ocotlán Red Rim.

The Graphite on Red Elegante subtype has graphite paint on the rim, but with elaborate painted decoration in a horizontal panel below the rim (figure 4.43f). Motifs are similar to those found on Ocotlán subtype Elegante, with codex-type representations painted in black, red, and orange over a white background. The most common vessel form found was the conical bowl.

The subtype Incised Black on Red is distinctive because it has black paint instead of the more common graphite paint. Decorative techniques include a panel of black paint below the rim, decorated with fine-line incising (figure 4.43g,h). Motifs are similar to the Incised subtypes of Cocoyotla Black on Natural and Ocotlán Red Rim.

The Shallow Grooved subtype has curvilinear motifs carved into the body as shallow grooves that were then covered by the red slip. Similar decorative techniques are seen on Fine Orange bowls and on small ollas found at the Altar of the Carved Skulls (Noguera 1937).

The Modeled subtype is characterized by an irregular vessel body, which was probably modeled in a naturalistic form such as a gourd shape. No other decoration is apparent. Only one example was found at UA-1, so the classification is tentative.

Vessel forms. San Pedro Polished Red occurs as both serving and ceremonial vessels, including conical bowls, subhemispherical bowls, sahumadores, and carved lattice censers.

Conical bowls measure 20 to 30 cm in diameter and 5

4.43 San Pedro Polished Red: *a,* Sencillo; *b,c,* Incised; *d,e,* Graphite on Red; *f,* Graphite on Red Banded; *g,h,* Incised Black on Red

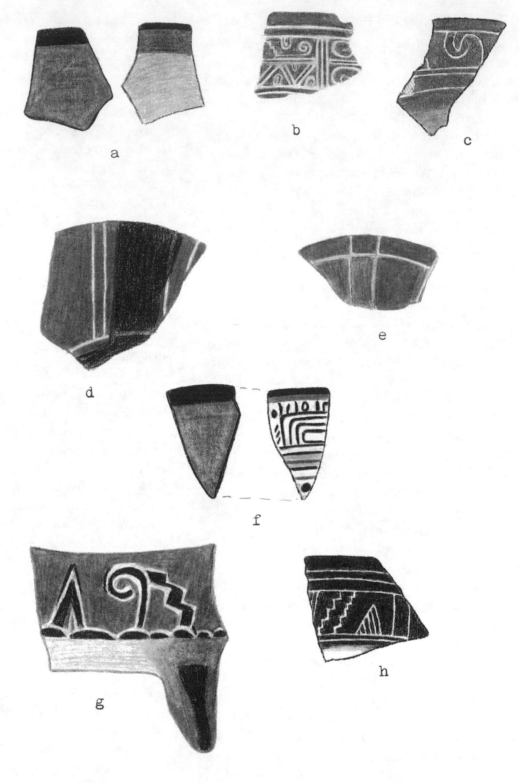

to 10 cm in vessel height. One large example of the sub-type Graphite on Red Elegante had an abraded interior base and lower walls, perhaps as the result of use as a spinning bowl or from whipping cacao.

Subhemispherical bowls are generally smaller and shallower than conical bowls.

Sahumadores are long-handled incense burners that can be compared to frying pans in form. The bowl section usually has a shallow outleaned wall and is unfinished and fire-blackened on the interior and decorated on the exterior. The handle is hollow and measures about 5 cm in diameter. Handles are occasionally decorated with zoomorphic representations on the end (Müller 1978).

Table 4.12 San Pedro Polished Red vessel-form frequencies

Vessel form	Well 1 n (%)	Well 2 n (%)	Midden n (%)	Well 3 n (%)	Totals n (%)
Sencillo subtype					
Plate/lid	...	2 (12)	...	...	13 (6)
Subhemispherical bowl	1 (50)	12 (75)	...	...	21 (9)
Hemispherical bowl	...	...	6 (9)	...	7 (3)
Conical bowl	1 (50)	...	6 (9)	...	37 (16)
SUBTOTALS	2 (100)	14 (88)	12 (18)	0	78 (34)
Incised subtype					
Hemispherical bowl	...	...	1 (1.5)	...	3 (1.3)
Conical bowl	...	...	6 (9)	1 (33)	22 (10)
SUBTOTALS	0	0	7 (11)	1 (33)	25 (11)
Graphite on Red subtype					
Subhemispherical bowl	...	...	...	...	4 (1.7)
Conical bowl	...	...	...	...	4 (1.7)
Cylindrical bowl	...	...	...	...	4 (1.7)
Carved lattice censer	...	...	7 (11)	...	19 (8)
SUBTOTALS	0	0	7 (11)	0	31 (13)
Incised Graphite on Red subtype					
Carved lattice censer	...	...	...	...	4 (1.7)
Sahumador	...	1 (6)	25 (38)	...	58 (25)
Florero	...	...	2 (3)	...	2 (0.9)
SUBTOTALS	0	1 (6)	27 (42)	0	64 (28)
Banded Graphite on Red subtype					
Hemispherical bowl	...	...	...	...	1 (0.4)
SUBTOTALS	0	0	0	0	1 (0.4)
Graphite on Red Elegante subtype					
Hemispherical bowl	...	...	5 (8)	...	5 (2)
Conical bowl	...	1 (6)	7 (11)	...	13 (6)
Hemispherical censer	...	...	...	2 (67)	2 (0.9)
SUBTOTALS	0	1 (6)	12 (18)	2 (67)	20 (9)
Incised Black on Red subtype					
Subhemispherical bowl	...	...	...	...	3 (1.3)
Hemispherical bowl	...	...	...	...	4 (1.7)
Conical bowl	...	...	...	...	2 (0.9)
SUBTOTALS	0	0	0	0	9 (4)
Shallow Grooved subtype					
Hemispherical bowl	...	...	...	...	2 (0.9)
SUBTOTALS	0	0	0	0	2 (0.9)
Modeled subtype					
(Unidentified form)	...	...	...	...	1 (0.4)
SUBTOTALS	0	0	0	0	1 (0.4)
TOTALS	2 (100) (0.6% of well 1)	16 (100) (4% of well 2)	65 (100) (2% of midden)	3 (100) (1.2% of well 3)	231 (100) (2% of total assemblage)

4.44 San Pedro Polished Red Incised Black on Red with feathered serpent motif (R-106 object)

Carved lattice censers resemble miniature ollas with a globular body, constricted orifice, and a low, flaring neck. The diagnostic attribute of this vessel form is the carving of the vessel walls, in which the clay was completely cut away to create a lattice-like pattern to allow the smoke from the incense to pass through the sides. The interior of the vessels is usually fire-blackened and unfinished. The exterior is well-burnished and often decorated. Complete examples of these censers usually have two short supports, and a longer third support that probably also served as a handle.

Discussion. San Pedro Polished Red is another enigmatic type, in part because it is relatively rare at UA-1, but also because various subtypes are found in contexts throughout the Postclassic sequence and into the Colonial/Historic period. In contrast to the relatively short periods of popularity exhibited by most polychrome types, San Pedro appears to have maintained a limited, probably specialized function over a long time. A second possibility, however, is that the San Pedro designation may include more than one type that shared basic similarities but have not as yet been distinguished because of the small sample sizes of individual collections.

Noguera (1954:113–115) described two variations of his *esgrafiada* type that correspond to the San Pedro classification. The first is most similar to the Incised Graphite on Red subtype in that the incising is used to outline the painted decoration; Noguera attributed this to Aztec influence. The second variation is more similar to the Incised and Incised Black on Red subtypes. Noguera described the quality of workmanship as among the finest in Cholula and identified several symbolic motifs, including serpents and birds similar to styles found in the codices. A sample found in an intrusive midden at the R-106 excavation (McCafferty, Suárez C., and Edelstein N.D.) featured an elaborate feathered serpent in black outlined with incising on a large olla (figure 4.44).

Polished red ceramics were identified by Müller as both "Azteca polícromo de Texcoco" and "*negro esgrafiado sobre rojo*" (1978:123–124). She interpreted both as intrusive pottery types.

Mountjoy and Peterson (1973: Fig. 23, k–l) identified this type as "Tlatoa Graphite on Red Engraved," which occurred in very low frequencies (2 to 3%) in their UA-70 trash deposits. As "Cuauhtli Red," it made up about 4% (*n*=139) of the midden assemblage at the UA-69 Faculty Housing Complex (Peterson 1972:200–201, Table 18). It was very rare (0.2%, *n*=7) in feature 10 at UA-79 (Barrientos 1980).

Regional similarities link San Pedro Polished Red with both the Valley of Mexico and the Gulf Coast. "Texcoco Black on Red" is a Middle and Late Postclassic diagnostic (Chadwick 1971a:252–254; Sanders, Parsons, and Santley 1979:467–473) that has often been used to infer Aztec influence in outlying regions (for example, Bernal 1949; MacNeish, Peterson, and Flannery 1970). Smith (1990:154) has recently criticized the use of "Guinda" ceramics as a means of identifying Aztec trade since the style is relatively abundant throughout the Central Highlands, probably as the result of local production. Polished red pottery with irridescent black paint, together with an incised variety, occurs on the Gulf Coast (García Payón 1971:542).

In summary, pottery similar to San Pedro Polished Red is found over a wide geographical area, and probably had a long temporal range. The UA-1 assemblage does little to clarify this situation since the type is found in very low frequencies in all Postclassic contexts (table 4.12). This is interpreted as an indication of the longevity of the type, perhaps because of ritual importance. The censer forms in particular seem to continue unchanged over a long time. Other subtypes, for example the Incised and Incised Black on Red subtypes, may have been restricted to the Early/Middle Postclassic.

◆ TORRE RED AND ORANGE ON WHITE POLYCHROME

Torre Polychrome is characterized by bold red and orange painted motifs on a white background. It is one of the most distinctive types in the Cholula ceramic complex, corresponding to Noguera's polícroma firme.

Paste and firing effects. The paste is a light brown to light reddish-brown color. It is compact and has a medium hardness. Firing anomalies are generally rare, but are most common on superhemispherical bowls that may have been heated during food preparation.

Surface treatment. Vessel surfaces are slipped and painted and are generally well-burnished. Decorated surfaces cover almost the entire vessel, and even the unpainted exterior base is often burnished. A characteristic of this type is the relatively good bond between the slip and vessel wall, the rationale behind Noguera's polícroma firme designation.

Two subtypes (Unburnished Matte and Polished Cream) are distinguished on the basis of variant surface treatment. The Unburnished Matte subtype is distinguished by a powdery surface finish similar to that of Cuaxiloa Matte Polychrome. The Polished Cream subtype was highly burnished to a luster, particularly on the whitish background. Both of these subtypes were rare at UA-1, and may represent either regional variation or perhaps idiosyncratic production.

Decoration. Painted decoration consists of red and orange painted motifs over a whitish background. The colors are bold and the application is solid, without streaks or brush strokes. Designs are usually in the form of alternating vertical bands, simple geometric motifs (especially xicalcoliuhquis), and concentric circles (figure 4.45). This type usually does not feature codex-style representations, with the exception of elaborately painted interior bases that are found more commonly on flared-rim, outleaned-wall dishes.

Depictions on the vessel bases are often very intricate and can resemble Codex Borgia-style representation (see Müller 1978:203, Fig. 2). Lind (1967, 1994) has illustrated a number of these with monkey (*ozomaztli*) heads. At UA-1, a set of four vessels were found in the trash midden with very similar depictions of a bald male figure with a large speech scroll coming from his mouth (figures 4.46, 4.47). A fifth vessel, from the floor of structure 1, featured an identical scene. In all five examples, and also on similar vessel bases from other collections, the image is bisected with the rear portion of the scene partially obscured by a reddish-orange wash.

A characteristic of the open vessel forms in which the major decoration occurs on the interior vessel walls is a standardized design configuration that occurs on the exterior rim (see figure 4.45d). Alternating groups of red and orange diagonal lines are painted over the whitish background. This pattern also occurs on Aquiahuac Polychromes and occasionally on Cuaxiloa Matte Polychrome.

The principal area for decoration on superhemispherical bowls was the exterior walls, although some examples also had horizontal painted lines on the interior (figure 4.48).

The Universidad subtype has a border around the rim decorated with a repeating eagle feather motif that resembles a white haystack with vertical hatching (figure 4.49). The consistent recurrence of the motif suggests a possible ritual function for these vessels, perhaps related to the eagle vessels used during heart sacrifices (Sahagún 1950–1982 [1547–1585], Book 9:64). This distinctive motif was identified by both Peterson (1972) and Caskey and Lind (N.D.) as the "Universidad Polychrome" type. The subtype is considered a variation of Torre Polychrome because of the use of white in the feathers, but among large examples found among the Proyecto Cholula collection, the pattern of four red circles on the interior surface was similar to traits found on Aquiahuac Sencillo.

Vessel forms. Torre Polychrome is predominantly a serving ware. The most common vessel forms include outleaned-wall dishes, conical bowls, superhemispherical bowls, and biconical copas. Outleaned-wall dishes feature horizontally flared rims so that they are relatively shallow measuring only about 2 to 4 cm in vessel height (figure 4.50). They measure about 15 to 30 cm in diameter. Conical bowls have either direct or flaring rims (figure 4.51). They measure 15 to 25 cm in diameter and 4 to 6 cm in vessel height. Conical bowls often have hollow, bulbous supports. Several examples have abraded interior surfaces, possibly the result of use as either spinning bowls or for whipping cacao. Superhemispherical bowls have rim diameters measuring between 15 to 20 cm and vessel height ranges from about 7 to 10 cm (figures 4.52, 4.53, 4.54).

Biconical copas are tall vessels that were probably used for consuming liquids, possibly pulque or chocolate. Copas consist of two elongated cones attached at their

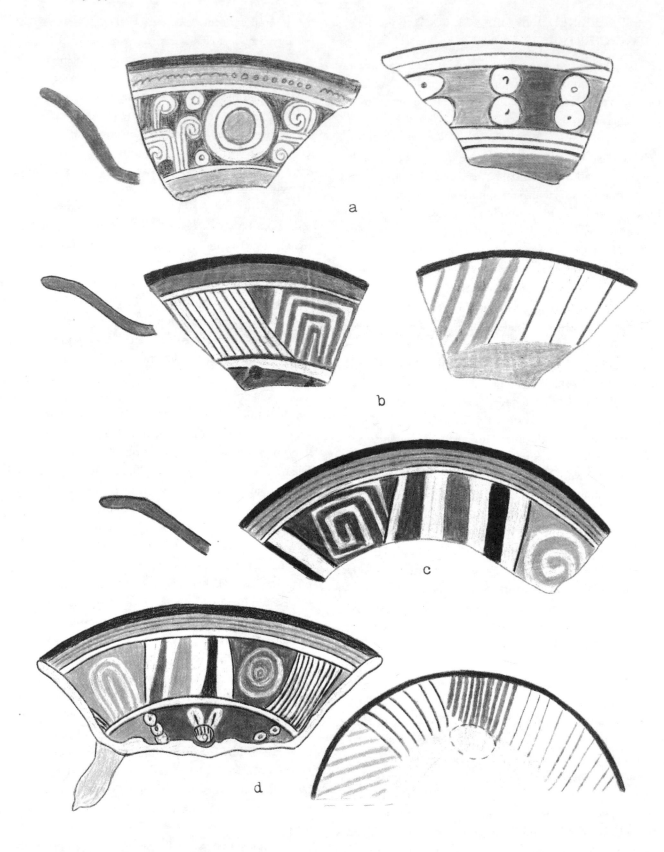

4.45 Torre Red and Orange on White Polychrome conical bowls and flared-rim outleaned-wall dishes (UA-1 9551)

4.46 Torre Red and Orange on White Polychrome flared-rim outleaned-wall dish with anthropomorphic "portrait" (UA-1 9551)

4.47 Torre Red and Orange on White Polychrome flared rim outleaned-wall dish with anthropomorphic "portrait" (UA-1 11872)

Table 4.13 Torre Red and Orange on White Polychrome vessel-form frequencies

Vessel form	Well 1 n (%)	Well 2 n (%)	Midden n (%)	Well 3 n (%)	Totals n (%)
Outleaned-wall dish	1 (50)	3 (75)	90 (39)	9 (33)	128 (35)
Subhemispherical bowl	...	...	10 (4)	...	12 (3)
Conical bowl	1 (50)	1 (25)	54 (24)	13 (48)	109 (30)
Superhemispherical bowl	...	...	26 (11)	4 (15)	36 (10)
Biconical copa	...	...	35 (15)	...	35 (10)
Sahumador	...	...	1 (0.4)	...	1 (0.3)
SUBTOTALS	2 (100)	4 (100)	216 (95)	26 (96)	321 (89)
Unburnished Matte subtype					
Subhemispherical bowl	...	...	2 (0.9)	...	2 (0.6)
Conical bowl	...	...	4 (1.8)	...	4 (1.1)
Superhemispherical bowl	...	...	6 (3)	...	6 (1.7)
SUBTOTALS	0	0	12 (5)	...	12 (3)
Polished Cream subtype					
Conical bowl	...	...	...	...	2 (0.6)
SUBTOTALS	0	0	0	0	2 (0.6)
Universidad subtype					
Outleaned wall dish	...	...	...	...	10 (3)
Conical bowl	...	...	...	1 (4)	5 (1.4)
Superhemispherical bowl	...	...	...	...	11 (3)
SUBTOTALS	0	0	0	1 (4)	26 (7)
TOTALS	2 (100)	4 (100)	228 (100)	27 (100)	361 (100)
	(0.6% of well 1)	(1.1% of well 2)	(8% of midden)	(11% of well 3)	(3.2% of total assemblage)

4.48 *a–e*, Torre Red and Orange on White Polychrome
superhemispherical bowls

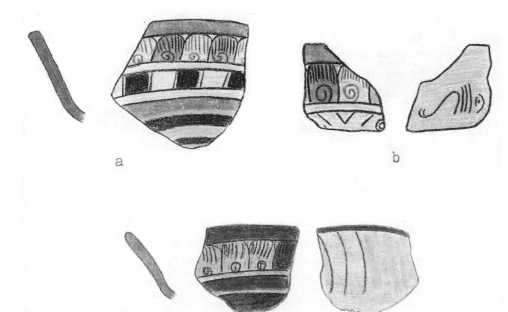

4.49 Torre Red and Orange on White Polychrome subtype Universidad conical bowls

a

b

c

4.50 Torre Red and Orange on White Polychrome flared-rim outleaned-wall dish fragments

4.51 Torre Red and Orange on White Polychrome conical bowl (UA-1 11856)

narrowest points to form an hourglass shape. The upper portion is finished on both the interior and exterior, while the base is only burnished on the exterior, with the interior left unfinished. The rim diameters vary between 7 and 15 cm. Vessel height is undetermined since no complete examples were found; whole pieces would probably measure between 20 and 40 cm in height.

Discussion. Torre Polychrome is one of the best known of the Cholula polychromes, but it is also one of the most problematic in terms of previous interpreta-

tions. Noguera (1954) classified it as polícroma firme and suggested that it was diagnostic of the Cholulteca III period. This periodization was based on its recovery in upper levels of the ceremonial center including the northeast platform of the Great Pyramid where the Altar of the Carved Skulls was found (Noguera 1954:226). Similar pottery was found in a large offering of vessels at the ex-Volador (now the Supreme Court building) in Mexico City (Noguera 1954:270–271; also Solís and Morales 1991). On that basis, Noguera interpreted firme as the polychrome

4.52 Torre Red and Orange on White Polychrome superhemispherical bowl (UA-1 11855)

4.53 Torre Red and Orange on White Polychrome superhemispherical bowl fragments

4.54 Torre Red and Orange on White Polychrome superhemispherical bowl (UA-1 bag 8539)

type that was contemporary with the Aztec empire at the time of the Conquest.

Wolfman (1968:8–9) correctly identified polícroma firme at UA-1 in association with structure 1. Using Noguera's ceramic sequence, he interpreted the structural compounds as dating to the Late Postclassic/Colonial period. On the basis of the UA-1 ceramic seriation discussed in chapter 5, this interpretation must now be revised.

Torre Polychrome was also a significant component of other excavations on the UDLA campus. "Torre Multichrome" made up 4% (n=165) of the pottery from the UA-69 Faculty Housing midden deposit, and "Universidad Multichrome" added another 2% (Peterson 1972:200–201, Table 18). Torre Polychrome was present as 15% (n=741) of another UA-69 midden that was located just south of the UA-1 compounds (Peterson 1972:200–201, Table 18). As "Cholula Polychrome D" it appeared as 10% (n=126) and 13% (n=451), respectively, in deposits 2 and 3 of UA-70 (Mountjoy and Peterson 1973:81, Table 8). It appeared in very low frequency (4%, n=168) in the Late Postclassic midden (F-10) from UA-79 (Barrientos 1980). Torre Polychrome was also an important component of the midden deposit found at the Transito site (R-106) in San Pedro Cholula (McCafferty, Suárez C., and Edelstein N.D.).

The relative frequencies of Torre Polychrome in different contexts at UA-1 display a similar pattern (table 4.13). In the late contexts represented by wells 1 and 2, it occurred as only a trace (0.8% and 1.1%, respectively). In the trash midden and well 3, however, it was more abundant (8% and 11%, respectively). It occurred as only a trace in association with structure 1, while it made up 5% of the structure 2 assemblage.

The UA-1 ceramic data, in combination with the other UDLA materials, indicate that Torre Polychrome was not as popular during the Late Postclassic or Colonial periods as it was earlier. It was probably near its peak popularity in the midden deposits from UA-69 and UA-70 and in the UA-1 midden and well 3. Precise dates for these features are not available, but they probably predate the 1250±95 CE radiocarbon date associated with the Faculty Housing deposit (Peterson 1972; Mountjoy and Peterson 1973:30). Torre Polychrome overlapped with Ocotlán Red Rim, particularly the Elegante subtypes, in the Late Tlachihualtepetl phase and on into the following Early Cholollan phase.

Table 4.14 Minor types and vessel-form frequencies: Colonial/Historical period

	Well 1 n (%)	Well 2 n (%)	Midden n (%)	Well 3 n (%)	Totals n (%)
COLONIAL SALT GLAZE	0	0	1 (0.03)	0	2 (0.018)
Conical bowl	0	0	1 (100)**	0	2 (100)**
POBLANO GLAZE WARE	0	67 (18)	0	0	106 (0.9)
White Glaze subtype	0	0	0	0	7 (7)*
Outleaned-wall dish	0	0	0	0	1 (14)**
Conical bowl	0	0	0	0	6 (86)**
Brown Glaze subtype	0	62 (93)*	0	0	77 (73)*
Comal	0	1 (1.6)**	0	0	1 (1.3)**
Subhemispherical bowl	0	25 (40)**	0	0	27 (35)**
Conical bowl	0	33 (53)**	0	0	40 (52)**
Wide-mouth olla	0	2 (3)**	0	0	3 (4)**
Conical cazuela	0	1 (1.6)**	0	0	6 (8)**
Green Glaze subtype	0	2 (3)*	0	0	16 (15)*
Conical bowl	0	0	0	0	7 (44)**
Wide-mouth olla	0	1 (50)**	0	0	3 (19)**
Conical cazuela	0	1 (50)**	0	0	6 (38)**
Yellow and Black/White subtype	0	3 (4)*	0	0	6 (06)*
Conical bowl	0	3 (100)**	0	0	6 (100)**
POBLANO WHITE WARE	0	8 (2)	0	0	14 (0.12)
Sencillo subtype	0	0	0	0	2 (14)*
Outleaned wall dish	0	0	0	0	1 (50)**
Conical bowl	0	0	0	0	1 (50)**
Green and Black/White subtype	0	7 (88)*	0	0	7 (50)*
Outleaned-wall dish	0	3 (43)**	0	0	3 (43)**
Subhemispherical bowl	0	3 (43)**	0	0	3 (43)**
Conical bowl	0	1 (14)**	0	0	1 (14)**
Blue and Black/White subtype	0	1 (12)*	0	0	5 (36)*
Outleaned-wall dish	0	1 (100)**	0	0	2 (40)**
Conical bowl	0	0	0	0	3 (60)**
PUEBLA BLUE/WHITE MAYOLICA	0	0	0	0	4 (0.04)
Outleaned-wall dish	0	0	0	0	1 (25)**
Conical bowl	0	0	0	0	3 (75)**
TOTALS	0	75	1	0	126

Note: Type frequencies are expressed as the proportion of the assemblage; subtype frequency (*) relates to the proportion of the corresponding type; and vessel-form frequency (**) relates to the proportion of the subtype.

MINOR TYPES

In addition to the major types described above, twenty-three Minor types were identified that either appeared in extremely low frequencies (each representing less than 2% of the total assemblage) or else are known from other Cholula ceramic assemblages from other time periods. Minor types were grouped into five categories based on temporal association: Colonial/Historic period, Late Postclassic period, Early Postclassic period, Classic period, and Preclassic period. These categories are discussed below, with brief descriptions of each of the component Minor types.

COLONIAL/HISTORIC PERIOD

Four Minor types were identified relating to the Colonial/Historic period (1520–present): Colonial Salt Glaze, Poblano Glaze Ware, Poblano White Ware, and Puebla Blue on White Mayolica. Since ceramic glazes were not used in the pre-Columbian era, the presence of glaze wares is an unambiguous indicator of post-Conquest site utilization.

Historical archaeology is a relatively new field of in-

Table 4.15 Minor Late Postclassic type and vessel-form frequencies

	Well 1 n (%)	Well 2 n (%)	Midden n (%)	Well 3 n (%)	Totals n (%)
AZTEC III BLACK/ORANGE	0	0	0	0	1 (0.009)
Superhemispherical bowl	0	0	0	0	1 (100)**
COXCATLAN GRAY	1 (0.3)	0	0	0	1 (0.009)
Conical bowl	1 (100)**	0	0	0	1 (100)**
MIXTECA BAJA BLACK/ORANGE	0	0	1 (0.03)	0	4 (0.04)
Hemispherical bowl	0	0	1 (100)**	0	2 (50)**
Superhemispherical bowl	0	0	0	0	2 (50)**
TECALI BLACK/ORANGE	6 (1.7)	0	0	0	15 (0.1)
Subhemispherical bowl	1 (17)**	0	0	0	3 (20)**
Conical bowl	0	0	0	0	1 (7)**
Superhemispherical bowl	5 (83)**	0	0	0	11 (73)**
TOTALS	7/ (2% of well 1)	0	1/ (0.03% of trash midden)	0	21/ (0.2% of total assemblage)

Note: Type frequencies are expressed as the proportion of the assemblage; subtype frequency (*) relates to the proportion of the corresponding type; and vessel-form frequency (**) relates to the proportion of the subtype.

Table 4.16 Minor Early Postclassic type and vessel-form frequencies

	Well 1 (n/%)	Well 2 (n/%)	Midden (n/%)	Well 3 (n/%)	Totals (n/%)
ISLA DE SACRIFICIOS WHITE/CREAM	0	0	1 (0.03)	0	4 (0.04)
Sencillo subtype	0	0	1 (100)*	0	3 (75)*
Subhemispherical bowl	0	0	0	0	2 (67)**
Hemispherical bowl	0	0	1 (100)**	0	1 (33)**
Incised subtype	0	0	0	0	1 (25)*
Subhemispherical bowl	0	0	0	0	1 (100)**
GULF COAST FINE ORANGE	0	0	1 (0.03)	0	1 (0.009)
Incised subtype	0	0	1 (100)*	0	1 (100)*
Subhemispherical bowl	0	0	1 (100)**	0	1 (100)**
IMITATION FINE ORANGE	0	0	3 (0.1)	0	3 (0.03)
Incised subtype	0	0	3 (100)*	0	3 (100)*
Conical bowl	0	0	1 (33)**	0	1 (33)**
Long neck olla	0	0	2 (67)**	0	2 (67)**
COMAC BUFF	0	0	6 (0.2)	1 (0.4)	13 (0.1)
Incised subtype	0	0	2 (33)*	0	2 (15)*
Hemispherical bowl	0	0	2 (100)**	0	2 (100)**
Red Rim subtype	0	0	4 (67)*	1 (100)*	11 (85)*
Outleaned wall bowl	0	0	0	1 (100)**	5 (45)**
Subhemispherical bowl	0	0	4 (100)**	0	4 (36)**
Hemispherical bowl	0	0	0	0	2 (18)**
TOTALS	0	0	11/ (0.4% of midden)	1/ (0.4% of well 3)	21/ (0.2% of total assemblage)

Note: Type frequencies are expressed as the proportion of the assemblage; subtype frequency (*) relates to the proportion of the corresponding type; and vessel-form frequency (**) relates to the proportion of the subtype.

vestigation in Mexico and with a few notable exceptions, post-Conquest ceramics are poorly documented from the Cholula region (but see Lister and Lister 1982; Müller 1981). The types described in this section represent provisional categories and should be developed further when more comprehensive collections are available.

At UA-1, Colonial/Historic period ceramics made up 1.1% of the total assemblage (table 4.14). The greatest concentration occurred in well 2, where more than half of all glazed pottery was recovered. No Colonial/Historic ceramics were found in either well 1 or well 3, and only one piece was recovered from the trash midden (and that was in level 2 where it probably related to the plow-zone level).

Colonial Salt Glaze is characterized by a light gray surface coated with a clear salt glaze, identified by its pockmarked surface (similar in texture to the skin of an orange). This type was very rare at UA-1, making up only .02% of the total assemblage.

Poblano Glaze Ware is characterized by a light brown to light reddish-brown paste, similar to the local paste used in pre-Columbian pottery. Four subtypes were identified on the basis of different colored glazes and painted decoration: White Glaze, Brown Glaze, Green Glaze, and Yellow and Black on White. This type usually occurs in serving wares, but some large utilitarian vessels were also found. Poblano Glaze Ware made up 18% of the well 2 assemblage, but less than 1% of the total assemblage.

Poblano White Ware is characterized by a white earthenware paste that is covered with a white glazed slip. Staffordshire White Ware from England is an important diagnostic of the nineteenth and twentieth centuries, and Mexico developed an imitation of this type in the mid-nineteenth century. One notable motif found on Mexican transfer-print vessels of this type features the Great Pyramid of Cholula. Based on the small sample and lack of makers' marks, it was impossible to accurately identify the sources of the UA-1 examples. Three subtypes were identified: Sencillo, Green and Black on White, and Blue and Black on White. Poblano White Ware always occurred in serving wares. It made up 2% of the well 2 assemblage, but only 0.1% of the total assemblage.

Puebla Blue on White Mayolica has a well-fired white paste, with a thick white glazed slip and blue painted decoration. A similar type ("Puebla azul/blanco") is described by Müller (1981:26) dating to her "Late Colonial period" (1700–1850). The type is also similar to traditional Talavera pottery still produced in Puebla. Remains of this type were very rare at UA-1 (.03% of the total assemblage).

LATE POSTCLASSIC PERIOD

Four minor types were identified from the Late Postclassic period (1200–1520 CE): Aztec III Black on Orange, Coxcatlán Gray, Mixteca Baja Black on Orange, and Tecali Black on Orange. These types are all foreign to the Cholula area and, therefore, their presence in the UA-1 assemblage indicates regional interaction. Identification of the types is the result of comparisons with other ceramic reports and personal observations.

Minor Late Postclassic types were very rare in the UA-1 assemblage as a whole (0.2% of the total), with the highest concentration found in well 1 where they made up 2% of the assemblage (table 4.15).

Aztec III Black on Orange is identified on the basis of its light orange slip color, painted with black fine-line decoration. These distinctive vessels have been described in numerous sources (Séjourné 1970, 1983; Vega Sosa 1975; Whalen and Parsons 1982; Evans 1988) and provide a useful artifact class for identifying and quantifying exchange with the Aztec empire (Smith 1990). In my experience working with Cholula ceramics from both surface and excavated contexts, this type is extremely rare at Cholula. Only one example of Aztec III Black on Orange was recovered at UA-1, representing 0.009% of the total assemblage.

Coxcatlán Gray is characterized by its polished surface and dark gray/black slip (MacNeish, Peterson, and Flannery 1970:189–196). It originated in the Tehuacán Valley, where it was most common in the Late Venta Salada phase. A related type, Miguelito Hard Fine Gray, was made in the Mixteca Alta during the Natividad phase (Spores 1972; Byland 1980; Lind 1987). Coxcatlán Gray occurs in serving wares, and occasionally includes stamp-bottom decoration. A single sherd of this type was found in the UA-1 assemblage (0.009%), in well 1.

Mixteca Baja Black on Orange is identified by a high proportion of mica temper in the paste. The type has an orange paste and surface color, with dark brown/black painted decoration (Gorenstein 1973). It occurs in serving wares, including superhemispherical bowls with a slightly everted rim. Four examples were found at UA-1

Table 4.17 Minor Classic period type and vessel-form frequencies

	Well 1 n (%)	Well 2 n (%)	Midden n (%)	Well 3 n (%)	Totals n (%)
TEOTIHUACAN THIN ORANGE	0	0	4 (0.1)	0	18 (0.2)
Subhemispherical bowl	0	0	3 (75)**	0	12 (86)**
Conical bowl	0	0	1 (25)**	0	1 (7)**
Superhemispherical bowl	0	0	0	0	1 (7)**
IMITATION THIN ORANGE	1 (0.3)	0	2 (0.07)	0	8 (0.07)
Thin Tan subtype	1 (100)*	0	0	0	4 (50)*
Subhemispherical bowl	1 (100)**	0	0	0	2 (33)**
Micaceous Orange subtype	0	0	2 (100)*	0	4 (50)*
Subhemispherical bowl	0	0	0	0	1 (25)**
Hemispherical bowl	0	0	0	0	1 (25)**
Conical bowl	0	0	2 (100)**	0	2 (50)**
TECOLA POLISHED	1 (0.3)	0	11 (0.4)	0	35 (0.3)
Sencillo subtype	1 (100)*	0	11 (100)*	0	32 (91)*
Outleaned wall dish	0	0	1 (9)**	0	1 (5)**
Subhemispherical bowl	1 (100)**	0	0	0	4 (19)**
Conical bowl	0	0	8 (73)**	0	13 (62)**
Superhemispherical bowl	0	0	2 (18)**	0	2 (10)**
Groove Incised subtype	0	0	0	0	3 (09)*
LOS TETELES GRAY/BROWN	0	0	3 (0.1)	0	13 (0.1)
Sencillo subtype	0	0	3 (100)*	0	11 (85)*
Plate/lid	0	0	1 (33)**	0	1 (33)**
Comal	0	0	2 (67)**	0	2 (67)**
Pinched Exterior	0	0	0	0	2 (15)*
MANZANILLA ORANGE	0	0	0	0	13 (0.1)
TOTALS	2 (0.6% of well 1)	0	20 (0.7% of trash midden)	0	87 (0.8% of total assemblage)

Note: Type frequencies are expressed as the proportion of the assemblage; subtype frequency (*) relates to the proportion of the corresponding type; and vessel-form frequency (**) relates to the proportion of the subtype.

Table 4.18 Minor Preclassic period type and vessel-form frequencies

	Well 1 n (%)	Well 2 n (%)	Midden n (%)	Well 3 n (%)	Totals n (%)
CHOLULA CREAM	1 (0.3)	0	3 (0.1)	0	12 (0.1)
Sencillo subtype	1 (100)*	0	3 (100)*	0	9 (75)*
Subhemispherical bowl	1 (100)**	0	0	0	3 (33)**
Superhemispherical bowl	0	0	0	0	2 (22)**
Composite silhouette bowl	0	0	3 (100)**	0	4 (44)**
Incised subtype	0	0	0	0	3 (25)*
Outleaned-wall bowl	0	0	0	0	1 (33)**
Composite silhouette bowl	0	0	0	0	2 (67)**
TOTIMEHUACAN BROWN	0	0	1 (0.03)	0	2 (0.02)
Incised subtype	0	0	1 (100)*	0	1 (50)*
Superhemispherical bowl	0	0	1 (100)**	0	1 (100)**
Red on Brown subtype	0	0	0	0	1 (50)*
Conical cazuela	0	0	0	0	1 (100)**
TOTALS	1 (0.3% of well 1)	0	4 (0.1% of trash midden)	0	14 (0.1 of total assemblage)

Note: Type frequencies are expressed as the proportion of the assemblage; subtype frequency (*) relates to the proportion of the corresponding type; and vessel-form frequency (**) relates to the proportion of the subtype.

(0.04% of the total assemblage), including one piece from the trash midden.

Tecali Black on Orange is characterized by fine gray paste that is fired until the pottery is quite brittle. Examples of this type are common on Late Postclassic sites southeast of Cholula, such as Tecali and Tepeaca. Tecali Black on Orange made up 0.1% of the UA-1 assemblage, including a partially reconstructable superhemispherical bowl from well 1.

EARLY POSTCLASSIC PERIOD

Four minor types were identified from the Early Post-classic period (700–1200 CE): Isla de Sacrificios White on Cream, Gulf Coast Fine Orange, Imitation Fine Orange, and Comac Buff. Early Postclassic types occurred as 0.2% of the total assemblage, but more than half of the examples were recovered from the trash midden (table 4.16).

Isla de Sacrificios White on Cream is characterized by very fine grain, cream color paste. It features painted decoration, usually in white, that includes curvilinear and codex-style motifs (García Payón 1971). Examples of this type were recovered in Cholula by Noguera, and also in recent excavations by the Centro Regional de Puebla where it was found in association with Ocotlán Red Rim and Cocoyotla Black on Natural (Cano 1993). A few sherds were also found at the Patio of the Carved Skulls in an Epiclassic context (McCafferty and Suárez C. 1995). Noguera (1954:208–210) suggested that although it originally came from the Gulf Coast, similarities with Cholula polychromes indicated that decorative motifs were adopted into the local ceramic tradition. I have already pointed out similarities between Isla de Sacrificios White on Cream with both Cuaxiloa Matte Polychrome and Ocotlán subtype Cristina Matte. Although these imitations were found in abundance at UA-1, only four examples (0.03%) of the imported type were recovered.

Gulf Coast Fine Orange is another import from the Gulf Coast region (Smith 1958). It is identified by a very fine grain paste and lustrous orange surface. In the only example recovered at UA-1 (from the trash midden), the sherd was decorated with groove incising.

Imitation Fine Orange is very similar to Gulf Coast Fine Orange in outer appearance, but is made with local paste that can be easily distinguished from the fine gray of the imported type. The surface treatment, however, is virtually identical. Three examples were found in the UA-1 assemblage, all from the trash midden.

Comac Buff is usually identifiable by a wide red band on the rim of a light-brown colored vessel. The red paint is usually made from specular hematite that glistens in the light. Garcia Cook (in Nagao 1989:86, n.7) described red-on-buff pottery as diagnostic of the Olmeca-Xicallanca occupation of the Puebla/Tlaxcala area in the Epiclassic period. It is possible, therefore, that this represents a local type that was more popular during an earlier period, with some vessels possibly still in use due to curation. Very few examples were found at the Patio of the Carved Skulls; however, so the periodization remains in question (McCafferty 1996a). This was the most numerous of the Minor Early Postclassic period types, comprising 0.1% of the total assemblage. Nearly half of the examples were recovered from the trash midden deposit.

CLASSIC PERIOD

Five minor types are associated with the Classic period (200–700 CE): Teotihuacan Thin Orange, Imitation Thin Orange, Tecola Polished, Los Teteles Gray/Brown, and Manzanilla Orange. These types account for 0.8% of the total UA-1 assemblage (table 4.17). In addition, Tepontla Burnished Gray/Brown (which occurred as more than 2% of the total assemblage) is primarily a Classic period type that apparently continued in use into the Early Postclassic period. Another type, Acozoc Tan/Orange, was not distinguished at UA-1 but has been identified as an important component of the Classic ceramic complex at both the Transito site (R-106) and the Patio of the Carved Skulls (McCafferty 1996a) and is defined here.

The greatest concentration of minor Classic period types occurred in bag 8153 from unit S8/E1 in level III of the trash midden area. This collection unit is discussed in chapter 5 and is interpreted as a discrete lens of Classic period refuse. Even discounting this anomalous deposit, however, the midden contained twenty Classic period sherds, for 0.7% of its total. A Terminal Formative/Classic period platform (structure 3) was located at the southern end of the UA-1 project area; two subsequent field seasons (UA-69 and UA-70) were devoted to further exploration of the area (Mountjoy and Peterson 1973). Materials from the Transito site (R-106) provide further details on the Classic period ceramic complex (McCafferty, Suárez C., and Edelstein N.D.).

Teotihuacan Thin Orange is one of the most famous pottery types in Mesoamerica, and has often been used

Table 4.19 Unidentified type frequencies

	Well 1 N (%)	Well 2 N (%)	Midden N (%)	Well 3 N (%)	Totals N (%)
"A" Stucco polychrome	0	0	1 (0.03)	0	1 (0.009)
"B" Red on cream	0	0	4 (0.1)	0	4 (0.04)
"C" Red on buff	0	0	1 (0.03)	0	1 (0.009)
"D" Incised gray	0	0	2 (0.07)	0	2 (0.02)
"E" Black on cream	0	0	2 (0.07)	0	2 (0.02)
"F" Black on orange	0	0	1 (0.03)	0	1 (0.009)
"G" Shallow-grooved gray	0	0	1 (0.03)	0	1 (0.009)
"H" Coarse gray	1 (0.2)	0	0	0	1 (0.009)
"I" Sandy gray	0	0	0	0	2 (0.02)
"J" Chalky gray incised	0	0	0	0	1 (0.009)
"K" Red on brown matte polychrome	0	0	0	0	1 (0.009)
"L" Reddish brown burnished	0	0	0	0	1 (0.009)
"M" Red and brown on tan	0	0	0	0	1 (0.009)
"N" Metallic gray grooved	0	0	0	0	1 (0.009)
"O" Red on orange	0	0	0	0	1 (0.009)
"P" Dark gray incised	0	0	0	0	1 (0.009)
"Q" Polished reddish brown	0	0	0	0	1 (0.009)
"R" Painted stucco	0	0	0	0	1 (0.009)
"S" Dark gray with punctates	0	0	0	0	1 (0.009)
TOTALS	1 (0.3% of well 1)	0	12 (0.4% of trash midden)	0	25 (0.2% of total assemblage)

to interpret regional interaction with the Teotihuacan empire (Rattray 1981; Kolb 1986). Recent studies indicate that the type did not originate at the Valley of Mexico center, but rather was imported in bulk from southern Puebla (Rattray 1990). The type is identified by its bright orange color, and especially by white calcite inclusions in the paste. It occurs in serving wares, usually with exceptionally thin vessel walls. Teotihuacan Thin Orange appeared as 0.2% of the UA-1 assemblage, with four pieces (0.1%) found in the trash midden deposit. At the Transito site, Teotihuacan Thin Orange comprised about 9% of the subfloor assemblage (McCafferty 1996a), but none was found at the Patio of the Carved Skulls, suggesting that Thin Orange was no longer part of the ceramic complex because of either temporal or social factors.

Imitation Thin Orange is similar to the type just described, but with distinctive differences in surface color and/or paste composition. Two subtypes were identified: Thin Tan has the diagnostic white inclusions but is tan to light gray/brown in color; Micaceous Orange has mica temper in place of calcite. Vessel forms are similar to those of Teotihuacan Thin Orange, although Micaceous Orange vessels are generally more crudely formed.

Tecola Polished is a locally produced type that was probably most popular during the Early Classic period. It is identified by a highly polished surface finish, which contrasts with the stick-burnished finish on Tepontla Burnished. In other respects, such as color and vessel form, the two types are very similar. Tecola Polished usually occurs in dark brown/black, but it is also found in light brown, gray/brown, and even red. A subtype was identified that had groove-incised decoration. After Tepontla Burnished, this was the most common of the Classic period types found at UA-1, comprising 0.3% of the total assemblage. It made up 0.4% of the trash midden deposit. Tecola Polished was not identified in the Middle Classic R-106 assemblage (McCafferty 1996a).

Los Teteles Gray/Brown is a poorly defined type that was found almost exclusively in bag 8153. It is characterized by a gray/brown color and occurs as large, coarsely made utilitarian vessels. The exterior of these vessels is often unfinished, reminiscent of the diagnostic G-35 type from the Valley of Oaxaca (Caso, Bernal, and Acosta 1967). Similar pottery was found at the Classic period site of Los Teteles, north of the city of Puebla, which William Reliford (1983) interpreted as including ethnic Zapotecs from Oaxaca.

Manzanilla Orange is another poorly defined type that was only recovered in bag 8153. It is identified by a bright orange slip over light brown paste. This type occurs in both serving and utilitarian vessels, including large outleaned-wall bowls. Similar pottery was found at the type site Manzanilla, located to the north of the city of Puebla and adjacent to Los Teteles, and also in Terminal Formative deposits at Amalucan.

A final Classic period type, Acozoc Tan/Orange, was not recognized during the UA-1 analysis, but has been identified as a major component of the Classic period ceramic complex at both the Transito site and the Patio of the Carved Skulls (McCafferty 1996a). It is defined by an unslipped surface that is tannish-orange in color, and smooth but not burnished. It occurs in thick-walled utilitarian vessels such as ollas and casuelas. Acozoc Tan/Orange was the major utilitarian ware of the Classic period and appeared in high frequency in both of these assemblages.

PRECLASSIC PERIOD

Two minor types were identified at UA-1 from the Preclassic period (1000 BCE–200 CE): Cholula Cream and Totimehuacan Brown. Two additional types, Amalucan Polished Black and Coapa Orange, were also important components of the Formative ceramic complex. These types have been found in previous investigations in Cholula and are described in greater detail in relation to a Middle Preclassic trash deposit from San Andrés Cholula (McCafferty 1984, 1996a). Preclassic ceramics were rare at UA-1, accounting for only 0.1% of the assemblage (table 4.18). More extensive Preclassic deposits have been found on the UDLA campus (Mountjoy and Peterson 1973; Baravalle and Wheaton 1974) and in scattered locations around San Andrés Cholula (Noguera 1956; McCafferty 1984; Caskey 1988).

Cholula Cream is the local variety of a kaolin-slipped ceramic type found throughout Mesoamerica during the Middle Formative period. This general style has been associated with Olmecoid traits in numerous areas of the central highlands, including Oaxaca, Tehuacán, Morelos, and the Valley of Mexico (Flannery 1968; MacNeish, Peterson, and Flannery 1970; Grove 1974; Niederberger 1976). Cholula Cream is identified by a light brown paste, covered with a thick cream-colored kaolin slip. It usually occurs in thick-wall serving vessels, especially composite silhouette forms. Decorative techniques include incising, excising, and the use of red paint; often, combinations of these techniques are employed. At UA-1, Cholula Cream occurred as 0.1% of the total assemblage.

Totimehuacan Brown is another local product, identified by a light to medium brown paste and burnished brown surface. It is often decorated with incising and/or red paint. Common vessel classes include both utilitarian and serving vessels. Only two examples were recovered at UA-1, representing 0.02% of the total assemblage.

Amalucan Polished Black was not identified at UA-1 but was found in both the San Andrés and Villas Arqueológicas trash deposits (McCafferty 1996a). It often occurs in serving wares with composite silhouette walls. Incised decoration in simple geometric patterns is characteristic.

Coapa Orange is also defined based on assemblages other than UA-1 (McCafferty 1996a). It has a moderately well-burnished exterior surface and occurs as the major utilitarian ware of the Middle Formative period.

UNIDENTIFIED TYPES

A few sherds were recovered that were sufficiently distinctive as to be classified, yet could not be assigned to either the Major or Minor types. These usually represented unique sets of attributes, identifiable as discrete types, but the identification was unknown. They probably relate to the same spatial and/or temporal differences that account for the low frequency of the Minor types. Nineteen of these Unidentified types were classified (table 4.19), and each was given a brief descriptive name.

5 Ceramic Analysis

A contextual analysis of the UA-1 ceramics provides important insights into site chronology and functional patterns. In this chapter, ceramic data from different depositional contexts are analyzed. In the first section, relative frequencies of types and subtypes are used to construct a ceramic sequence for Postclassic Cholula and to group contemporaneous assemblages for interpretations of the occupational context of the site. The second section focuses on vessel form, as well as the larger groupings of vessel type and vessel class to reconstruct the ceramic "tool kits" represented by the different contexts.

SERIATION ANALYSIS OF UA-1 CERAMICS

The refinement of the Postclassic Cholula ceramic sequence was one of the principal objectives of the UA-1 ceramic analysis. Clear differences emerge from a seriation analysis of relative ceramic frequencies from the various depositional contexts and lead to the definition of five distinct ceramic complexes. These correspond to the Colonial/Historical period, the Early and Late Cholollan phases (1200–1400 CE and 1400–1520 CE, respectively), and the Middle and Late Tlachihualtepetl phases (900–1050 CE and 1050–1200 CE, respectively).

The seriation analysis was multifaceted because of the number of depositional contexts present. This section is divided into six parts:

- stratigraphic analysis of the trash midden and well 3;
- detailed analysis of the four primary depositional contexts (that is, the trash midden and wells 1, 2, and 3);
- analysis of stratigraphic contexts associated with structure 1;

- analysis of additional features associated with structure 1;
- analysis of stratigraphic contexts associated with structure 2; and
- the stratigraphic analysis of selected units not significantly affected by construction disturbance.

Finally, these data on ceramic type frequencies are seriated to construct a sequence of the UA-1 features, and consequently, a revised ceramic chronology for Postclassic Cholula.

STRATIFIED CERAMICS FROM THE TRASH MIDDEN AND WELL 3

Layered deposits of ash and organic soils located in units S7/E1, S7/W1, S8/E1, and S8/W1 (and intervening balks) provided the richest source of material culture at the UA-1 excavation. In addition to the many other artifact classes recovered, a total of 4095 rim sherds were analyzed from these units. Unfortunately, the deposit was not excavated as a discrete feature, so there was the potential for mixing because of arbitrary unit boundaries, particularly in the uppermost levels. This section considers the evidence for homogeneity through a detailed analysis of ceramic frequencies from distinct stratigraphic levels of the feature.

The units were excavated in arbitrary 25-cm levels. The balks, on the other hand, were usually excavated by natural levels. Using information recorded on the pit forms and in the original field notes, all collection units were clustered into five "strata" (I, II, III, IV, and V), with each representing a 25-cm level. Stratum I was not analyzed because it consisted of mixed plow zone. Stratum II was analyzed in this area because the field records indicated that the midden feature began in this level. This was the most contaminated of the analyzed strata since it also included the bottom of the plow zone.

One collection unit in the midden area stood out because it contained an unusually high concentration of Classic-period ceramics. Bag 8153, from S8/E1 level III, had a total of 186 identifiable rim sherds. Classic-period types included Tecola Polished ($n= 14$, 8%), Los Teteles Gray/Brown ($n=10$, 5%), Manzanilla Orange ($n=13$, 7%), Teotihuacan Thin Orange ($n=4$, 2%), and Imitation Thin Orange ($n=2$, 1%). In addition, Tepontla Burnished accounted for 15% of the assemblage, far more than its usual frequency in Postclassic contexts. Notably, these vessel fragments had a generally high degree-of-arc value, indicating that they were relatively large sherds and therefore probably from a primary depositional context of secondary refuse. The field notes from this level did not mention any anomalous features other than ash lenses, but it appears that this collection unit intersected a Classic-period trash lens. For the purpose of further analysis of the Postclassic midden deposit, these six types were eliminated from subsequent analyses of the bag 8153 collection unit.

The midden deposit ended at a depth of 125 cm below the ground surface. Three shallow borrow pits were found dug into sterile soil, and in the bottom of unit S7/E1 an oval stain indicated the presence of well 3. Well 3 was filled with dirt and cultural remains to a depth of 277 cm below ground surface. The stratigraphic relationship between the midden and well is problematic because although the initial report describes the well deposit as sealed beneath the midden deposit (Wolfman 1968), the original site map indicates that it was located to the side.

The ceramic frequencies from the trash midden and well 3 are presented in table 5.1. The most significant observation is the relative scarcity of Apolo, Aquiahuac, and Coapan Polychromes. These never occur as more than a trace, and are most common in stratum II, the most likely stratum to contain mixed deposits. This is consistent with the absence below stratum II of Minor types from either the Colonial/Historic period or Late Postclassic period.

A comparison of type frequencies from the different stratigraphic levels reveals that Torre and Cuaxiloa Polychromes were slightly more abundant in stratum II

than in the lower strata, while Ocotlán Red Rim, Tepontla Burnished, and Xicalli Plain were slightly less common in stratum II. This contrast also appeared in the relative frequencies of subtypes of Cocoyotla Black on Natural and Ocotlán Red Rim. Cocoyotla subtype Banded was predominant in stratum II, but less common in lower strata, while subtypes Sencillo and Chalco Black on Orange were more common in the deeper strata. Ocotlán subtypes Elegante and Cristina Matte were slightly more common in stratum II, while subtype Sencillo was more common in the lower strata.

These differences might reflect temporal change or could be the result of contamination with later materials from the plow zone. The relative frequencies of other types (particularly utilitarian wares) remained fairly consistent throughout the stratigraphic levels.

Curiously, type frequencies in well 3 were most similar to those of stratum II, even though the well deposit was stratigraphically beneath stratum V. One possible explanation is that the observed differences do not exceed the normal range of variation of ceramic frequencies, therefore reflecting behavioral rather than temporal differences. An alternative interpretation, however, is that the well deposit was contemporary with the upper stratum and intruded into the the lower strata. If the well passed through the midden and was not recognized until it was outlined in the natural layer beneath stratum V, it would have passed through unit S7/E1; by extension the ceramic frequencies of deposits from unit S7/E1 should resemble stratum II and well 3. This is not borne out in the individual bags from S7/E1, which do not differ significantly from the general pattern for the midden strata.

The Kolmogorov-Smirnov test (Shennan 1988:55–61) was used to determine the significance of differences between the different strata. In this method, the totals of two samples are used to derive a minimum level of significant difference. In other words, a threshold of dissimilarity is estimated mathematically, with the data then compared to that figure to determine if and where it exceeds the threshold. The formula used is

$$1.36 \sqrt{\frac{n_1 + n_2}{n_1 n_2}}$$

where n_1 and n_2 are the number of individuals in samples 1 and 2 and 1.36 is the theoretically derived multiplication factor used to obtain a significance level of 0.05.

Applying the Kolmogorov-Smirnov test to the ceramic

Table 5.1 Trash midden and Well 3 stratified ceramics

Stratum	II	III	IV	V	Well 3
	n (%)	*n* (%)	*n* (%)	*n* (%)	*n* (%)
Major Decorated Types					
APOLO BLACK & RED/ORANGE	9 (1.5)	0	1 (0.1)	2 (.3)	0
AQUIAHUAC BURNT ORANGE	3 (0.5)	2 (0.2)	0	2 (.3)	0
COAPAN LACA	0	0	0	0	0
COCOYOTLA BLACK/NATURAL	42 (7)	55 (6)	51 (7)	49 (8)	20 (8)
Sencillo	4 (10)*	24 (44)*	16 (31)*	21 (43)*	0
Incised	0	1 (1.8)*	0	4 (8)*	0
Banded	37 (88)*	27 (49)*	29 (57)*	13 (27)*	17 (85)*
Banded Elegante	**	**	**	**	3 (15)*
Chalco Black/Orange	1 (2)*	3 (5)*	6 (12)*	11 (22)*	0
CUAXILOA MATTE	76 (13)	68 (8)	49 (6)	42 (07)	62 (25)
OCOTLAN RED RIM	48 (8)	112 (13)	101 (13)	66 (10)	21 (8)
Sencillo	26 (54)*	79 (71)*	81 (80)*	55 (83)*	16 (76)*
Elegante	5 (10)*	9 (8)*	3 (3)*	2 (3)*	2 (10) *
Cristina Matte	13 (27)*	22 (20)*	15 (15)*	5 (8)*	1 (5)*
Other subtypes	4 (8)*	2 (1.8)*	2 (2)*	4 (6)*	2 (10)*
SAN PEDRO POLISHED	20 (3)	7 (0.8)	21 (3)	16 (2)	3 (1.2)
TORRE RED & ORANGE (WHITE	71 (12)	58 (7)	52 (7)	43 (7)	27 (11)
Major Undecorated Types					
CERRO ZAPOTECAS SANDY PLAIN	21 (4)	25 (3)	25 (3)	26 (4)	4 (1.6)
MOMOXPAN METALLIC ORANGE	123 (21)	183 (21)	141 (18)	124 (19)	39 (16)
SAN ANDRES RED	52 (9)	52 (6)	58 (8)	49 (8)	25 (10)
TEPONTLA BURNISHED	8 (1.3)	14 (1.6)	24 (3)	25 (4)	3 (1.2)
XICALLI PLAIN	116 (19)	286 (33)	229 (30)	186 (29)	44 (18)
Minor Types					
COLONIAL/HISTORICAL	1 (0.2)	0	0	0	0
LATE POSTCLASSIC	1 (0.2)	0	0	0	0
EARLY POSTCLASSIC	1 (0.2)	3 (0.3)	5 (0.7)	2 (0.3)	1 (0.4)
CLASSIC	4 (0.7)	6 (0.7)	5 (0.7)	5 (0.8)	0
PRECLASSIC	1 (0.2)	1 (0.1)	1 (0.1)	1 (0.2)	0
UNIDENTIFIED	0	1 (0.1)	5 (0.7)	5 (0.8)	0
IDENTIFIABLE	597 (100)	873 (100)	768 (100)	643 (100)	249 (100)
	(71% of	(72% of	(82% of	(80% of	(95% of
	total)	total)	total)	total)	total)
UNIDENTIFIABLE					
ERODED/BURNT	14 (1.7)	22 (1.8)	16 (1.7)	15 (1.9)	3 (1.1)
TOO SMALL	225 (27)	321 (26)	148 (16)	148 (18)	10 (4)
TOTAL RIM SHERDS	836 (100)	1216 (100)	932 (100)	806 (100)	262 (100)

* Type frequencies are expressed as the proportion of the Identifiable subtotal; subtype frequency (*) relates to the proportion of the corresponding type.

** Subtype Banded Elegante was not recognized in the trash midden analysis.

data from the trash midden as a whole and well 3, where $n_1=2881$ and $n_2=249$, the threshold of significant difference is 9%. In this case, if any specific type comparison between the two samples exceeds 9%, then the two assemblages cannot be considered similar at the 0.05 level. In this comparison, the proportions for both Cuaxiloa Matte and Xicalli Plain exceed the 9% threshold, and therefore the two assemblages are considered significantly different.

The same comparative test when run on stratum II versus stratum III also shows significant differences for Xicalli Plain and, within the Cocoyotla type, subtypes Sencillo and Banded. Comparisons between strata III, IV, and V do not show significant differences. When comparing stratum II with well 3, a significant difference still exists in the Cuaxiloa type, but these two strata are more similar than either is to the other strata.

In summary, of the possible explanations for the apparent pattern in ceramic frequencies between the midden strata and well 3, neither is particularly satisfying. There is no evidence that the well was intrusive, yet the differences between the assemblages are statistically significant. Based on this discussion, I tentatively conclude that the trash midden and well 3 deposits were approximately contemporary, with the observed differences in ceramic frequencies within the normal range of variation. The possibility remains, however, that these differences do reflect slight chronological change, with Cuaxiloa Matte, Torre Polychrome, Cocoyotla subtype Banded, and Ocotlán subtypes Elegante and Cristina Matte occurring slightly later than Cocoyotla subtypes Sencillo and Chalco, Ocotlán subtype Sencillo, and Xicalli Plain. This trend is supported by stratified ceramics from structure 1.

The proportion of Unidentifiable Eroded/Burnt sherds was remarkably consistent throughout the midden strata and dropped slightly in well 3. In contrast, strata II and III contained higher amounts of Unidentifiable-Too Small sherds than strata IV and V, while well 3 contained a very low 4% of the category. Based on the suggestion that the relative frequency of small sherds compared to the total assemblage can be used to infer the degree of postdepositional disturbance, this indicates that the lower strata, and especially well 3, probably experienced relatively little disturbance.

The integrity of the assemblage is also reflected in the average of the degree-of-arc measurements, where values for the four strata of the midden are virtually identical at 21 degrees of arc, while well 3 had a higher value (27 degrees of arc). This supports the observation that the well was relatively less disturbed, but is in contrast with the possibility of different degrees of disturbance in the midden strata. This will be discussed further in the section on Vessel Form Analysis (below).

COMPARATIVE ANALYSIS OF PRIMARY CONTEXTS

Four depositional contexts are considered "primary" in the sense that they represent intentional refuse disposal in discrete features that have undergone minimal postdepositional disturbance. These contexts include well 1, well 2, the trash midden, and well 3. A comparative analysis of these ceramic assemblages provides a foundation for constructing a revised ceramic sequence.

Table 5.2 presents a detailed summary of all significant types and subtypes, including significant vessel forms for the Undecorated types. All Major types are included, with Minor types lumped into the temporal categories defined in chapter 4. All subtypes that made up at least 0.1% of the total assemblage are included, and vessel forms that constituted at least 0.5% of the total are listed. Note that rare subtypes and vessel forms are not included in the tabulated data. Type totals are summed as Total Identifiable, while subtypes (with single asterisk) are indicated as percentage of each individual type. Vessel form frequencies (with double asterisk) are also tabulated in reference to type.

Well 1 ceramics were dominated by a very high frequency (49%) of Apolo Polychrome, distributed evenly between the Sencillo and Geométrico subtypes. The only other decorated type that occurred as more than a trace was Aquiahuac Burnt Orange (4%), with the Zócalo subtype most common. Momoxpan Metallic Orange was the most common undecorated type (25%), while San Andrés Red appeared in moderate frequency (15%) and Xicalli Plain made up a very low (4%) proportion of the assemblage.

The well 2 assemblage differed markedly in terms of the decorated types. Apolo Polychrome made up a low percentage (6%) of the assemblage, while Aquiahuac, Cocoyotla, and San Pedro Polished were all present in very low frequency. The most abundant decorated category was the minor type Poblano Glaze Ware and the Colonial/Historical category made up 20% of the well 2 assemblage. San Andrés Red was the most common un-

Table 5.2 Ceramic frequencies from primary contexts

	Well 1 n (%)	Well 2 n (%)	Trash midden n (%)	Well 3 n (%)
Major Decorated Types				
APOLO BLACK & RED/ORANGE	163 (49)	24 (6)	12 (0.4)	0
Sencillo	73 (45)*	11 (46)*	10 (83)*	0
Geométrico	75 (46)*	9 (38)*	2 (17)*	0
Elegante	15 (9)*	3 (12)*	0	0
Other subtypes	0	1 (4)*	0	0
AQUIAHUAC BURNT ORANGE	14 (4)	16 (4)	7 (0.2)	0
Sencillo	5 (36)*	5 (31)*	2 (29)*	0
Santa Catarina	2 (14)*	1 (6)*	2 (29)*	0
Zócalo Black (Orange	7 (50)*	10 (62)*	3 (43)*	0
COAPAN LACA	1 (0.3)	0	0	0
COCOYOTLA BLACK/NATURAL	0	9 (2)	204 (7)	20 (8)
Sencillo	0	7 (78)*	65 (32)*	0
Incised	0	0	5 (2)*	0
Banded	0	1 (11)*	110 (54)*	17 (85)*
Banded Elegante	0	1 (11)*	0	3 (15)*
Chalco Black/Orange	0	0	24 (12)*	0
CUAXILOA MATTE	6 (1.8)	7 (1.9)	237 (8	62 (25)
Sencillo	2 (33)*	6 (86)*	199 (84)*	39 (63)*
Polished Cream	2 (33)*	1 (14)*	31 (13)*	20 (32)*
Xicotenco Black & Red/Orange	2 (33)*	0	0	1 (1.6)*
Other subtypes	0	0	7 (3)*	2 (3)*
OCOTLAN RED RIM	1 (0.3)	6 (1.6)	332 (11)	21 (8)
Sencillo	0	4 (67)*	246 (74)*	16 (76)*
Incised	0	0	6 (1.8)*	1 (5)*
Banded	0	0	5 (1.5)*	0
Banded Elegante	0	0	19 (6)*	1 (5)*
Elegante	1 (100)*	1 (17)*	0	2 (10)*
Cristina Matte	0	1 (17)*	56 (17)*	1 (5)*
SAN PEDRO POLISHED	2 (0.6)	16 (4)	65 (2)	3 (1.2)
Sencillo	2 (100)*	14 (88)*	12 (18)*	0
Incised	0	0	7 (11)*	1 (33)*
Graphite on Red	0	0	7 (11)*	0
Graphite on Red Incised	0	1 (6)*	27 (42)*	0
Graphite on Red Elegante	0	1 (6)*	12 (18)*	2 (67)*
TORRE RED & ORANGE/WHITE	2 (0.6)	4 (1.1)	228 (8)	27 (11)
Sencillo	2 (100)*	4 (100)*	216 (95)*	26 (96)*
Universidad	0	0	0	1 (4)*
Other subtypes	0	0	12 (5)*	0
Major Undecorated Types				
CERRO ZAPOTECAS SANDY PLAIN	3 (0.9)	14 (4)	97 (3)	4 (1.6)
Conical cazuela	1 (33)**	4 (29)**	28 (29)**	2 (50)**
Bracero	1 (33)**	0	34 (35)**	1 (25)**
Other forms	0	10 (71)**	35 (36)**	1 (25)**
MOMOXPAN METALLIC ORANGE	84 (25)	75 (20)	587 (20)	39 (16)
Comal	74 (88)**	71 (95)**	488 (83)**	38 (97)**
Subhemispherical bowl	4 (5)**	1 (1.3)**	25 (4)**	0
Conical bowl	3 (4)**	3 (4)**	66 (11)**	1 (3)**
Other forms	3 (4)**	0	8 (1.4)**	0

continued

Table 5.2 Ceramic frequencies from primary contexts, *continued*

	Well 1 n (%)	Well 2 n (%)	Trash midden n (%)	Well 3 n (%)
SAN ANDRES RED	50 (15)	108 (29)	216 (7)	25 (10)
Comal	11 (22)**	8 (7)**	1 (0.5)**	1 (4)**
Long-neck olla	17 (34)**	12 (11)**	45 (21)**	5 (20)**
Small-mouth olla	2 (4)**	8 (7)**	42 (19)**	1 (4)**
Wide-mouth olla	12 (24)**	12 (11)**	37 (17)**	4 (16)**
Hemispherical cazuela	4 (8)**	12 (11)**	23 (11)**	6 (24)**
Conical cazuela	0	13 (12)**	24 (11)**	2 (8)**
Cylindrical maceta	1 (2)**	10 (9)**	0	1 (4)**
Other forms	0	12 (11)**	44 (20)**	4 (16)**
Dark Red	3 (6)*	21 (19)*	0	1 (4)*
TEPONTLA BURNISHED	3 (0.9)	2 (0.5)	75 (3)	3 (1.2)
Subhemispherical bowl	0	1 (50)**	16 (21)**	0
Conical bowl	3 (100)**	1 (50)**	32 (43)**	2 (67)**
Other forms	0	0	23 (31)**	1 (33)**
Incised	0	0	0	0
Red Rim	0	0	4 (5)*	0
XICALLI PLAIN	15 (4)	21 (6)	841 (29)	44 (18)
Comal	1 (7)**	4 (19)**	91 (11)	16 (36)**
Outleaned-wall dish	5 (33)**	5 (24)**	295 (35)	11 (25)**
Shallow bowl	4 (27)**	2 (10)**	6 (0.7)	3 (7)**
Subhemispherical bowl	2 (13)**	8 (38)**	430 (51)	9 (20)**
Conical bowl	1 (7)**	0	**	4 (9)**
Lantern censer	1 (7)**	2 (10)**	16 (1.9)**	1 (2)**
Other forms	1 (7)**	0	3 (0.4)**	0
Minor Types				
COLONIAL/HISTORICAL	0	75 (20)	1 (0.03)	0
LATE POSTCLASSIC	7 (2)	0	1 (0.03)	0
EARLY POSTCLASSIC	0	0	11 (0.4)	1 (0.4)
CLASSIC	2 (0.6)	0	20 (0.7)	0
PRECLASSIC	1 (0.3)	0	4 (0.1)	0
UNIDENTIFIED	1 (0.3)	0	11 (0.4)	0
TOTAL IDENTIFIABLE	355 (100) (80% of total)	377 (100) (70% of total)	2949 (100) (76% of total)	249 (100) (95% of total)
UNIDENTIFIABLE				
ERODED/BURNT	17 (4)	36 (7)	67 (1.7)	3 (1.1)
TOO SMALL	73 (16)	129 (24)	842 (22)	10 (4)
TOTAL SHERDS	445 (100)	542 (100)	3858 (100)	262 (100)

Note: Type frequencies are expressed as the proportion of the Total Identifiable sherds; subtype frequency (*) relates to the corresponding type; and vessel-form frequency (**) relates to the proportion of the type.

** Subtype Banded Elegante was not recognized in the trash midden analysis.

decorated type (29%), but Momoxpan Metallic Orange was present in high frequency (20%). Cerro Zapotecas Sandy Plain and Xicalli Plain were both present in very low frequency.

Ocotlán Red Rim was the most abundant (11%) decorated type found in the trash midden, with Sencillo as its most common subtype. Also present in low frequencies were Cocoyotla Black on Natural (7%), Cuaxiloa Matte (8%), and Torre Polychrome (8%), with San Pedro Polished Red present in very low frequency (2%). In contrast to that found in wells 1 and 2, Xicalli Plain was the most common undecorated type (29%), although Momoxpan Orange was again present in high frequency (20%). San Andrés Red made up only 7% of the assemblage, and Cerro Zapotecas Sandy Plain (3%) and Tepontla Burnished (3%) were each present in very low frequencies.

Well 3 has a particularly high frequency of Cuaxiloa Matte (25%). Torre Polychrome was present in moderate frequency (11%), and both Cocoyotla (8%) and Ocotlán (8%) occurred in low frequencies. Xicalli Plain was the most abundant of the undecorated types at 18%, and Momoxpan Orange (16%) and San Andrés Red (10%) were present in moderate amounts.

To summarize, the ceramic assemblages from the trash midden and well 3 share the most similarities, although they are not identical. On the basis of the high frequency of Minor Colonial/Historical types, well 2 clearly dates to the post-Conquest era. The frequencies found in well 1 are very similar to those found in midden F-10 at UA-79 (Barrientos 1980) that Lind (1994) attributed to the Late Postclassic period. General similarities between well 1 and well 2, particularly in the relative abundance of Apolo and Aquiahuac Polychromes and the scarcity of other decorated types and Xicalli Plain, suggest that these two contexts were probably more similar to one another than either was to the trash midden and well 3 assemblages. It should be noted, however, that no Colonial/Historical types were recovered from well 1, and it is therefore likely that the well 1 deposit was pre-Conquest. Based on these primary assemblages, the most likely sequence for the primary contexts is that the trash midden and well 3 assemblages were the earliest, followed by well 1, with well 2 as the latest.

In terms of specific decorated types, Cocoyotla Black on Natural, Cuaxiloa Matte, Ocotlán Red Rim, and Torre Polychrome were all most common early in the sequence, with Apolo Polychrome and Aquiahuac Burnt Orange more abundant in excavated deposits from the Late Postclassic period. The frequency of San Pedro Polished Red remained very low but relatively consistent in all four contexts. Among the undecorated types, Xicalli Plain was predominant at the beginning of the sequence, but declined markedly in relative frequency, while San Andrés Red increased. The proportion of Momoxpan Metallic Orange increased slightly through time, although it was one of the most consistent of all of the major types. The evidence for Cerro Zapotecas Sandy Plain and Tepontla Burnished is less clear, in part because of the relative scarcity of these types in all four contexts. The importance of these two types in the Classic and Epiclassic periods, however, suggests that they had already declined in popularity before the UA-1 occupations.

Turning to diachronic changes in vessel form, particularly for utilitarian wares, Momoxpan Orange comales were the most common form in all contexts. Other comal types, however, varied in the different deposits, with Xicalli Plain comales common in the trash midden and well 3, San Andrés Red comales common in well 1, and San Andrés subtype Dark Red comales most numerous in well 2.

Some minor variation occurs in relation to the different forms of San Andrés ollas; long-neck ollas and wide-mouth ollas were most abundant in well 1, while small-mouth ollas were more common in the trash midden. Cazuelas, on the other hand, were relatively rare in well 1 and most abundant in well 3. These and other aspects of vessel form are discussed in greater detail below.

In considering the relative frequencies of the total Identifiable versus Unidentifiable types in relation to the total number of sherds, it has already been observed that well 3, with 95% Identifiable sherds, was probably relatively undisturbed. Well 2 had the lowest proportion of Identifiable sherds, with the highest frequencies of both Eroded/Burnt sherds and Too Small sherds. This evidence for disturbance may account for some of the anomalous values for early types such as Cocoyotla, Cerro Zapotecas, and Xicalli that may have been redeposited as mixed fill during the deposition of the midden refuse.

In summary, the ceramic frequencies from the four primary depositional contexts indicate significant differences relating to both Decorated and Undecorated types. Based on this data, Apolo Polychrome and Aquiahuac

Burnt Orange are tentatively identified as diagnostics of the Late Postclassic period, while Cocoyotla Black on Natural, Cuaxiloa Matte, Ocotlán Red Rim, Torre Polychrome, and Xicalli Plain occurred earlier. Further refinement of the sequence depends upon clarifying the relationship between Ocotlán and Cocoyotla on the one hand, and Torre and Cuaxiloa on the other.

STRUCTURE 1 DEPOSITIONAL CONTEXTS

Five depositional contexts were associated with structure 1, including materials from

- beneath the floor,
- beneath the porch areas,
- floor contact,
- porch contact, and
- fill from above the floor but sealed beneath and in association with the collapsed adobe walls.

A comparison of ceramic frequencies from these contexts helps to refine the ceramic sequence, particularly in relation to the ceramic complex associated with the occupation of structure 1 (table 5.3).

A small sample ($n=29$) of sherds was recovered from beneath the floor because in most units excavation stopped at the plaster surface. More than half were Unidentifiable, mainly due to their small size. Of the Identifiable pottery, more than half were either of the Ocotlán Red Rim ($n=3$, 21%) or Xicalli Plain ($n=6$, 43%), types that have been suggested as diagnostic of the earlier Postclassic occupation phase. Because of the small sample size, however, this evidence is tenuous.

The sample size for materials from below the porch is much larger ($n=1,112$), in part because the earthen walking surfaces were probably more difficult to identify during excavation and were often dug through. Levels from below the porch were arbitrarily defined as those more than 80 cm below the surface, but because these were usually not sealed deposits, there was a greater potential for postdepositional mixing. Evidence for a high level of disturbance appears in the very high proportion (33%) of Unidentifiable-Too Small sherds.

The most common Decorated type found below the porch was Ocotlán Red Rim (24%), with Sencillo as the most common of its subtypes. Cocoyotla Black on Natural occurred in low frequency (6%), with its Sencillo subtype as the most common. Xicalli Plain occurred in very

high frequency (35%), while Momoxpan Orange (12%) was present in moderate frequency, San Andrés Red (9%) and Tepontla Burnished (5%) occurred in low amounts, and Cerro Zapotecas Sandy Plain (3%) was present in very low frequency.

Ceramic frequencies from the floor contact deposit ($n=517$) again contained Ocotlán (27%) and Cocoyotla (11%) as the most abundant decorated types, and Xicalli Plain (23%) and Momoxpan Orange (19%) as the most common undecorated types. Cuaxiloa Matte occurred in very low frequency (3%). Notably, 84% of the sherds found in direct association with the floor were Identifiable, one of the highest ratios of any context found at UA-1. This high frequency contrasts with the expectation of floor areas being regularly maintained to remove debris and supports the interpretation that the structure was destroyed catastrophically with artifacts left in situ. The relatively low frequency of Burnt/Eroded sherds, however, is not consistent with the interpretation that structure 1 was destroyed by fire.

Ceramic frequencies from the porch contact ($n=77$) resembled the general trend for structure 1, with the exception of relatively more Apolo Polychrome (7%). Ocotlán Red Rim remained the most common decorated type (20%), and Xicalli Plain occurred in very high frequency (36%). In part because of difficulties in recognizing the porch surface, there were relatively few sherds in this assemblage; thus, problems of integrity as well as sample size make this a less reliable context for further analysis.

The largest sample ($n=4,234$) came from above the floor, including materials deposited after the abandonment of the structure, but before the adobe walls had completely collapsed. The ceramic assemblage from this context was more diverse than those from lower levels. Ocotlán was still the most common decorated type, occurring in moderate frequency (15%). Apolo Polychrome was present in low frequency (9%), and Cocoyotla (4%), Aquiahuac (3%), Cuaxiloa (3%) and San Pedro (2%) were all found in very low frequencies. In this context Cocoyotla subtype Sencillo was only represented as 44% of the type total in contrast to its much higher proportion in lower levels, and subtypes Banded Elegante (29%) and Chalco Black on Orange (11%) were relatively more common. Among the undecorated types, the relative frequencies of Xicalli and Momoxpan were both 21%, while San Andrés Red was found in moderate frequency (13%).

Table 5.3 Structure 1 Ceramics

	Below floor n (%)	Below porch n (%)	Floor contact n (%)	Porch contact n (%)	Above floor n (%)
Major Decorated Types					
APOLO BLACK & RED/ORANGE	0	10 (1.4)	7 (1.6)	4 (7)	252 (9)
AQUIAHUAC BURNT ORANGE	0	4 (0.6)	3 (0.7)	0	93 (3)
COAPAN LACA	0	0	0	0	16 (0.5)
COCOYOTLA BLACK/NATURAL	0	42 (6)	47 (11)	1 (1.7)	111 (4)
Sencillo	0	35 (83)*	39 (83)*	1 (100)	49 (44)*
Incised	0	0	0	0	10 (9)*
Banded	0	2 (5)*	5 (11)*	0	8 (7)*
Banded Elegante	0	2 (5)*	1 (2)*	0	32 (29)*
Chalco Black/Orange	0	3 (7)*	2 (4)*	0	12 (11)*
CUAXILOA MATTE	0	9 (1.3)	15 (3)	0	80 (3)
OCOTLÁN RED RIM	3 (21)	169 (24)	118 (27)	12 (20)	439 (15)
Sencillo	3 (100)*	127 (75)*	91 (77)*	9 (75)	(340 (77)
Elegante	0	15 (9)*	16 (14)*	2 (17)	(36 (8)
Cristina Matte	0	15 (9)*	3 (3)*	1 (8)	(41 (9)
Other subtypes	0	12 (7)*	8 (7)*	0	(22 (5)
SAN PEDRO POLISHED	2 (14)	13 (1.8)	10 (2)	1 (1.7)	60 (2)
TORRE RED & ORANGE/WHITE	0	3 (0.4)	2 (0.5)	1 (1.7)	38 (1.3)
Major Undecorated Types					
CERRO ZAPOTECAS SANDY PLAIN	0	21 (3)	5 (1.2)	3 (5)	110 (4)
MOMOXPAN METALLIC ORANGE	3 (21)	88 (12)	84 (19)	8 (14)	618 (21)
SAN ANDRÉS RED	0	63 (9)	32 (7)	6 (10)	396 (13)
TEPONTLA BURNISHED	0	34 (5)	11 (3)	1 (1.7)	80 (3)
XICALLI PLAIN	6 (43)	246 (35)	98 (23)	21 (36)	624 (21)
Minor Types					
COLONIAL/HISTORICAL	0	1 (0.1)	0	0	16 (0.5)
LATE POSTCLASSIC	0	1 (0.1)	0	0	4 (0.1)
EARLY POSTCLASSIC	0	3 (0.4)	0	0	3 (0.1)
CLASSIC	0	2 (0.3)	1 (0.2)	1 (1.7)	8 (0.3)
PRECLASSIC	0	0	1 (0.2)	0	4 (0.1)
UNIDENTIFIED	0	1 (0.1)	0	0	1 (0.03)
IDENTIFIABLE	14 (100) (48% of total)	710 (100) (64% of total)	434 (100) (84% of total)	59 (100) (77% of total)	2953 (100) (70% of total)
UNIDENTIFIABLE					
ERODED/BURNT	1 (3)	32 (3)	11 (2)	0	166 (4)
TOO SMALL	14 (48)	370 (33)	72 (14)	18 (23)	1115 (26)
TOTAL SHERDS	29 (100)	1112 (100)	517 (100)	77 (100)	4234 (100)

Note: Type frequencies are expressed as the proportion of the Total Identifiable sherds, and subtype frequency (*) relates to the corresponding type.

In summary, the ceramic frequencies from structure 1 show a high degree of consistency, with Ocotlán Red Rim and Cocoyotla Black on Natural as the predominant decorated types, and Xicalli Plain, Momoxpan Orange, and San Andrés Red the principal undecorated types. The higher proportions of types such as Apolo Polychrome and Aquiahuac Burnt Orange in the fill above the floor suggests that the occupation predated the Late Postclassic period, when these types predominated. Cuaxiloa Matte and Torre Polychrome were not well represented in the structure 1 contexts, indicating that they, too, probably postdate the occupation. There is relatively little difference in the frequencies of Ocotlán Red Rim subtypes among these contexts, whereas the proportion of Cocoyotla subtype Sencillo is very high in the floor contact level but drops sharply relative to the other subtypes in the fill level above the floor.

STRUCTURE 1 FEATURES

Several additional features were excavated in association with structure 1 that provide discrete depositional contexts. One was the oval structure located south of room 1 that has been identified tentatively as a temazcal. The other features include two group burials: in room 4 at unit N2/W1 and south of the structure at unit S6/W3 (table 5.4).

Stratigraphic evidence indicated that the temazcal was built and used at the same time as structure 1. Wolfman (1968:11) observed that the oval structure was constructed through an existing stucco floor associated with porch area C, but that it was probably abandoned at the same time as structure 1. Analysis of ceramics from the collapsed structure support the interpretation that the temazcal was used at the same time as structure 1.

Pottery from the temazcal (*n*=113) included a high frequency of Ocotlán Red Rim (21%), with low frequencies of Cocoyotla Black on Natural (6%) and Cuaxiloa Matte (5%), and a very low amount of Torre Polychrome (4%). Undecorated types included a very high frequency of Xicalli Plain (33%), moderate amount of Momoxpan Orange (18%), and low amounts of San Andrés Red (9%) and Tepontla Burnished (4%). Based on these frequencies, the temazcal assemblage is roughly contemporary with the ceramic complex of the trash midden and structure 1.

Excavations at unit N2/W1 encountered burials 4, 5, 6, 7, 11, and 12 in the northwest corner of room 4. The burials were placed in a walled chamber excavated through the structure floor (figure 5.1). The burials were obviously interred after the abandonment of the struc-

Table 5.4 Ceramics from structure 1 features

	Temazcal n (%)	N2/W1 burials n (%)	S6/W3 burials n (%)
Major Decorated Types			
APOLO BLACK & RED/ORANGE	0	2 (5)	0
AQUIAHUAC BURNT ORANGE	0	0	0
COAPAN LACA	0	0	0
COCOYOTLA BLACK/NATURAL	5 (6)	3 (7)	9 (8)
Sencillo	3 (60)*	1 (33)*	5 (56)*
Incised	0	1 (33)*	1 (11)*
Banded	1 (20)*	0	0
Banded Elegante	1 (20)*	0	0
Chalco Black/Orange	0	1 (33)*	3 (33)*
CUAXILOA MATTE	4 (5)	0	0
OCOTLÁN RED RIM	17 (21)	6 (15)	37 (33)
Sencillo	16 (94)*	5 (83)*	30 (81)*
Elegante	0	0	2 (5)*
Cristina Matte	1 (6)*	1 (17)*	5 (14)*
SAN PEDRO POLISHED RED	1 (1.2)	0	4 (4)
TORRE RED & ORANGE/WHITE	3 (4)	0	0
Major Undecorated Types			
CERRO ZAPOTECAS SANDY PLAIN	0	4 (10)	5 (4)
MOMOXPAN METALLIC ORANGE	15 (18)	7 (17)	17 (15)
SAN ANDRES RED	7 (9)	2 (5)	15 (13)
TEPONTLA BURNISHED	3 (4)	3 (7)	0
XICALLI PLAIN	27 (33)	13 (32)	26 (23)
Minor Types			
COLONIAL/HISTORICAL	0	0	0
LATE POSTCLASSIC	0	0	0
EARLY POSTCLASSIC	0	0	0
CLASSIC	0	1 (2)	0
PRECLASSIC	0	0	0
UNIDENTIFIED	0	0	0
IDENTIFIABLE	82 (100) (73% of total)	41 (100) (57% of total)	113 (100) (74% of total)
UNIDENTIFIABLE			
ERODED/BURNT	4 (4)	3 (4)	3 (2)
TOO SMALL	27 (24)	28 (39	37 (24)
TOTAL SHERDS	113 (100)	72 (100)	153 (100)

Note: Type frequencies are expressed as the proportion of the Total Identifiable sherds, and subtype frequency (*) relates to the corresponding type.

5.2 Burial 9 in S6/W3

ture because some of the bones were actually located above floor level. It is likely, however, that the burial occurred before the complete collapse of the adobe walls since no intrusive burial pit was noticed in the collapsed adobe. Ceramics from the burial context (n=72) included a moderate amount of Ocotlán Red Rim (15%), and low frequencies of Cocoyotla Black on Natural (7%) and Apolo Polychrome (5%). Undecorated types included a very high proportion of Xicalli Plain (32%), moderate amounts of Momoxpan Orange (17%) and Cerro Zapotecas Sandy Plain (10%), and low frequencies of Tepontla Burnished (7%) and San Andrés Red (5%). A complete Cocoyotla subtype Sencillo vessel (UA-1 10147) was associated with burial 4. The general characteristics of this assemblage resemble the ceramic complex of structure 1 and the trash midden, although the low frequency of Apolo Polychrome would indicate that it was later than either of those assemblages. It should also be noted that this was a relatively small sample, with an above average number of Unidentifiable-Too Small sherds suggesting the

possibility of postdepositional disturbance.

The second burial context was located south of structure 1 in unit S6/W3. It was adjacent to the extension of the main north/south structure wall and was above the stucco floor layers associated with the wall. Five burials (9, 10, 14, 16 and 17) were found in this unit (figure 5.2) and burial 18 was located in the adjoining unit S5/W3. Since these burials were placed above a stucco floor it was inferred that they postdated structure 1 (Wolfman 1968). Ceramics from this burial context (n=153) included a very high proportion of Ocotlán Red Rim (33%), and a low amount of Cocoyotla Black on Natural (8%). Undecorated types included a high frequency of Xicalli Plain (23%) and moderate amounts of Momoxpan Orange (15%) and San Andrés Red (13%). These frequencies are consistent with the overall ceramic complex associated with structure 1, although the absence of either Cuaxiloa or Torre polychromes may indicate that these features predate the midden.

The ceramic data from these features conform to the general ceramic complex related with structure 1, the trash midden, and well 3. The temazcal was probably contemporary with the final occupation of the structure, and perhaps the filling of the trash midden. The burial deposit at N2/W1 followed the abandonment of structure 1, although probably not by a long time. The S6/W3 burials may have been interred before the final occupation of structure 1 or perhaps even at the time of the early structural remains found beneath the floor of structure 1.

STRUCTURE 2 CERAMICS AND SHERD CONCENTRATIONS

The limited excavations at structure 2 yielded ceramics from the floor contact and above floor deposits that provide a notable contrast to those from other contexts (table 5.5). Similar patterns are apparent in ceramics from an intrusive midden that passed through the floor of structure 2 and two sherd concentrations located between structures 1 and 2.

The ceramic frequencies associated with the floor contact of Structure 2 are tenuous because of the small sample size of analyzed sherds (n=21). The most common decorated types were Apolo Polychrome and Aquiahuac Burnt Orange. Xicalli Plain was the most common undecorated type, and Momoxpan Orange was present in moderate amount. The relatively high proportions of Apolo and Aquiahuac contrast with the patterns

Table 5.5 Structure 2 Ceramics and Associated Sherd Concentrations

	Floor contact n (%)	Above floor n (%)	Intrusive midden n (%)	Sherd conc. 1 n (%)	Sherd conc. 2 n (%)
Major Decorated Types					
APOLO BLACK & RED/ORANGE	2 (14)	43 (11)	6 (4)	14 (18)	101 (12)
Sencillo	1 (50)*	19 (44)*	2 (33)*	6 (43)*	56 (55)*
Geometrico.	1 (50)*	16 (37)*	2 (33)*	6 (43)*	28 (28)*
Elegante	0	8 (19)*	2 (33)*	2 (14)*	17 (17)*
AQUIAHUAC BURNT ORANGE	2 (14)	30 (8)	36 (21	7 (9)	79 (10)
Sencillo	2 (100)*	13 (43)*	18 (50)*	1 (14)*	37 (47)*
Santa Catalina	0	1 (3)*	0	0	3 (4)
Zócalo	0	16 (53)*	18 (50)*	6 (86)*	(39 (49)*
COAPAN LACA	0	4 (1.0)	1 (0.6)	1 (1.3)	8 (0.1)
COCOYOTLA BLACK/NATURAL	0	8 (2)	10 (6)	0	13 (1.6)
Sencillo	0	2 (25)*	4 (40)*	0	3 (23)*
Banded	0	4 (50)*	3 (30)*	0	4 (31)*
Banded Elegante	0	0	3 (30)*	0	3 (23)*
Chalco Black on Orange	0	2 (25)*	0	0	3 (23)*
CUAXILOA MATTE	0	19 (5)	7 (4)	4 (5)	24 (03)
OCOTLÁN RED RIM	1 (7)	33 (8)	11 (6)	1 (1.3)	55 (7)
Sencillo	1 (100)*	21 (64)*	6 (55)*	1 (100)*	39 (71)*
Elegante	0	4 (12)*	2 (18)*	0	9 (16)*
Cristina Matte	0	6 (18)*	1 (9)*	0	7 (13)*
Other subtypes	0	2 (6)*	2 (18)*	0	0
SAN PEDRO POLISHED	1 (7)	6 (1.5)	4 (2)	0	20 (2)
TORRE RED & ORANGE/WHITE	0	16 (4)	6 (4)	1 (1.3)	14 (1.7)
Major Undecorated Types					
CERRO ZAPOTECAS SANDY PLAIN	1 (7)	12 (3)	2 (1.2)	5 (6)	24 (3)
MOMOXPAN METALLIC ORANGE	2 (14)	81 (20)	42 (25)	21 (27)	216 (27)
SAN ANDRÉS RED	1 (7)	52 (13)	17 (10)	11 (14)	133 (16)
TEPONTLA BURNISHED	1 (7)	9 (2)	4 (2)	0	15 (1.9)
XICALLI PLAIN	3 (21)	81 (20)	22 (13)	13 (17)	84 (10)
Minor Types					
COLONIAL/HISTORICAL	0	4 (1.0)	0	0	16 (2)
LATE POSTCLASSIC	0	0	1 (0.6)	0	3 (0.4)
EARLY POSTCLASSIC	0	1 (0.2)	0	0	1 (0.1)
CLASSIC	0	1 (0.2)	1 (0.6)	0	2 (0.2)
PRECLASSIC	0	0	0	0	0
UNIDENTIFIED	0	0	0	0	1 (0.1)
IDENTIFIABLE	14 (100)	400 (100)	170 (100)	78 (100)	809 (100)
	(67% of total)	(68% of total)	(68% of total)	(76% of total)	(73% of total)
UNIDENTIFIABLE					
ERODED/BURNT	1 (5)	31 (5)	14 (6)	17 (17)	66 (6)
TOO SMALL	6 (29)	160 (27)	65 (26)	8 (8)	226 (21)
TOTAL SHERDS	21 (100)	591 (100)	249 (100)	103 (100)	1101 (100)

Note: Type frequencies are expressed as the proportion of the Total Identifiable sherds, and subtype frequency (*) relates to the corresponding type.

associated with structure 1, suggesting that the two compounds were not contemporary.

Ceramics collected above the floor provide a more extensive sample (*n*=591), and the relative proportions are very similar to the floor contact deposit. Apolo Polychrome again occurs in moderate amounts (11%), with low frequencies of Aquiahuac (8%), Ocotlán (8%), and Cuaxiloa Matte (5%). Torre Polychrome (4%) and Cocoyotla Black on Natural (2%) were present in very low frequencies. High frequencies of both Momoxpan Orange (20%) and Xicalli Plain (20%) were recovered, and San Andrés Red appeared in a moderate amount (13%). This assemblage probably relates to a fairly late period of deposition, but it represents a more varied ceramic complex than well 1, for example, where Apolo was the predominant type present. The relatively high frequencies of Aquiahuac, Cuaxiloa, and Torre suggest that these types relate to an intermediate period between the structure 1 and well 1 ceramic complexes.

The intrusive midden deposit (*n*=249) passed through the north side of structure 2 and was in turn sealed beneath the stone wall that passed along the north side of the structural remains. Since this deposit was not securely identified during the excavation, it is difficult to relate it stratigraphically to the above floor deposit. The most common decorated type found was Aquiahuac Burnt Orange (21%), with low to very low amounts of Apolo (4%), Cocoyotla (6%), Cuaxiloa (4%), Ocotlán (6%), and Torre (4%). Momoxpan Orange was the most common undecorated type (25%), with moderate amounts of Xicalli Plain (13%) and San Andrés Red (10%).

Concentration 1 (*n*=103) was recovered from unit S2/E4 where a sherd lens was found beneath a section of a north/south adobe wall that was stratigraphically later than the occupation of structure 2. Ceramics included a moderate amount (18%) of Apolo Polychrome and small quantities of Aquiahuac (9%) and Cuaxiloa (5%). Momoxpan Orange was the most abundant of the undecorated types (27%), with moderate amounts of Xicalli (17%) and San Andrés (16%).

Concentration 2 (*n*=1,101) may represent the northern extension of the concentration 1 sherd lens and was again found in stratigraphic association beneath the wall. Apolo was the most common decorated type found (12%), although Aquiahuac was also found in moderate frequency (10%), with a low amount of Ocotlán also present (7%). A high proportion of Momoxpan Orange

was found (27%), with moderate amounts of San Andrés Red (16%) and Xicalli Plain (10%). The similarities in relative ceramic frequencies between the two sherd concentrations support the possibility that they relate to the same extensive sheet midden.

Ceramic frequencies from these contexts are substantially different from those associated with structure 1 and the trash midden. The relatively large amounts of Apolo Polychrome, Aquiahuac Burnt Orange, and Momoxpan Orange are balanced by the decrease in Ocotlán Red Rim, Cocoyotla Black on Natural, and Xicalli Plain. This evidence suggests that the two structural compounds were not contemporary. The abundance of Aquiahuac, and the relatively high frequencies of Cuaxiloa and Torre, however, contrast with the well 1 ceramic assemblage where Apolo predominated. Although the structure 2 ceramic complex is still not very well represented, I suspect that it and these associated features relate to an intermediate phase between the Early Postclassic structure 1 ceramic complex and the Late Postclassic well 1 assemblage.

SELECTED STRATIFIED UNITS

Two units, N4/E1 and N5/E1, were located north of structure 1 and its associated architectural features and produced stratified remains that were not severely impacted by construction disturbances. In these units, sterile soil was usually encountered at depths between 130 and 150 cm below ground surface. Note that this is approximately 50 cm lower than the plaster floors, indicating that structure 1 was built about 0.5 m above the natural surface.

Four levels were analyzed from unit N4/E1, ranging from 60 to 155 cm below the surface (the two plow-zone levels, 0 to 60 cm, were not analyzed). Levels III and IV (60 to 120 cm) contained large quantities of pottery mixed with fallen wall material. At a depth ranging from 130 to 137 cm, a layer of black muck was encountered that was culturally sterile.

Ceramic frequencies from unit N4/E1 are differentiated by level in table 5.6. In level III, Ocotlán Red Rim (12%) and Aquiahuac Burnt Orange (12%) were found in moderate proportions, while Apolo Polychrome was present in low frequency (8%). Undecorated types Momoxpan Orange (18%), Xicalli Plain (18%), and San Andrés Red (14%) were all found in moderate amounts. In level IV, the proportions of Aquiahuac (7%) and Apolo

Table 5.6 N4/E1 stratified ceramics (by level)

	III (60-87) n (%)	IV (87-120) n (%)	V (120-130) n (%)	VI (130-150) n (%)
Major Decorated Types				
APOLO BLACK & RED/ORANGE	13 (8)	12 (3)	0	0
Sencillo	7 (54)*	6 (50)*	0	0
Geometrico	2 (15)*	1 (8)	0	0
Elegante	4 (31)*	5 (42)*	0	0
AQUIAHUAC BURNT ORANGE	20 (12	33 (7)	0	1 (8)
Sencillo	2 (10)*	6 (18)*	0	0
Santa Catalina	0	1 (3)*	0	0
Zócalo	18 (90)*	26 (79)*	0	1 (100)*
COAPAN LACA POLYCHROME	5 (3)	1 (0.2)	0	0
COCOYOTLA BLACK/NATURAL	3 (1.8)	22 (5)	2 (4)	0
Sencillo	2 (67)*	14 (64)*	2 (100)*	0
Incised	0	3 (14)*	0	0
Banded	0	3 (14)*	0	0
Banded Elegante	1 (33)*	1 (5)*	0	0
Chalco Black on Orange	0	1 (5)*	0	0
CUAXILOA MATTE	4 (2)	7 (1.5)	1 (2)	0
OCOTLAN RED RIM	20 (12	69 (15)	13 (28)	6 (46)
Sencillo	15 (75)*	50 (72)*	10 (77)*	5 (83)*
Elegante	3 (15)*	9 (13)*	2 (15)*	0
Cristina Matte	1 (5)*	7 (10)*	0	1 (17)*
Other subtypes	0	3 (4)*	1 (8)*	0
SAN PEDRO POLISHED	1 (0.6)	5 (1.1)	3 (6)	0
TORRE RED & ORANGE/WHITE	3 (1.8)	7 (1.5)	0	0
Major Undecorated Types				
CERRO ZAPOTECAS SANDY PLAIN	5 (3)	9 (1.9)	1 (2)	0
MOMOXPAN METALLIC ORANGE	30 (18)	86 (18)	5 (11)	0
SAN ANDRÉS RED	23 (14)	46 (10)	3 (6)	1 (8)
TEPONTLA BURNISHED	5 (3)	23 (5)	2 (4)	2 (15)
XICALLI PLAIN	29 (18)	141 (30)	16 (34)	3 (23)
Minor Types				
COLONIAL/HISTORICAL	2 (1.2)	0	0	0
LATE POSTCLASSIC	0	1 (0.2)	0	0
EARLY POSTCLASSIC	0	1 (0.2)	0	0
CLASSIC	0	2 (0.4)	0	0
PRECLASSIC	0	1 (0.2)	1 (2)	0
UNIDENTIFIED	0	0	0	0
IDENTIFIABLE	163 (100) (65% of total)	466 (100) (78% of total)	47 (100) (77% of total)	13 (100) (76% of total)
UNIDENTIFIABLE				
ERODED/BURNT	9 (3)	11 (1.8)	1 (1.6)	0
TOO SMALL	77 (31)	120 (20)	13 (21)	4 (24)
TOTAL SHERDS	249 (100)	597 (100)	61 (100)	17 (100)

Note: Type frequencies are expressed as the proportion of the Total Identifiable sherds, and subtype frequency (*) relates to the corresponding type.

(3%) both decreased, with slight increases in the relative frequencies of Ocotlán (15%) and Cocoyotla (5%). The most dramatic increase was in the percentage of Xicalli Plain, which is present in very high frequency (30%). In levels V and VI Apolo was completely absent, while only one example of Aquiahuac was found in level VI. High to very high frequencies of Ocotlán Red Rim (28% and 46%) and Xicalli Plain (34% and 23%) were present in these two levels. A dramatic decrease in sample size in levels V and VI accentuates the differences in ceramic frequencies, but also introduces a potential for error.

Unit N5/E1 was also excavated in six levels to sterile soil reached at a depth of 137 cm. The bottom four levels were analyzed. The field notes from this excavation unit describe a high quantity of fallen adobe material in levels III to V, and a possible wall alignment in the northeast section of the unit. Beneath the collapsed wall at a depth of 125 cm, an adobe semicircle filled with charcoal was found immediately above sterile soil.

Other than levels III and IV, relatively few sherds were found in the analyzed levels, so sample size is a problem in the analysis of this unit (table 5.7). In level III there was an unusually high amount of the category "Unidentifiable-Too Small" (60% of total), so that even here the number of identifiable examples was relatively low. Decorated types included Aquiahuac, Coapan, and San Pedro Polished Red, and Minor types included examples from the Colonial/Historical and Late Postclassic periods. San Andrés Red was the most common undecorated type. In levels IV to VI, Ocotlán Red Rim was the most abundant of the decorated types, with Cocoyotla present in low frequencies. Xicalli Plain was present in high to very high proportions (20–30%).

Both of these stratified deposits contained mixed contents of collapsed adobe wall material approximately 50 to 120 cm below the surface and sterile soil at about 130 cm. Since no floors or walking surfaces were found associated with the mixed adobe, it is likely that the units were located outside of the walled area associated with the structure 1 compound, with the walls collapsing outward. The stratified ceramics have a similar pattern of Apolo and Aquiahuac polychromes in the upper levels of the wall debris but few examples of these types in the lower levels and beneath it. Instead, Ocotlán Red Rim and Xicalli Plain were the major types found, with a small amount of Cocoyotla Black on Natural. This pattern is consistent with the ceramic complex associated with structure 1, suggesting the possibility that the wall debris was associated with the compound, perhaps as part of the northern compound wall.

A second observation based on the analysis of these two stratified units is that the structure 1 compound (including the earlier structural remains) was built directly over natural soil. No evidence was found for occupation associated with the Terminal Formative/Classic-period platform found in the southern portion of the UA-1 project area (structure 3) and further exposed in the UA-69 and UA-70 excavations (Mountjoy and Peterson 1973).

SERIATION OF UA-1 CERAMIC ASSEMBLAGES

The analyses of the different depositional contexts produced varied distributions of relative ceramic frequencies, probably relating at least in part to temporal change. Since polychrome types made up significant portions of all of the major assemblages, they relate to the Postclassic period or later. Despite this basic similarity, however, distinctive patterns in the ceramic frequencies were apparent in the initial interpretations of the contexts. Thirteen assemblages were identified from discrete depositional contexts that contained a relatively high sample size (that is, at least seventy-five identifiable rim sherds). These assemblages are tabulated in table 5.8, using only the percentage of each type.

To order these assemblages into a linear series based on similarity, each pair of assemblages was converted into similarity coefficients using the Brainerd-Robinson Index of Agreement (Brainerd 1951; Robinson 1951; Marquardt 1982[1978]; Shennan 1988; Cowgill 1990). In this system, the total difference between the percentages of each type is calculated, and this total is subtracted from 200% (the maximum possible level of disagreement). This is expressed in the formula

$$IA_{jk} = 200 - \left(\sum_{i=1}^{m} | X_{ji} - X_{ki} | \right)$$

where the Index of Agreement (IA) of two assemblages (j and k) is 200 minus the sum of the absolute values of the differences between the percentages for each type. Thus a high index value will show greater similarity, and a low value will represent greater dissimilarity. For example,

Table 5.7   N5/E1 Stratified ceramics (by level)

	III (50–80) n (%)	IV (80–100) n (%)	V (100–112) n (%)	VI (112–137) n (%)
Major Decorated Types				
APOLO BLACK & RED/ORANGE	1 (1.6)	0	1 (3)	0
Sencillo	1 (100)*	0	0	0
Geométrico	0	0	0	0
Elegante	0	0	1 (100)*	0
AQUIAHUAC BURNT ORANGE	2 (3)	1 (1.4)	1 (3)	0
Sencillo	0	1 (100)*	1 (100)*	0
Santa Catalina	0	0	0	0
Zócalo	2 (100)*	0	0	0
COAPAN LACA POLYCHROME	2 (3)	0	0	0
COCOYOTLA BLACK/NATURAL	0	2 (3)	2 (6)	2 (7)
Sencillo	0	2 (100)*	1 (50)*	2 (100)*
Incised	0	0	1 (50)*	0
Banded	0	0	0	0
Banded Elegante	0	0	0	0
Chalco Black on Orange	0	0	0	0
CUAXILOA MATTE	0	1 (1.4)	0	0
OCOTLÁN RED RIM	0	16 (23)	7 (21)	8 (29)
Sencillo	0	13 (81)*	4 (57)*	6 (75)*
Elegante	0	0	1 (14)*	2 (25)*
Cristina Matte	0	2 (12)*	0	0
Other subtypes	0	1 (6)*	2 (29)*	0
SAN PEDRO POLISHED	2 (3)	3 (4)	1 (3)	0
TORRE RED & ORANGE/WHITE	0	1 (1.4)	0	0
Major Undecorated Types				
CERRO ZAPOTECAS SANDY PLAIN	3 (5)	6 (9)	2 (6)	3 (11)
MOMOXPAN METALLIC ORANGE	12 (19)	13 (19)	2 (6)	3 (11)
SAN ANDRÉS RED	22 (34)	9 (13)	6 (18)	1 (4)
TEPONTLA BURNISHED	4 (6)	3 (4)	1 (3)	3 (11)
XICALLI PLAIN	11 (17)	14 (20)	10 (30)	7 (25)
Minor Types				
COLONIAL/HISTORICAL	3 (5)	0	0	0
LATE POSTCLASSIC	2 (3)	0	0	0
EARLY POSTCLASSIC	0	0	0	0
CLASSIC	0	0	0	1 (4)
PRECLASSIC	0	0	0	0
UNIDENTIFIED	0	0	0	0
IDENTIFIABLE	64 (100) (33% of total)	69 (100) (64% of total)	33 (100) (75% of total)	28 (100) (80% of total)
UNIDENTIFIABLE				
ERODED/BURNT	13 (7)	10 (9)	3 (7)	0
TOO SMALL	116 (60)	29 (27)	8 (18)	7 (20)
TOTAL SHERDS	193 (100)	108 (100)	44 (100)	35 (100)

Note: Type frequencies are expressed as the proportion of the Total Identifiable sherds, and subtype frequency (*) relates to the corresponding type

Table 5.8 UA-1 Ceramic frequencies from major depositional contexts (by percentage)

	A	B	C	D	E	F	G	H	I	J	K	L	M
APOLO	46	6	0	0	1	2	9	0	0	11	4	18	12
AQUIAHUAC	4	4	0	0	1	1	3	0	0	8	21	9	10
COAPAN	0	0	0	0	0	0	1	0	0	1	1	1	1
COCOYOTLA	0	2	7	8	6	11	4	6	8	2	6	0	2
CUAXILOA	2	2	8	25	1	3	3	5	0	5	4	5	3
OCOTLÁN	0	2	11	8	24	27	15	21	33	8	4	1	7
SAN PEDRO	1	4	2	1	2	2	2	1	4	2	2	0	2
TORRE	1	1	8	11	0	1	1	4	0	4	4	1	2
C ZAPOTECAS	1	4	3	2	3	1	4	0	4	3	1	6	3
MOMOXPAN	24	20	20	16	12	19	21	18	15	20	25	27	27
SAN ANDRÉS	14	29	7	10	9	7	13	9	13	13	10	14	16
TEPONTLA	1	1	3	1	5	3	3	4	0	2	2	0	2
XICALLI	4	6	29	18	35	23	21	33	23	20	13	17	10
COLONIAL/ HISTORIC	0	20	0	0	0	0	1	0	0	1	0	0	2
LATE POSTCLASSIC	2	0	0	0	0	0	0	0	0	0	1	0	0
EARLY POSTCLASSIC	0	0	0	0	0	0	0	0	0	0	0	0	0
CLASSIC	1	0	1	0	0	0	0	0	0	0	1	0	0
PRECLASSIC	0	0	0	0	0	0	0	0	0	0	0	0	0
UNIDENTIFIED	0	0	0	0	0	0	0	0	0	0	0	0	0
TOTALS	100	100	100	100	100	100	100	100	100	100	100	100	100

Key: A = well 1; B = well 2; C = trash midden; D = well 3; E = below porch; F = structure 1 floor contact; G = structure 1 above floor; H = temazcal; I = S6/W3 burial ; J = structure 2 above floor; K = intrusive midden; L = sherd concentration 1; M = sherd concentration 2

Table 5.9 Similarity Matrix of UA-1 Assemblages

	A	B	C	D	E	F	G	H	I	J	K	L	M
1. A	200	106	76	71	62	77	110	70	67	115	108	136	128
2. B	106	200	92	85	80	91	124	82	91	125	110	116	134
3. C	76	92	200	153	150	155	150	168	137	147	130	110	118
4. D	71	85	153	200	117	128	127	135	124	134	121	105	109
5. E	62	80	150	117	200	163	144	174	159	123	106	92	102
6. F	77	91	155	128	163	200	157	165	166	136	123	107	115
7. G	110	124	150	127	144	157	200	148	147	175	138	146	156
8. H	70	82	168	135	174	165	148	200	149	137	122	102	108
9. I	67	91	137	124	159	166	147	149	200	126	103	101	105
10. J	115	125	147	134	123	136	175	137	126	200	151	161	171
11. K	108	110	130	121	106	123	138	122	103	151	200	140	154
12. L	136	116	110	105	92	107	146	102	101	161	140	200	164
13. M	128	134	118	109	102	115	156	108	105	171	154	164	200

comparing the well 1 assemblage (A) with the well 2 assemblage (B) produces these results:

$$| 46 - 6 | = 40$$
$$| 4 - 4 | = 0$$
$$| 0 - 0 | = 0$$
$$| 0 - 2 | = 2$$
$$| 2 - 2 | = 0$$
$$| 0 - 2 | = 2$$
$$| 1 - 4 | = 3$$
$$| 1 - 1 | = 0$$
$$| 1 - 4 | = 3$$
$$| 24 - 20 | = 4$$
$$| 14 - 29 | = 15$$
$$| 1 - 1 | = 0$$
$$| 4 - 6 | = 2$$
$$| 0 - 20 | = 20$$
$$| 2 - 0 | = 2$$
$$| 0 - 0 | = 0$$
$$| 1 - 0 | = 1$$
$$| 0 - 0 | = 0$$
$$| 0 - 0 | = 0$$

$$\overline{}$$
94

$$IA_{AB} = 200 - (94)$$
$$IA_{AB} = 106$$

The Brainerd-Robinson Index of Agreement values for the thirteen assemblages are recorded in a "similarity matrix" (table 5.9), where each line represents the similarity coefficient of that assemblage compared with the assemblage of the corresponding column. The principal diagonal maintains a constant value of 200, since any assemblage compared to itself will be perfectly similar.

In simple, well-behaved data sets, this matrix can be rearranged heuristically to construct a seriation where the similarity coefficients decrease as they move away from the principal diagonal. A more rigorous and replicable method for generating a seriation has been suggested by Renfrew and Sterud (1969) and elaborated by Gelfand (1971). In Gelfand's Method II (see Marquardt 1982[1978]:419–421), the Brainerd-Robinson values are systematically sorted by order of similarity and then the rankings of each row are averaged to produce the best possible seriation. The actual ordering of the assemblages is done by pairing the two highest values on the line (one of which is always 200). The next step is to select the next highest value and place it next to the initial value with which it has the highest similarity coefficient. The process continues until all values on a line have been placed in order.

In reference to row 1, the greatest similarity is between A (200) and L (136). The next highest value is for M (128). To determine where M should be placed in rela-

tion to the initial pair, its coefficient of similarity is compared for MA (128) and ML (164). Since ML is greater, M is placed next to L, so that the string becomes A - L - M. The next highest value is J (115). The comparison is now made between JA (115) and JM (171), with the greatest value that of JM. The seriation is expanded to A - L - M - J. This systematic ordering continues until the entire row is complete, and is then repeated for each of the remaining rows. For the UA-1 data, the corrected seriation orders by row are:

1. A - L - M - J - G - K - B - F - C - D - H - I - E
2. A - K - L - G - J - M - B - C - F - I - D - H - E
3. A - B - L - M - K - D - C - H - F - E - G - J - I
4. A - B - L - M - K - D - C - H - J - F - G - I - E
5. A - B - L - M - K - D - J - G - C - E - H - F - I
6. A - B - L - M - K - D - J - C - G - I - F - H - E
7. A - B - D - K - L - M - J - G - F - C - H - I - E
8. A - B - L - M - K - D - J - G - C - H - E - F - I
9. A - B - L - K - M - D - J - C - G - H - E - F - I
10. A - B - K - L - M - J - G - C - H - F - D - I - E
11. A - B - K - M - J - L - G - C - F - H - D - E - I
12. A - G - J - M - L - K - B - C - F - D - H - I - E
13. A - K - L - M - J - G - B - C - F - D - H - I - E

The final step is to calculate the average rank order for the thirteen different seriations. This is done by assigning a numerical rank to each assemblage per row and then totaling that rank for all rows. For example, in Row 1, A = 1, L = 2, M = 3, J = 4, and so on. The rank average is determined by dividing the rank totals by 13 (the number of assemblages). The rank average for each assemblage is: A=1; B=3.5; C=8.2; D=7.8; E=12.2; F=9.9; G=7.3; H=10.3; I=12.1; J=6.5; K=4.2; L=3.5; and M=4.4.

These rank averages can be graphed (figure 5.3) to show not only the order of the assemblages, but also clusters based on similarity. At the far left, is the well 1

5.3 Graph of averaged rank order of UA-1 ceramic assemblages

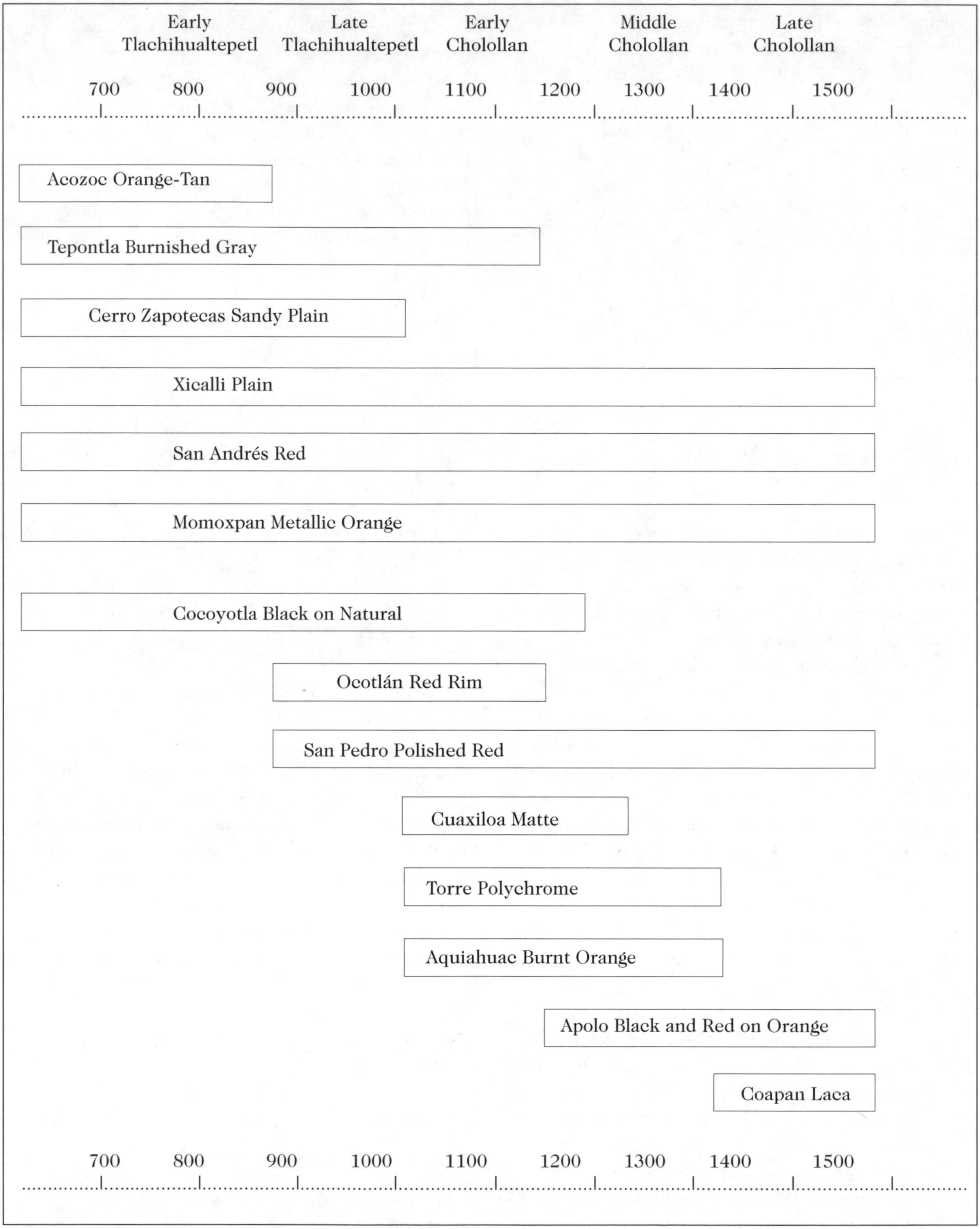

	Early Tlachihualtepetl	Late Tlachihualtepetl	Early Cholollan	Middle Cholollan	Late Cholollan

700   800   900   1000   1100   1200   1300   1400   1500

Acozoc Orange-Tan

Tepontla Burnished Gray

Cerro Zapotecas Sandy Plain

Xicalli Plain

San Andrés Red

Momoxpan Metallic Orange

Cocoyotla Black on Natural

Ocotlán Red Rim

San Pedro Polished Red

Cuaxiloa Matte

Torre Polychrome

Aquiahuac Burnt Orange

Apolo Black and Red on Orange

Coapan Laca

700   800   900   1000   1100   1200   1300   1400   1500

5.4 Battleship graph of Postclassic ceramic chronology

assemblage (A), which was the most dissimilar because of its exceptionally high concentration of Apolo Polychrome. The first cluster includes well 2 (B), concentrations 1 and 2 (L and M), and the intrusive midden (K). A more dispersed cluster includes the fill deposits from above the two floors (J and G), and the well 3 (D) and trash midden (C) assemblages. Another grouping is formed by the structure 1 floor contact deposit (F) and temazcal (H) materials. Finally, nearly identical rank averages were produced for the assemblages from the S6/W3 burials (I) and from below the structure 1 porch (E).

This ranking correlates well with an intuitive ranking based on stratigraphic relationships and diagnostic artifacts, with one significant exception. Well 2, with its high concentration of Colonial/Historic period ceramics (and other evidence for post-Conquest deposition), was clustered with assemblages of probable pre-Columbian origin, and appears earlier than well 1. A plausible explanation for this apparent error is that, with the exception of glazed serving wares, traditional pottery types continued in use, particularly as utilitarian types. Colonial/Historic pottery, possibly used for purposes of display, took the place of Apolo Polychrome, the predominant Late Postclassic serving type. I suspect that this assemblage may have also contained a small amount of redeposited fill based on the fairly high number of small sherds and the persistent presence of Early Postclassic types such as Xicalli Plain, Cocoyotla Black on Natural, and Ocotlán Red Rim.

Other aspects of the rank order, however, do correspond well with the stratigraphy. For example, the intrusive midden (K) and the sherd concentrations (L and M) fall to the left of, or later than, the structure 2 fill deposits; and the structure 1 fill (G) falls later than the floor contact (F), which in turn was later than the materials from below the porch (E). The relationship between the trash midden (C) and well 3 (D) is interesting because, although they are very close on the scale, the well assemblage is later than the midden. Based on this grouping, the temazcal assemblage was closely associated with the materials from the structure 1 floor contact, and the burials found at S6/W3 date to a period before the abandonment of structure 1.

To orient this seriation in time relative to the chronological framework suggested in chapter 2, the rank order and corresponding ceramic frequencies are used to construct a series of "battleship" curves (figure 5.4). This graphic presents an idealized perspective and future analyses of additional ceramic assemblages will further refine the sequence; note that recently analyzed assemblages such as the San Pedro well and R-106 (McCafferty 1996a) tend to support the current scheme. In general terms the pattern that emerges is of relatively rapid change in the popularity of decorated serving types, while undecorated utilitarian types undergo relatively little change. During the Middle Tlachihualtepetl phase (900–1050 CE), the principal serving wares were Xicalli Plain, Ocotlán Red Rim, and Cocoyotla Black on Natural, with utilitarian vessels of the types Momoxpan Orange, San Andrés Red, and Cerro Zapotecas Sandy Plain. By the Late Tlachihualtepetl phase (1050–1200 CE), Cuaxiloa Matte and Torre Polychrome were introduced as serving wares, and Cocoyotla subtype Banded became more common than the Sencillo subtype. During the Early Cholollan phase (1200–1400 CE), the proportions of Xicalli, Ocotlán, and Cocoyotla were reduced, and Aquiahuac Burnt Orange and Apolo Black and Red on Orange Polychrome were introduced. The utilitarian types remained fairly constant. Finally, in the Late Cholollan phase (1400–1520 CE) Apolo Polychrome was the predominant decorated type, with a minor presence of Aquiahuac and Coapan Laca. Momoxpan Orange and San Andrés Red remained as the major utilitarian types.

On the basis of this reconstruction of the Postclassic ceramic sequence, the materials from structures 1 and 2 are not contemporary. Structure 1 and its associated features (including the temazcal and the S6/W3 burials) date to the Middle Tlachihualtepetl phase, while the trash midden and well 3 date to the Late Tlachihualtepetl phase. Structure 2 was occupied several centuries later, in the Early Cholollan period. The well 1 assemblage, with its very high proportion of Apolo Polychrome, dates to the Late Cholollan period and passed intrusively through the structure 1 occupation levels.

VESSEL-FORM ANALYSIS OF UA-1 CERAMICS

This section focuses on vessel form as a means of inferring vessel function. The analysis combines specific forms into functional vessel types and vessel classes for subsequent interpretations. These include a comparison of vessel-form frequencies from the trash midden, using both sherd counts and degree-of-arc measurements; a comparison of vessel-form frequencies from the four pri-

Table 5.10 Vessel-form analysis from the UA-1 trash midden

Vessel form	Sherd count n (%)	Degree of arc n (%)	Min. # of vessels
Plate	13 (0.5)	276 (0.5)	0.77
Comal	571 (20)	7981 (13)	22.2
Outleaned-wall dish	429 (15)	11051 (19)	30.7
Flared rim	181 (42)*	4358 (39)*	12.1*
Subhemispherical dish	6 (0.2)	160 (0.3)	0.44
Outleaned-wall bowl	8 (0.3)	114 (0.2)	0.32
Everted lip	1 (12)*	15 (13)*	0.04*
Subhemispherical bowl	657 (23)	13156 (22)	36.5
Everted "L" lip	3 (0.5)*	(63 (0.5)*	0.18*
Hemispherical bowl	40 (1.4)	722 (1.2)	2.0
Flared rim	1 (2)*	20 (3)*	0.06*
Conical bowl	522 (18)	10636 (18)	29.5
Finger-impressed rim	1 (0.2)*	20 (0.2)*	0.06*
Flared rim	214 (41)*	4414 (42)*	12.3*
Everted lip	19 (4)*	340 (3)*	0.94*
Cylindrical bowl	2 (0.07)	46 (0.08)	0.13
Flared rim	2 (100)*	46 (100)*	0.13*
Superhemispherical bowl	269 (9)	6025 (10)	16.7
Composite silhouette bowl	3 (0.1)	44 (0.07)	0.12
Long-neck olla	51 (1.8)	1839 (03)	5.1
Everted "L" lip	7 (14)*	198 (11)*	0.55
Small-mouth olla	43 (1.5)	978 (1.6)	2.7
Wide-mouth olla	37 (1.3)	850 (1.4)	2.4
Hemispherical cazuela	23 (0.8)	343 (0.6)	0.95
Flared rim	8 (35)*	170 (50)*	0.47*
Conical cazuela	52 (1.8)	830 (1.4)	2.3
Flared rim	27 (52)*	405 (49)*	1.1*
Everted lip	25 (48)*	425 (51)*	1.2*
Conical maceta	26 (0.9)	382 (0.6)	1.1
Brasero	34 (1.2)	781 (1.3)	2.2
Tecomate	9 (0.3)	238 (0.4)	0.66
Inverted rim	6 (67)*	130 (55)*	0.36*
Vertical rim	2 (22)*	95 (40)*	0.26*
Biconical copa	34 (1.2	1362 (2)	3.8
Tripod incense burner	7 (0.2)	275 (0.5)	0.76
Sahumador	26 (0.9)	674 (1.1)	1.9
Florero	2 (0.07)	255 (0.4)	0.71
Ladle	1 (0.03)	**	**
Miniature vessel	1 (0.03)	8 (0.01)	0.02
Lantern censer	15 (0.5)	345 (0.6)	0.96
TOTALS	2881 (100)	59371 (100)	165.49

* Form frequencies are expressed as the proportion of the total, and rim form frequency relates to the corresponding vessel form.

** Degree-of-arc measurement could not be made for the elongated ladle form.

mary depositional contexts;the combination of vessel forms into vessel types and classes for the primary contexts; and the tabulation of vessel type and class frequencies in other depositional contexts.

TRASH MIDDEN VESSEL FORMS

The extensive trash midden located south of structure 1 contained the highest concentration of vessel fragments of any of the primary contexts. Furthermore, since artifactual evidence links the midden with the terminal occupation phase of structure 1, it therefore provides a potential source for comparing an assemblage of secondary refuse with materials from the same behavioral system that were either abandoned as de facto refuse or dropped as primary refuse (Schiffer 1987).

Table 5.10 presents the distribution of different vessel forms found in the trash midden using two distinct methods for characterizing the amount present. In the first column vessel forms are listed together with rim form variants. The second column provides the number of sherds present per form, as well as its proportion in the total assemblage. For example, 429 sherds were identified as outleaned-wall dishes, or 15% of the total assemblage. For alternative rim forms, the number in parenthesis represents the count and percentage of the total form. Again using the outleaned-wall dish vessel form, 181 examples were identified with a flared rim, making up 42% of the form total.

Based on sherd counts, subhemispherical bowl fragments were the most abundant vessel form present, occurring as 23% of the total assemblage. Comal fragments were also found in high proportion (20%). Conical bowl (18%) and outleaned-wall dish (15%) fragments were present in moderate amounts, and superhemispherical bowl fragments were found in low frequency (9%). Surprisingly, other than comales, utilitarian vessel forms were rare, with long-neck ollas (1.8%), small-mouth ollas (1.5%), wide-mouth ollas (1.3%), and conical cazuelas (1.8%) each present as less than 2% of the total assemblage.

A second measure of vessel-form frequency was determined based on the total degrees of arc for each vessel form. Degree-of-arc measurements have potential for controlling bias introduced by vessel forms with unusually large or small orifice dimensions (for example, comales versus copas). In the third column of the table, the degree-of-arc total is given, followed by its percent-

age of the total assemblage. Thus, for the outleaned-wall dish category, the degree-of-arc total was 11,051, making up 19% of the total assemblage.

In comparing the degree-of-arc totals with the sherd counts, the most obvious difference is, as expected, in the relative frequency of comal fragments. Based on degrees of arc, this form made up only 13% of the total assemblage as opposed to 20% based on sherd count. The other significant difference is in terms of outleaned-wall dish fragments, as noted. Other than these two exceptions, the results of the different methods of analysis were quite similar.

The fourth column of table 5.10 presents the minimum number of vessels for each form. Using the degree-of-arc measurement, it is possible to estimate the minimum number of individual vessels for each form by dividing the total degree-of-arc value by 360, the number of degrees in a complete rim. The 11,051 degrees of arc for the outleaned-wall dish form can therefore be reduced to a minimum of 30.7 vessels. Based on the figures in column four, the trash midden contained a minimum of 166 vessels; this total does not include the eighty-one complete or reconstructable vessels that were not available for analysis, but were identified in the original object cards.

Relating the minimum number of vessels to the kitchen tool kit assumes a constant breakage rate. For example, the high relative frequency of serving wares in contrast to utilitarian wares (121:38) does not necessarily imply the actual proportion of these vessel classes in the average kitchen assemblage because the breakage rates may have varied considerably (Isaac 1986). A comparison of the trash midden ratio with one from the structure 1 floor contact (discussed below) provides a means for evaluating the breakage rate.

George Foster (1960) studied the ethnographic use life of pottery vessels from Tzintzuntzan, Michoacan. One notable result was an estimate that comales were replaced approximately once every six months. A similar rate was calculated for modern comal users from the Cholula area (Mountjoy and Peterson 1973:35). Peterson (1972; Mountjoy and Peterson 1973:35–36) used this rate to calculate the possible duration of midden use (based on varying number of households sharing a single midden) for the Faculty Housing Complex trash pit.

Comal fragments from the UA-1 trash midden can also be used cautiously to estimate the duration of deposi-

Table 5.11 Vessel forms from primary contexts

Vessel form	Well 1 n (%)	Well 2 n (%)	Trash midden n (%)	Well 3 n (%)
Plate	6 (1.7)	2 (0.5)	13 (0.5)	1 (0.4)
Comal	89 (25)	105 (28)	571 (20)	56 (22)
Outleaned-wall dish	55 (15)	18 (5)	429 (15)	23 (9)
Flared rim	55 (100)*	16 (89)*	181 (42)*	16 (70)*
Subhemispherical dish	4 (1.1)	2 (0.5)	6 (0.2)	3 (1.2)
Outleaned-wall bowl	0	1 (0.3)	8 (0.3)	2 (0.8)
Flared rim	0	0	0	1 (50)*
Everted lip	0	0	1 (12)*	0
Subhemispherical bowl	21 (6)	69 (18)	657 (23)	34 (14)
Flared rim	0	1 (1.4)*	0	0
Everted lip	1 (5)*	3 (4)*	0	0
Everted "L" lip	0	0	3 (0.5)*	0
Hemispherical bowl	13 (4)	0	40 (1.4)	12 (5)
Flared rim	0	0	1 (2)*	3 (25)*
Conical bowl	109 (31)	73 (19)	522 (18)	48 (19)
Finger-impressed rim	0	0	1 (0.2)*	0
Flared rim	3 (3)*	7 (10)*	214 (41)*	23 (48)*
Everted lip	0	2 (3)*	19 (4)*	0
Cylindrical bowl	0	0	2 (0.07)	0
Flared rim	0	0	2 (100)*	0
Superhemispherical bowl	12 (3)	15 (4)	269 (9)	41 (16)
Composite silhouette bowl	0	0	3 (0.1)	0
Long-neck olla	17 (5)	12 (3)	51 (1.8)	5 (2)
Ridged neck	(11 (65)	(6 (50)	0	0
Flanged neck	(6 (35)	(1 (8)	0	1 (20)*
Everted "L" lip	0	0	7 (14)*	0
Small-mouth olla	2 (0.6)	8 (2)	43 (1.5)	1 (0.4)
Conical neck	1 (50)*	0	**	0
Short neck	0	2 (25)*	**	0
Flared rim	1 (50)*	4 (50)*	**	1 (100)*
Bolstered lip	0	2 (25)*	**	0
Wide-mouth olla	12 (3)	16 (4)	37 (1.3)	4 (1.6)
Flanged neck	0	4 (25)*	**	0
Flared rim	4 (33)*	3 (19)*	**	4 (100)*
Everted rim	8 (67)*	5 (31)*	**	0
Bolstered rim	0	1 (6)*	**	0
Outleaned-wall cazuela	1 (0.3)	6 (1.6	0	0
Hemispherical cazuela	4 (1.1)	12 (3)	23 (0.8)	6 (2)
Flared rim	1 (25)*	6 (50)*	8 (35)*	3 (50)*
Conical cazuela	1 (0.3)	19 (5)	52 (1.8)	4 (1.6)
Square lip	0	2 (11)*	0	0
Flared rim	0	0	27 (52)*	1 (25)*
Everted lip	1 (100)*	5 (26)*	25 (48)*	1 (25)*
Conical maceta	0	1 (0.3)	26 (0.9)	2 (0.8)
Cylindrical maceta	1 (0.3)	10 (3)	0	1 (0.4)
Low wall	0	5 (50)*	0	0
Square lip	1 (100)*	5 (50)*	0	1 (100)*
Superhemispherical Maceta	0	3 (0.8)	0	0
Bracero	1 (0.3)	0	34 (1.2)	1 (0.4)
Tecomate	0	0	9 (0.3)	1 (0.4)
Inverted rim	0	0	6 (67)*	0
Vertical rim	0	0	2 (22)*	0
Biconical copa	1 (0.3)	1 (0.3)	34 (1.2)	2 (0.8)
Biconical bowl	0	1 (0.3)	0	1 (0.4)
Tripod incense burner	0	0	7 (0.2)	0
Sahumador	1 (0.3)	1 (0.3)	26 (0.9)	0
Florero	0	0	2 (0.07)	0
Ladle	0	0	1 (0.03)	0
Miniature vessel	4 (1.1)	0	1 (0.03)	0
Lantern censer	1 (0.3)	2 (0.5)	15 (0.5)	1 (0.4)
TOTALS	355 (100)	377 (100)	2881 (100)	249 (100)

Note: Form frequencies are expressed as the proportion of the total, and rim form frequency (*) relates to the corresponding vessel form.
Rim form not distinguished during trash midden analysis (**).

tion. Based on an estimated minimum of twenty-two comales in the deposit, it could have accumulated over a period of eleven years if the deposit was used exclusively by a single nuclear family, 5.5 years if used by two families, or a single year if used by eleven families. A variety of variables could affect this estimate, including the presence of additional comales among the missing vessels. Nevertheless, the estimated duration of the UA-1 midden deposit suggests a relatively short use life for the feature, on the order of less than a single generation. Evidence from mendable vessels with pieces found in different levels of the feature supports this estimate.

VESSEL-FORM ANALYSIS
FROM PRIMARY CONTEXTS

Detailed vessel-form analysis of the four primary contexts relating to secondary refuse disposal provides an opportunity to study possible diachronic changes in kitchen assemblages during the Postclassic and Early Colonial periods. Table 5.11 presents the sherd count data and relative frequencies for well 1, well 2, the trash midden, and well 3.

In well 1 conical bowls were the most abundant vessel form present (31% of the total assemblage). Comales were also present in high proportion (25%), and outleaned-wall dishes were moderately common (15%). Forms present in low and very low amounts included subhemispherical bowls (6%), hemispherical bowls (4%), superhemispherical bowls (3%), long-neck ollas (5%), and wide-mouth ollas (3%).

Well 2 was distinctive in that comal fragments made up the most abundant vessel form (28% of the total). Subhemispherical bowls (18%) and conical bowls (19%) were both present in moderate amounts, and other forms found in low and very low percentages included outleaned-wall dishes (5%), superhemispherical bowls (4%), long-neck ollas (3%), small-mouth ollas (2%), wide-mouth ollas (4%), hemispherical cazuelas (3%), conical cazuelas (5%), and cylindrical macetas (3%).

As described above, subhemispherical bowls (23%) and comales (20%) were the most common vessel forms found in the trash midden on the basis of sherd count. Outleaned-wall dishes (15%), conical bowls (18%), and superhemispherical bowls (9%) were also common.

The well 3 assemblage had a high proportion of comal fragments (22%). Forms present in moderate amounts included conical bowls (19%), subhemispherical bowls (14%), and superhemispherical bowls (16%). Outleaned-wall dishes (9%) and hemispherical bowls (5%) were found in low proportions, and long-neck ollas (2%) and hemispherical cazuelas (2%) were both present in very low percentages.

Comparison of the vessel forms from these primary depositional contexts indicates a general consistency in the abundance of comales and scarcity of other utilitarian forms. This is most apparent in the trash midden deposit, where no other utilitarian forms accounted for more than 2% of the assemblage. The well 2 deposit had the highest relative frequency of utilitarian forms. The low proportions of utilitarian forms, however, may relate to longer use life of these vessel types and also to the very high proportions of serving wares. It should be noted that the general forms found remain fairly constant, with the possible exception of outleaned-wall cazuelas and conical and cylindrical macetas, which are not found in all assemblages.

The primary contexts also displayed variation in the specific forms of serving wares. Conical bowls, for example, were most common in wells 1, 2, and 3, while subhemispherical bowls were more abundant in the trash midden. While direct rim conical bowls were predominant from wells 1 and 2, nearly half of the conical bowls from the trash midden and well 3 had flared rims. Superhemispherical bowls were more common in the trash midden and well 3 than in the other contexts. Outleaned-wall dishes were fairly consistent in the well 1, trash midden, and well 3 deposits, but the percentage dropped dramatically in well 2.

Several possible explanations can be suggested for these observed differences. Changing cultural foodways in the types of foods prepared and the manner of consumption may account for the higher numbers of superhemispherical bowls in the earlier trash midden and well 3 assemblages. This form may have been used for drinking liquid foods such as atole, and the evidence for burning that was common on this vessel form indicates that it may also have been used for heating liquids. In contrast, the decline in outleaned-wall dishes in well 2 may indicate a reduction in the consumption of dry foods in favor of a greater reliance on stews eaten out of bowls.

Other variations in specific vessel forms may not represent functional differences in cultural foodways, but instead may be evidence of isochrestic variation in morphology, perhaps related to changing social definitions of

Table 5.12 Vessel types from primary contexts

Vessel form	Well 1 n (%)	Well 2 n (%)	Trash midden n (%)	Well 3 n (%)
UTILITARIAN WARES				
Comal	89 (25)	105 (28)	571 (20)	56 (22)
Olla	31 (9)	36 (10)	131 (5)	10 (4)
Cazuela	6 (1.7)	37 (10)	75 (3)	10 (4)
Maceta	1 (0.3)	14 (4)	26 (0.9)	3 (1.2)
Tecomate	0	0	9 (0.3)	1 (0.4)
SERVING WARES				
Plato	65 (18)	22 (6)	448 (16)	27 (11)
Cajete	155 (44)	158 (42)	1501 (52)	137 (55)
Copa	1 (0.3)	2 (0.5)	34 (1.2)	3 (1.2)
CEREMONIAL WARES				
Brasero	1 (0.3)	0	34 (1.2)	1 (0.4)
Tripod censer	0	0	7 (0.2)	0
Sahumador	1 (0.3)	1 (0.3)	26 (0.9)	0
Lantern censer	1 (0.3)	2 (0.5)	15 (0.5)	1 (0.4)
Miniature vessel	4 (1.1)	0	1 (0.03)	0
TOTALS	355 (100)	377 (100)	2878 (100)	249 (100)

Table 5.13 Vessel class analysis from primary contexts

Vessel class	Well 1 n (%)	Well 2 n (%)	Trash midden n (%)	Well 3 n (%)
Utilitarian wares	127 (36)	192 (51)	812 (28)	80 (32)
Serving wares	221 (62)	182 (48)	1983 (69)	167 (67)
Ceremonial wares	7 (2)	3 (0.8)	83 (3)	2 (0.8)
TOTALS	355 (100)	377 (100)	2878 (100)	249 (100)

Table 5.14 Vessel types from additional contexts

Vessel form	Structure 1 floor contact n (%)	Structure 2 intrusive midden n (%)	Concentrations 1 & 2 n (%)
UTILITARIAN WARES			
Comal	87 (20	40 (24	259 (29)
Olla	19 (4	7 (4	63 (7)
Cazuela	9 (2	7 (4	59 (7)
Maceta	0	1 (0.6	17 (1.9)
Tecomate	0	0	5 (0.6)
Serving wares			
Plato	9 (2	31 (18	114 (13)
Cajete	303 (70	83 (49	349 (39)
Copa	0	0	2 (0.2)
CEREMONIAL WARES			
Brasero	3 (0.7)	0	6 (0.7)
Tripod censer	1 (0.2)	1 (0.6)	0
Sahumador	2 (0.5)	0	4 (0.5)
Lantern censer	1 (0.2)	0	4 (0.5)
Miniature vessel	0	0	5 (0.6)
TOTALS	434 (100)	170 (100)	887 (100)

prototypical vessel forms (Kempton 1981). Examples of this kind of change might be seen in the shifting importance of superhemispherical and conical bowls, both of which would be used for consuming liquid foods such as stews, and also in the changing ratios of direct and flared rim conical bowls. Variation between these forms may not necessarily relate to changes in foodways, but could be sensitive to other aesthetic principles that structured ceramic consumption.

ANALYSIS OF VESSEL TYPE AND CLASS FROM PRIMARY CONTEXTS

The detailed analysis of vessel forms from the four primary contexts identified variations in specific forms, particularly serving wares. Lumping forms into functional vessel types provides a means of eliminating isochrestic variation from the analysis. This step is important for generalizing a kitchen tool kit for functional interpretations of different features. Vessel type data from the primary contexts are summarized in table 5.12.

The most significant differences in the relative frequencies of vessel types involve the utilitarian types olla, cazuela, and maceta. There were roughly twice as many of these types in well 2 as in either the trash midden or well 3. Ollas occurred in well 1 in comparable proportion to those in well 2, but the number of cazuelas and macetas were relatively low. Among the serving wares, well 2 had a notably low percentage of platos in contrast to the other assemblages. In addition, the trash midden and well 3 had larger amounts of cajetes and copas than the other assemblages. The relatively low number of copa fragments, and also ceremonial types, makes sample size a potential bias for interpreting the quantitative significance of these vessel types.

Overall, the distribution of vessel types was relatively consistent among the primary contexts. The greatest differences occurred in well 2 especially in the types cazuela, maceta, and plato. Assuming that breakage rates remained constant, this suggests that the well 2 kitchen tool kit contained relatively more of the utilitarian types but fewer platos. Functionally, this difference may again be related to an increased importance of foods of stew-like consistency. As the deposit that differs most from the other assemblages, well 2 can be interpreted as the greatest example of discontinuity in cultural foodways in this sequence. Because well 2 dated to the Colonial/Historical period, the kitchen tool kit probably reflects changes related to the introduction of new foods, food customs, and/or access to food goods, and therefore hints at the potential significance of studying foodways in relation to culture contact.

The relative frequency of serving to utilitarian wares is more clearly revealed when types are collapsed into vessel classes. This quantification is shown in table 5.13. Here the obvious feature is that more than half of the fragments from well 2 were utilitarian wares, in contrast to the other assemblages where utilitarian types made up 28 to 36% of the assemblage. The proportion of ceremonial wares remained relatively constant in all of these contexts.

Several possible explanations could account for this pattern. If these contexts all represent domestic refuse rather than deposits from other specialized activities, then it could suggest that these represent differences in socioeconomic status (Drennan 1974; Smith 1987b). Following this approach, household units of higher status consume relatively greater amounts of serving wares through ritual and social obligations such as feasting. The relatively low ratio of serving wares to utilitarian wares in well 2 may therefore be an indication of reduced status in the Colonial/Historical period. Alternatively, it may reflect changes in the display of status vis-à-vis group consumption, or even a change in household organization and consumption patterns. Obviously additional research is needed to investigate these aspects of cultural foodways.

VESSEL TYPE AND CLASS FROM ADDITIONAL DEPOSITS

The vessel type and vessel class data from the four primary deposits can be contrasted with that of other deposits, including the structure 1 floor contact, the intrusive midden in structure 2, and the extensive sheet midden identified as sherd concentrations 1 and 2. These data are presented in table 5.14.

The structure 1 floor contact deposit is of interest because of the potential for comparing secondary refuse from the trash midden with remains of primary and possible de facto refuse relating to the structure floor. This potential is enhanced by the possibility that the two contexts relate to the same systemic context.

The most significant difference between the two assemblages is in the very low percentage of platos in the floor contact collection. There is an increase, however, in the number of cajetes. This may indicate a ritual role for platos that created a specialized depositional pattern in the trash midden that was not reflected in the floor contact assemblage. Although only present as a trace in relation to other vessel forms in the trash midden, a relatively large number of copa fragments (1.2%, $n=34$) were found, in contrast to the absence of copas from the floor contact assemblage. Apart from these differences, however, the assemblages are quite similar.

The intrusive midden and sherd concentration deposits were both associated with the well 2 deposit in the seriation analysis, although it was noted that this association may reflect a degree of mixing of earlier material into the Colonial/Historical deposit. In comparing these features to wells 1 and 2, the percentages of platos are more similar to well 1. This may indicate that these additional features predate the change in socioeconomic status and/or food practice suggested by the decrease in this vessel type in the Colonial/Historic assemblage. The frequencies of cazuelas were intermediate between the two values from the well deposits.

6 Summary and Discussion

The UA-1 ceramic analysis concentrated on assemblages from thirteen depositional contexts relating to the two Postclassic structures and stratigraphically associated features such as the intrusive wells 1 and 2. These ceramic remains were analyzed by type and subtype, and the contexts were seriated to construct a diachronic sequence for the Middle and Late Tlachihualtepetl phases, Early and Late Cholollan phases, and Colonial/Historic period. The deposits were also analyzed by vessel form to interpret differences in consumption practices through time and between specific contexts.

Decorated serving ware types went through relatively rapid changes in terms of consumption patterns. Polychrome ceramics were not present at the Early Tlachihualtepetl phase (700–900 CE) assemblage from the Patio of the Carved Skulls at the Great Pyramid of Cholula where the predominant serving wares were Tepontla Burnished and Cocoyotla Black on Natural (McCafferty and Suárez C. 1995; McCafferty 1996a). Utilitarian wares also included a combination of Classic (Acozoc Tan/Orange) and Postclassic diagnostics (Momoxpan Metallic Orange and San Andrés Red).

The Middle Tlachihualtepetl phase (900–1050 CE) assemblages found at UA-1, including the structure 1 floor contact, temazcal, and S6/W3 burials, featured Ocotlán Red Rim and Cocoyotla Black on Natural (especially the Sencillo subtype) as the principal decorated types. Xicalli Plain, an undecorated serving ware, was the most abundant type used. Postclassic utilitarian types Momoxpan Orange and San Andrés Red were already well-established elements of the kitchen tool kit. This complex of types compares closely with the ceramic assemblage found at the San Pedro Cholula well from which two C14 dates were recovered: 892 –1018 CE (INAH 1102) and 905–1220 CE (INAH 1103; McCafferty 1996a).

The Torre and Cuaxiloa Matte polychrome types, as well as different subtypes of Ocotlán Red Rim (subtype Cristina Matte) and Cocoyotla Black on Natural (subtype Banded), are diagnostic of the Late Tlachihualtepetl phase (1050–1200 CE). This ceramic complex is represented at UA-1 by the trash midden and well 3 deposits. A similar assemblage was found in a midden deposit at the Transito site (R-106) in San Pedro Cholula (McCafferty, Suárez C., and Edelstein N.D.).

The Early Cholollan phase (1200–1400 CE) featured a diversity of polychrome types, including Aquiahuac, Apolo, and Torre. At UA-1 it was best represented by an intrusive midden that passed through the floor of structure 2, but also by deposits above the structure 2 floor and a sherd concentration found between structures 1 and 2. The Early Cholollan ceramic complex was also encountered at the UA-70 Faculty Housing Complex midden that produced a single C14 date of 1250 ± 95 CE (Mountjoy and Peterson 1973:30).

The Late Cholollan phase (1400–1520 CE) was represented by the assemblage from well 1 that passed through the floor of structure 1, room 4. It is characterized by a very high proportion of Apolo Polychrome, almost to the exclusion of any other decorated types. This is the period to which the famous Coapan Laca Polychrome belongs although it was rare at UA-1, perhaps because it was used by a more elite segment of Cholula society. This ceramic complex has also been found at

UA-79 (Lind 1979; Barrientos 1980), the San Andrés Cholula mass burial (Suárez C. 1989, 1994), and in a well from the UDLA campus that produced a date of 1450±80 CE (Uruñuela and Alvarez-Méndez 1989:70; in Lind 1994:81, n. 4).

A final depositional context, well 2, featured a high frequency of glazed ware and therefore represents a post-Contact assemblage.

Notably, whereas the decorated ceramics changed stylistically throughout the Postclassic period, utilitarian wares such as Momoxpan Orange and San Andrés Red remained relatively consistent. This would suggest a general cultural continuity on a fundamental level, but it is in contrast to the relatively rapid changes in the more symbolically charged serving ware types. It is likely that the polychrome serving vessels may have functioned symbolically to signal ethnic, status, and political boundaries within a complex, plural society (Wobst 1977). This would fit with the ethnohistoric accounts of successive in-migrations of Tolteca-Chichimeca groups that overlaid, rather than replaced, the original Olmeca-Xicallanca population (Olivera and Reyes 1969; Carrasco 1971; McCafferty 1989).

Based on the relative stability of the forms of utilitarian ware, there were few changes in foodways during the Postclassic period. Use of the comal was already well established at UA-1 by the Middle Tlachihualtepetl phase, while recent discoveries at the Patio of the Carved Skulls indicate that comales were introduced in the preceding Early Tlachihualtepetl phase. The use of superhemispherical bowls was more common in the Tlachihualtepetl period, perhaps relating to the preparation and consumption of a particular variety of liquid food. Platos became more common in the Cholollan period, suggesting an increased importance of dry foods.

The ceramic complexes defined herein require further investigation of additional assemblages from discrete depositional contexts. The fundamental problem faced, however, is the need for additional chronometric dates with which to calibrate the ceramic sequence (McCafferty 1996a).

The development of a revised ceramic classification and sequence provides an opportunity for analyzing and interpreting culture change at Postclassic Cholula. As a result of the UA-1 analysis, previous interpretations of the culture history of Cholula can be challenged. In the remainder of this chapter the UA-1 data are used to re-evaluate the Classic to Postclassic transition, particularly

in reference to the contradictory "histories" produced from archaeological and ethnohistoric sources. Second, the UA-1 data are related to ongoing debate about the origin and development of the Mixteca-Puebla stylistic tradition.

CULTURE HISTORY OF POSTCLASSIC CHOLULA

Information on the culture history of Cholula is available both from extensive archaeological excavations (Noguera 1954; Marquina 1970a; Mountjoy and Peterson 1973; Suárez C. 1985, 1989; Suárez C. and Martínez A. 1993; summarized in McCafferty 1996a), and from an equally detailed ethnohistorical record (Cortés 1986 [1519–1521]; Motolinía 1951 [1540]; Sahágun 1950-82 [1547 –1585]; Historia Tolteca-Chichimeca 1976 [ca. 1550]; Durán 1971 [1576–1579]; Diáz del Castillo 1963 [1580]; Rojas 1927 [1581]; Ixtlilxochitl 1975–1977 [1615]; Torquemada 1975–1983 [1625]). Since most of the excavations have concentrated on the early architectural features of the Great Pyramid, however, the combination of these two data sets have often been more confusing than helpful. Whereas the ethnohistorical accounts have usually been interpreted as indicating a continuous occupation of the city following the Classic period (Jiménez Moreno 1966; Chadwick 1966, 1971b; Weaver 1972), the archaeological evidence has been interpreted as indicating at least a temporary site abandonment at the end of the Classic period (Dumond and Müller 1972; Dumond 1972; Davies 1977; Weaver 1981, 1993; Mountjoy 1987; but see Sanders 1989; McCafferty 1996a).

As a result of recent reinterpretations of the construction history of the Great Pyramid of Cholula (McCafferty 1996b), I suggest that the pyramid continued in use into the Early Postclassic period (see also Sanders 1989). In fact, construction activity was possibly at its peak during the Epiclassic period, when stages 3 and 4 of the Great Pyramid were built (McCafferty 1996b, 2000), and the Patio of the Altars complex was built in a sequence of six successive stages (Acosta 1970). If this historical reconstruction is accurate, then the archaeological evidence for continuous occupation would become more consistent with the ethnohistorical record.

While the UA-1 data do not necessarily contribute specific information relating to the alleged abandonment of Cholula, revision of the Postclassic chronology and evaluation of the diagnostic ceramics from the different phases can be used to interpret possible cultural traditions or changes that may have occurred. By extending the origin of the polychrome ceramic tradition to as early as 900 CE, and through the recent discovery of an Early Tlachihualtepetl occupation at the Patio of the Carved Skulls (McCafferty and Suárez C. 1995), the cultural divide between the Epiclassic and Early Postclassic periods disappears (McCafferty 1996a, 2000).

Second, the ethnohistorical "invasion" of Cholula by Nahua Tolteca-Chichimeca in the late twelfth/early thirteenth centuries would be expected to have resulted in changes in the material culture (Olivera and Reyes 1969; McCafferty 1989). Ceramics and other remains predating the ethnohistoric event should relate to the Olmeca-Xicallanca occupation of the site. UA-70 artifacts associated with the radiocarbon date of 1250 ± 95 CE (Mountjoy and Peterson 1973:30) possibly relate to this period of transition, while those recovered from UA-79 (Barrientos 1980) would certainly postdate it. By organizing the UA-1 ceramic data around these two assemblages through seriation, comparisons of how and approximately when changes in the ceramic assemblage took place may be used to interpret possible cultural changes.

The Middle and Late Tlachihualtepetl phase occupation of structure 1 predated both of these previously described ceramic complexes. Similarities link the structure 1 ceramic complex with materials from the San Pedro well, especially through the importance of Ocotlán Red Rim and Cocoyotla Black on Natural. It may also relate to the final occupation of the Great Pyramid, which featured polychrome pottery on its surface (Noguera 1937, 1954:225–226).

Ethnohistorical accounts of the Epiclassic and Early Postclassic period occupation by the Olmeca-Xicallanca also suggest that this ethnic group (or confederation of ethnic groups) had close affilations with the Gulf Coast. Stylistic motifs diagnostic of the Gulf Coast are prominent in the architecture and carved stone monuments at the Great Pyramid, especially after stage 3A, and at the Patio of the Altars (McCafferty 1996b). Evidence for the Olmeca-Xicallanca occupation of Cholula is also present at the household level, as seen in the material culture found at UA-1. Gulf Coast influences were found in pottery decoration, particularly on Cuaxiloa Matte Polychrome and Ocotlán Red Rim subtype Cristina Matte; in plastered architectural façades; in the use of bitumen coating on spindle whorls; in the use of shell ornaments; and in a figurine that included blue paint (McCafferty 1992a).

CHOLULA AND THE MIXTECA-PUEBLA STYLISTIC TRADITION

One aspect of Mesoamerican history in which Cholula has often been discussed is in speculation about the development of the Postclassic Mixteca-Puebla horizon. Since the initial formulation of the Mixteca-Puebla concept in the 1930s (Vaillant 1938, 1941; Nicholson 1960, 1982, 1994; Nicholson and Quiñones Keber 1994), Cholula has been considered the point of origin of the style. Jiménez Moreno (1942:128–129) and Nicholson (1982) have suggested the possibility that the Mixteca-Puebla style was developed by the Olmeca-Xicallanca ethnic group in the Cholula region.

Michael Smith and Cynthia Heath-Smith (1980) advanced an important critique of the Mixteca-Puebla concept in which they argued that instead of being indicative of an overarching "culture complex," the Mixteca-Puebla concept combined three distinct elements:

> (1) the *Postclassic Religious Style,* a collection of standardized religious symbols that were popular throughout Mesoamerica, beginning in the Early Postclassic period;
>
> (2) the *Mixtec Codex Style,* a highly-distinctive Late Postclassic polychrome narrative style most commonly associated with codices, murals and ceramics of the Mixteca-Puebla region; and
>
> (3) the *Mixteca-Puebla Regional Ceramic Sphere,* the local ceramic complexes of the Mixteca-Puebla which share several stylistic features (Smith and Heath-Smith 1980:15).

In distinguishing these three phenomena, Smith and Heath-Smith suggested that while the Postclassic Religious Style was relatively widespread, the other elements were local developments that retained a high degree of regional specificity. The significance of the critique is the suggested model for the transmission of the Religious Style, that is, through "processes of trade, communication and religious interpretation" (Smith and Heath-Smith 1980:39), and especially for the critical evaluation of often simplistic ascriptions of cultural contact.

In evaluating this model, Cholula is central to all three of these phenomena. As the center of the Quetzalcoatl cult, it was at the origin of the Postclassic Religious

Style. As the probable source for the *Codex Borgia* and other pre-Columbian codices, as well as *tipo codice* polychrome pottery, Cholula was an important center for the Mixtec Codex Style, or at least the Borgia-group branch of it. And Cholula was certainly a major source for the production of Mixteca-Puebla polychrome ceramics.

One of the pervasive themes of the Postclassic Religious Style is the prevalence of iconographic elements of the Quetzalcoatl cult, including feathered serpent motifs and *xicalcoliuhqui* patterns (McCafferty 1999; Nicholson 1960, 1982). Ethnohistoric sources clearly place Cholula at the center of this religious movement (Durán 1971 [1576–1579]:133; Rojas 1927 [1581]:160–161; Torquemada 1975–1983 [1615], Book 1:387). Quetzalcoatl was a deity whose priesthood preserved sacred knowledge, and the temple complex at Cholula may have housed a vast library and university where scribes trained in codex-style painting.

The mechanism for the diffusion of the Postclassic Religious Style remains to be explicated. In addition to the possibility of religious souvenirs carried back from pilgrimages (Ringle, Gallareta Negrón, and Bey III 1998), the iconography of Quetzalcoatl may have been transmitted by the pochteca, professional merchants affiliated with their patron, Quetzalcoatl/Yacatecuhtli, and their cult centered in Cholula (Durán 1971 [1576–1579]:262; Rojas 1927 [1581]).

A possible ethnographic analogue of this process may be found in the spread of Islam in Africa by ethnically organized Hausa merchants (Cohen 1969; Curtin 1984; Helms 1993). The Hausa established a trading diaspora based on concepts of ethnic and religious identity. The network was maintained through the distribution of religious icons, forming a safety net of religious partisans.

In regard to the Mixtec Codex Style, Nicholson (1960, 1982:229) suggested that the *Codex Borgia* was the definitive example of the Mixteca-Puebla style, based on its use of glyphic symbols relating to the religious pantheon and calendrical system. The *Codex Borgia* and related texts are distinguishable from examples of the Mixtec group of codices (Nicholson 1966), probably relating to both regional differences in provenience and thematic differences in content. Yet, Nowotny claimed that the *Codex Becker II* originated "in the neighborhood of Cholula" (1961: 27), even though it is stylistically a member of the Mixtec-group of codices. The Mixtec codices themselves refer to the Cholula area, with depictions of

the snow-covered volcanoes and references to a ceremonial nose-piercing at the site of the Cattail-Frieze, which may have been Cholula itself (Smith 1973; Byland and Pohl 1995).

Architectural features of the Great Pyramid provide evidence of the Mixtec Codex Style, for example, in the diagonal painted bands on murals from the Patio of the Altars, the woven *petate* (mat) motif on stage 3C of the pyramid and structure 3-1 of the Patio of the Altars, and the greca-frieze motif that occurs on the *talud* (sloped facade) around the Patio of the Altars (McCafferty 1996b, 2001). The use of the petate and greca-frieze motifs as architectural elements on the Great Pyramid are evidence that its architects shared a similar vocabulary of symbolic meaning with the artists who painted the Mixtec codices. Not only were the motifs similar but the contexts in which they were used were stylistically or grammatically appropriate. The possibility is consistent with the concept of a Mixteca-Puebla culture complex because it implies an eclectic blending of culture traits from the central highlands, the Mixteca Alta, and includes the Gulf Coast and Maya region. The use of the petate mat motif as an architectural feature is closely parallel to the Mat House discovered at Copán (Fash 1991:130–134), interpreted as a council house associated with the ruler.

The final aspect of Smith and Heath-Smith's (1980) model involves the identification of "Mixteca-Puebla Regional Ceramic Spheres," with the implication that a variety of distinctive subtraditions should co-occur. The famous Cholula polychrome pottery is the classic example of this overarching polychrome style (Smith and Heath-Smith 1980:35–37; Nicholson 1982:243); yet, contradictions between the two previous ceramic studies conducted at Cholula (Noguera 1954; Müller 1978) created problems relating to the developmental sequence of Cholula polychrome pottery. When Müller claimed that all Cholula polychromes dated to post-1325, Cholula became one of the last sites in the central highlands to use Mixteca-Puebla polychrome pottery. This position can now be challenged by the UA-1 ceramic sequence and the chronometric evidence associated with early polychromes from the UA-70 midden (Mountjoy and Peterson 1973) and the San Pedro Cholula well (Suárez C. 1994; McCafferty 1996a).

What, then, can the UA-1 excavation contribute to an understanding of a Mixteca-Puebla culture complex of shared religious ideology and stylistic traits? In refer-

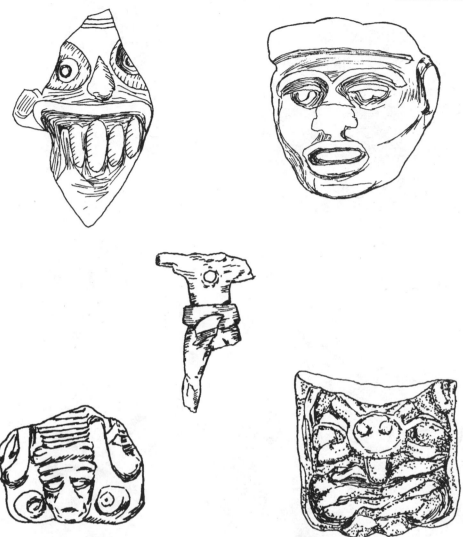

ence to the tripartite model proposed by Smith and
Heath-Smith (1980), the UA-1 material culture does in
varying degrees indicate Mixteca-Puebla traits in each of
the three categories.

Smith and Heath-Smith (1980:19–20) suggested that
the xicalcoliuhqui pattern and variations of the feathered
serpent motif may be considered symbolic manifesta-
tions of the "Postclassic Religious Style." Examples of
these stylistic motifs occur frequently on polychrome ceramics at UA-1, particularly Cuaxiloa Matte and Ocotlán
subtype Elegante. While evidence for the cult of
Quetzalcoatl was not identified among the figurines,
other central Mexican deities that were present included
Tlaloc, Xipe Totec, and members of the Mother Goddess
complex (figure 6.1).

Examples of the Mixtec Codex Style occurred in what
Müller (1978) called the tipo codice style, incorporating
stylistic elements similar to those found in the codices.
In addition to the xicalcoliuhqui and feathered serpent
motifs, other symbolic elements included crossed bones,
eagle feathers, and tule grass. Figurines also represent
the Codex Style, especially in the stylization of specific
deities such as Tlaloc.

The most significant example of the Codex Style is the
set of five Torre Polychrome dishes found both in the
trash midden and in association with the structure 1
house floor (figure 6.2). Although these figures were not
painted in a style clearly identifiable with either Mixtec
or Borgia Group codices, they do comply with what
Nicholson (1960, 1982:229) referred to as a "Disney type"

6.2 *a-e*, Torre Polychrome
platos with anthropomorphic
motif on interior base

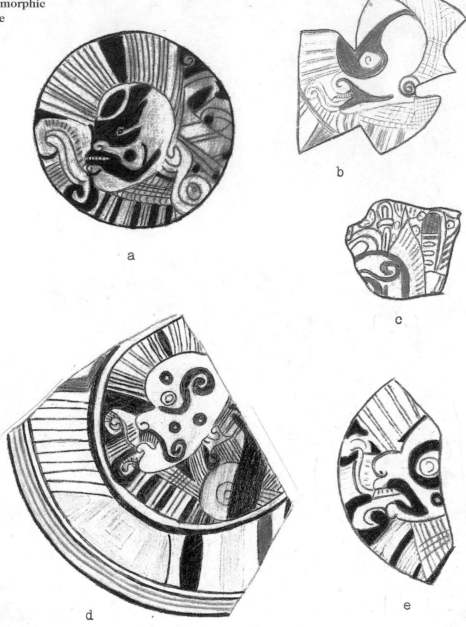

a

b

c

d

e

caricature and may represent an early stage in the development of the style. Other examples from decorated Torre Polychrome bases conform closely to codex-style figures, for example depictions of Macuilxochitl and a monkey as illustrated in Müller (1978).

Finally, the quantity and diversity of polychrome pottery found in association with Middle Tlachihualtepetl contexts suggests a relatively early presence of the Mixteca-Puebla Regional Ceramic Style. The predominant type found in association with the floor of structure 1 was Ocotlán Red Rim, including examples of the subtypes Elegante and Cristina Matte. The trash midden and well 3 from the Late Tlachihualtepetl phase had more diverse polychrome assemblages, with moderate amounts of Torre Polychrome and Cuaxiloa Matte, in addition to Ocotlán Red Rim.

Comparisons of the Tlachihualtepetl period ceramic complex with ceramics from other regions provides useful information for interpreting the cultural interactions that may have contributed to the early Mixteca-Puebla ceramic assemblage found at Cholula. Cocoyotla Black on Natural has parallels with Early Postclassic pottery from the southern Valley of Mexico (Noguera 1954:282–283; Hodge and Minc 1991), but it is also similar to X-Fine Orange from the Gulf Coast. Pottery similar to Torre Polychrome is also found in the Valley of Mexico (Séjourné 1983).

Other types with similarities to pottery of the Gulf Coast include Cuaxiloa Matte Polychrome and Ocotlán subtype Cristina Matte. Illustrated examples of Isla de Sacrificios pottery are virtually indistinguishable from pottery found at UA-1 (García Payón 1971:535–536). This possible Gulf Coast connection is further supported by decorative motifs that include marine animals as well as an individual in elaborate feathered headdress painted on the base of an Ocotlán subtype Cristina Matte bowl (figure 6.3). Further evidence for the possible importance of Gulf Coast ceramics in the development of the Early Postclassic ceramic complex comes from the Patio of the Carved Skulls, where several examples of Isla de Sacrificios White on Cream were found in the Early Tlachihualtepetl assemblage (McCafferty and Suárez C. 1995).

CONCLUSION

Analysis of the UA-1 material culture sheds light on the culture history of Early Postclassic Cholula and particularly on its role in the development of the Mixteca-Puebla stylistic tradition. Cholula had a vibrant polychrome tradition in the Middle and Late Tlachihualtepetl phases and some of the closest stylistic similarities were with the Gulf Coast. This conclusion seems to support Jiménez Moreno's (1942) and Nicholson's (1982) hypotheses that the Mixteca-Puebla horizon may have originated during the Olmeca-Xicallanca occupation of Cholula in the Epiclassic/Early Postclassic period. It further supports the architectural evidence from the Great Pyramid for Gulf Coast interaction during the Epiclassic period and strengthens assertions that Cholula was never abandoned.

Cholula was one of the major urban centers of pre-Columbian Mexico, with important religious, economic, cultural, and artistic contributions to Mesoamerican civilization. At the same time, however, Cholula remains one of the most enigmatic sites in terms of its culture history. The abundant archaeological record is poorly understood, with broad gaps in the sequence still to be

a

b

6.3 Ocotlán Red Rim subtype Cristina Matte plates: *a*, octopus motif (UA-1 bag 8076); *b*, anthropomorphic motif of figure with feathered headdress (UA-1 10927)

bridged. In order to move on to more anthropologically interesting questions involving social organization, economic production, and religious hegemony of the Cholula empire, a solid foundation in chronology is needed. This study of ceramics from UA-1 is intended as a stepping stone to more theoretically significant investigations. Without such basic information, however, higher level inferences would be tenuous.

Bibliography

Acosta Jorge R.

1970   Sección 3. In *Proyecto Cholula*, edited by I. Marquina, 47–56. Serie Investigaciones 19. Mexico, DF: Instituto Nacional de Antropología e Historia.

1975   La cerámica de Cholula. In *Los pueblos y senorios teocráticos: El período de las ciudades urbanas, primera parte*, by E. Matos M. et al., 123–134. Mexico, DF: Departamento de Investigaciones Historicos, Instituto Nacional de Antropología e Historia.

Bandelier, Adolph E.

1976 [1884]   *Report of an archaeological tour of Mexico, in 1881*. NewYork: AMS Press.

Baravalle, Richard, and Thomas R. Wheaton

1974   Preliminary site report: UA-73F fall and winter seasons, 1973–1974. Report submitted to the Departamento de Monumentos Prehispanicos of the Instituto Nacional de Antropología e Historia, Mexico, DF.

Barrientos, Catalina

1980   Análisis de la cerámica del elemento 10 de UA-79. Licenciatura thesis, Department of Anthropology, Universidad de las Américas, Cholula, Puebla, Mexico.

Bernal, Ignacio

1949   Exploraciones en Coixtlahuaca, Oaxaca. *Revista Mexicana de Estudios Antropológicos* 10:5–76.

Blanton, Richard E., Stephen A. Kowalewski, Gary Feinman, and Jill Appel

1981   *Ancient Mesoamerica: A comparison of change in three regions*. Cambridge, UK: Cambridge University Press.

Bonfil Batalla, Guillermo

1973   *Cholula: la ciudad sagrada en la era industrial*. Mexico, DF: Instituto de Investigaciones Historicas, Universidad Nacional Autonoma de México,

Bourdieu, Pierre

1984   *Distinction: A social critique of the judgement of taste*. Translated by R. Nice. Cambridge, MA: Harvard University Press.

Bradley, Richard, and Michael Fulford

1980   Sherd size in the analysis of occupation debris. *Bulletin* 17:85–94. London, UK: Institute of Archaeology, University of London.

Brainerd, G.W.

1951   The place of chronological ordering in archaeological analysis. *American Antiquity* 16:301–313.

Brumfiel, Elizabeth

1991   Weaving and cooking: Women's production in Aztec Mexico. In *Engendering archaeology: Women and prehistory*, edited by J.M. Gero and M.W. Conkey, 224–251. Oxford, UK: Basil Blackwell.

1992   Early postclassic dates for Aztec I ceramics at Xaltocan. Paper presented at the fifteenth Annual Meeting, Midwest Mesoamericanists, Indianapolis, IN.

Byland, Bruce E.

1980   Political and economic evolution in the Tamazulapan Valley, Mixteca Alta, Oaxaca, Mexico. Ph.D dissertation, Department of Anthropology, Pennsylvania State University, University Park, PA. Ann Arbor, MI: University Microfilms.

Byland, Bruce E. and John M.D. Pohl

1995   *In the Realm of Eight Deer: The Archaeology of the Mixtec Codices*. University of Oklahoma Press, Norman, OK.

Cano, Lucero Morales

2000   Personal communication. Conversation at the Regional Center Archaeology Lab, July 2000

Carrasco, David

1982   *Quetzalcoatl and the Irony of Empire: Myths and Prophecies of the Aztec Tradition*. University of Chicago Press, Chicago, IL.

Carrasco, Pedro

1971   Los barrios antiguos de Cholula. *Estudios y documentos de la región de Puebla-Tlaxcala* III: 9–87. Puebla, Mexico: Instituto Poblano de Antropología e Historia.

Caskey, Charles R.

1982a   Segundo informe preliminar sobre el análisis de cerámica de Cholula, Fonatur. Report submitted to the Centro Regional de Puebla, Instituto Nacional de Anthropología e Historia, Puebla, Mexico.

1982b   Tercera informe preliminar sobre el análisis de
cerámica de Cholula, Fonatur. Report submitted to the
Centro Regional de Puebla, Instituto Nacional de
Antropología e Historia, Puebla, Mexico.

1988   Two archaeological discoveries at Cholula, Puebla,
Mexico. Master's thesis, Department of Anthropology,
University of the Americas, Cholula, Puebla, Mexico.

Caskey, Charles, and Michael Lind

N.D.   Late Postclassic Cholula ceramic typology, annex IV.
Manuscript (1979) on file at the Department of
Anthropology, University of the Americas, Cholula,
Puebla, Mexico.

Caso, Alfonso, Ignacio Bernal, and Jorge R. Acosta

1967   *La cerámica de Monte Albán.* Memorias del INAH, no.
13. Mexico, DF: Instituto Nacional de Antropología e
Historia.

Castro Morales, Efrain, and Roberto Garcia Moll

1972   Un entierro colectivo en la Ciudad de Cholula, Puebla.
In *Religión en Mesoamérica*, edited by J. Litvak King
and N. Castillo Tejero, 381–384. Mexico, DF: Sociedad
Mexicana de Antropología.

Chadwick, Robert

1966   The "Olmeca-Xicallanca" of Teotihuacan: A preliminary study. *Mesoamerican Notes* 7/8:1–24.

1971a   Postclassic pottery of the Central Valleys. In *Handbook
of Middle American Indians, Volume 10: Archaeology
of Northern Mesoamerica, Part 1*, edited by R.
Wauchope, G.F. Ekholm, and I. Bernal, 228–257.
Austin, TX: University of Texas Press.

1971b   Native Pre-Aztec history of Central Mexico. In *Handbook of Middle American Indians, Volume 11:
Archaeology of Northern Mesoamerica, Part 2*, edited
by R. Wauchope, G.F. Ekholm, and I. Bernal, 474–504.
Austin, TX: University of Texas Press.

Codex Borgia

1963   *Codice Borgia* (facsimile). Fondo de Cultura
Economica. Mexico, D.F.

Codex Nuttall

1975   *The Codex Nuttall. A Picture Manuscript from Ancient
Mexico.* The Peabody Museum Facsimile edited by
Zelia Nuttall (introduction by A.G. Miller). Dover
Publications, Inc, New York, NY

Cohen, Abner

1969   *Custom and politics in urban Africa.* Berkeley, CA:
University of California Press.

Cortés, Hernan

1986 [1519–1521]   *Letters from Mexico.* Translated and
edited by A. Pagden. New Haven, CT: Yale University
Press.

Covarrubias, Miguel

1957   *Indian Art of Mexico and Central America.* New York:
Knopf.

Cowgill, George L.

1990   Why Pearson's *r* is not a good similarity coefficient for
comparing collections. *American Antiquity* 55(3):512–
521.

Curtin, Phillip D.

1984   *Cross-cultural trade in world prehistory.* Cambridge,
UK: Cambridge University Press.

Davies, Nigel

1973   *The Aztecs: A history.* London: Macmillan.

1977   *The Toltecs, until the fall of Tula.* Norman, OK:
University of Oklahoma Press.

Diáz del Castillo, Bernal

1963 [1580]   *The Conquest of New Spain.* Translated by
J.M. Cohen. Harmondsworth, Middlesex, England:
Penguin Books.

Douglas, Mary

1979   *The anthropology of food.* New York: Russel Sage
Foundation.

Drennan, Robert D.

1976   *Prehistory and human ecology of the Valley of Oaxaca,
Vol. 4: Fábrica San José and Middle Formative Society
in the Valley of Oaxaca.* Ann Arbor, MI: Memoirs of the
Museum of Anthropology no. 8, University of Michigan.

Dumond, Don

1972   Demographic aspects of the Classic Period in Puebla/
Tlaxcala. *Southwestern Journal of Anthropology*
28:101–130.

Dumond, Don, and Florencia Müller

1972   Classic to Post-Classic in Highland Central Mexico.
Science 175:1208–1215.

Durán, Diego

1971 [1576–1579]   *The book of the Gods and rites and
the ancient calendar.* Translated by F. Horcasitas and
D. Heyden. Norman, OK: University of Oklahoma Press.

Evans, Susan T.

1988   Cihuatecpan: The village in its ecological and historical
context. In *Excavations at Cihuatecpan: An Aztec
village in the Teotihuacan Valley*, edited by S.T. Evans,
1–49. Nashville, TN: Vanderbilt University Publications
in Anthropology, no. 36.

Fajardo, Carmen

1985   *Análisis de tres basureros del sitio arqueológico de
Cholula.* Licenciatura thesis. Mexico DF: Escuela
Nacional de Antropología e Historia.

Fash, William L.

1991   *Scribes, warriors and kings: The city of Copán and
the ancient Maya.* London: Thames and Hudson.

Feinman, Gary

1986   The emergence of specialized ceramic production in
formative Oaxaca. In *Research in economic anthropology, Supplement 2: Economic aspects of Prehispanic
Highland Mexico*, edited by B.L. Isaac, 347–373.
Greenwich, CT: JAI Press.

Feinman, Gary, Steadman Upham, and Kent Lightfoot

1981   The production step measure: An ordinal index of labor
input in ceramic manufacture. *American Antiquity*
46(4):871–884.

Flannery, Kent V.

1968   The Olmec and the valley of Oaxaca: A model for inter-
regional interaction in formative times. In *Dumbarton
Oaks Conference on the Olmec*, edited by E.P. Benson,
119–130. Washington, DC: Dumbarton Oaks.

Flannery, Kent V., and Marcus Winter

1976   Analyzing household activities. In *The early
Mesoamerican village*, edited by K.V. Flannery, 34–47.

New York: Academic Press.

Foster, George
1960 Life expectancy of utilitarian pottery in Tzintzuntzan, Michoacan, Mexico. *American Antiquity* 25(4):606–608.

Fowler, William R., Jr.
1989 *The evolution of ancient Nahua civilizations: The Pipil-Nicarao of Central America.* Norman, OK: University of Oklahoma Press.

Friedrich, Margaret Hardin
1970 Design structure and social interaction: Archaeological implications of an ethnographic analysis. *American Antiquity* 35:332–343.

García Cook, Angel
1981 *The Historical Importance of Tlaxcala in the Cultural Development of the Central Highlands. In Handbook of Middle American Indians, Supplement 1: Archaeology,* edited by V.R. Bricker and J.A. Sabloff, pp. 244-276. University of Texas Press, Austin, TX.

García Cook, Angel, and Beatriz Leanor Merino Carrión
1990 El "epiclásico" en la region Poblano-Tlaxcalteca. In *Mesoamerica y Norte de México: Siglo IX-XII,* edited by F. Sodi Miranda, 257–280. Mexico, DF: Instituto Nacional de Antropología e Historia.

García Payón, José
1971 Archaeology of Central Veracruz. In *Handbook of Middle American Indians, Vol. 11, part 2: Archaeology of Northern Mesoamerica,* edited by R. Wauchope, G. Ekholm, and I. Bernal, 505–543. Austin, TX: University of Texas Press.

Gelfand, A.E.
1971 Seriation methods for archaeological materials. *American Antiquity* 36:263–274.

Gifford, J.C.
1960 The type-variety method of ceramic classification as an indicator of cultural phenomena. *American Antiquity* 25 (3):341–347.

Gorenstein, Shirley
1973 *Tepexi El Viejo: A Postclassic fortified site in the Mixteca-Puebla region of Mexico.* Transactions of the American Philosophical Society, New Series, Volume 63, Part 1. Philadelphia, PA: American Philosophical Society.

Grove, David C.
1974 The Highland Olmec manifestation: A consideration of what is and what isn't. In *Mesoamerican archaeology: New approaches,* edited by N. Hammond, 109–128. Austin, TX: University of Texas Press.

Halley, David J.
1986 The identification of vessel function: A case study from Northwest Georgia. *American Antiquity* 51(2):267–295.

Hardin, Margaret Ann
1984 Models of decoration. In *The many dimensions of pottery: Ceramics in archaeology and anthropology,* edited by S.E. van der Leeuw and A.C. Pritchard, 573–614. Cingula 7. Amsterdam, The Netherlands: Amsterdam: Institute for Pre- and Proto-History, University of Amsterdam.

Helms, Mary W.
1993 *Craft and the kingly ideal: Art, trade, and power.* Austin, TX: University of Texas Press.

Henrickson, Elizabeth F., and Mary M.A. McDonald
1983 Ceramic form and function: An ethnographic search and an archaeological application. *American Anthropologist* 85(3):630–643.

Hernandez R., Carlos
1970 Restos arquitectonicos del horizonte Postclasico en Cholula. In *Proyecto Cholula,* edited by I. Marquina, 89–92. Serie Investigactiones No. 19. Mexico, DF: Inst nal de Antropología e Historia.

Historia Tolteca-Chichimeca
1976 [ca. 1550] *Historia Tolteca-Chichimeca,* edited and translated by P. Kirchhoff, L. Odena G., and L. Reyes G. Mexico, DF: Instituto Nacional de Antropología e Historia.

Hodge, Mary G., and Leah D. Minc
1990 The spatial patterning of Aztec ceramics: Implications for understanding prehispanic exchange systems in the Valley of Mexico. *Journal of Field Archaeology* 17:415–437.
1991 *Aztec-period ceramic distribution and exchange systems.* Report submitted to the National Science Foundation, Arlington, VA.

Hoopes, John W., and Geoffrey G. McCafferty
1989 Out of Mexico: An archaeological evaluation of the migration legends of Greater Nicoya. Paper presented at the Annual Meeting of the Society for American Archaeology, Atlanta, GA.

Isaac, Barry L.
1986 Notes on obsidian, the Pochteca, and the position of Tlatelolco in the Aztec Empire. In *Research in Economic Anthropology, Supplement 2: Economic Aspects of Prehispanic Highland Mexico,* edited by B.L. Isaac, 319–343. Greenwich, CT: JAI Press.

Ixtlilxochitl, Fernando de Alva
1975–1977 *Obras Historicas,* 2 volumes. Edited and with introduction by E. O'Gorman. Mexico, DF: Instituto de Investigaciones Historicas, Universidad Nacional Autonoma de México.

Jiménez Moreno, Wigberto
1942 El enigma de los Olmecas. *Cuadernos Americanos* I (5):113–145.
1966 Mesoamerica before the Toltecs. Translated by M. Bullington and C.R. Wicke. In *Ancient Oaxaca: Discoveries in Mexican archeology and history,* edited by J. Paddock, 3–82. Stanford, CA: Stanford University Press.

Johnsson, Mick
1986 *Food and culture among the Bolivian Aymara: Symbolic expressions of social relations.* Uppsala Studies in Cultural Anthropology, no. 7. Stockholm, Sweden: Almquist and Wiksell International.

Joy, Michael
N.D. *Type-variety and the ceramics of Jesús-Tlatempa, Cholula, Puebla, Mexico.* Manuscript on file in the Laboratorio de Arqueología, University of the Americas, Cholula, Puebla, Mexico.

Kaplan, Flora S.
1980   *Una tradicion Alfarera: Conocimiento y estilo*. Mexico, DF: Instituto Nacional Indigenista.

Kaplan, Flora S., and David M. Levine
1981   Cognitive mapping of a folk taxonomy of Mexican pottery: A multivariate approach. *American Anthropologist* 83:868–884.

Kempton, Willett
1981   *The folk classification of ceramics: A study of cognitive prototypes*. New York: Academic Press.

Kolb, Charles
1986   Commercial aspects of Classic Teotihuacan period "Thin Orange" Ware. In *Research in Economic Anthropology, Supplement 2*, edited by B. Isaac, 155–205. Greenwich, CT: JAI Press.

Krotser, Paula Homberger
1974   Country potters of Veracruz, Mexico: Technological survivals and culture change. In *Ethnoarchaeology*, edited by C.B. Donnan and C.W. Clewlow, 131–146. Institute of Archaeology, Monograph 4. Los Angeles, CA: UCLA Institute of Archaeology.

Lackey, Louana
1981   *The pottery of Acatlán: A changing Mexican tradition*. Norman, OK: University of Oklahoma Press.

Lind, Michael
1967   *Mixtec polychrome pottery: A comparison of the Late Preconquest polychrome pottery from Cholula, Oaxaca, and the Chinantla*. Master's thesis, Department of Anthropology, University of the Americas, Mexico, DF.
1979   Excavaciones de Salvamiento: UA-79-SP. Report submitted to the Centro Regional Puebla-Tlaxcala, Instituto Nacional de Antropología e Historia, Puebla, Mexico.
1982   Personal communication. Class lecture, ceramics seminar, February 1982
1987   *The sociocultural dimensions of Mixtec ceramics*. Vanderbilt University Publications in Anthropology, No. 33. Nashville, TN: Vanderbilt University.
1990   The great city square: Government in ancient Cholula. Paper presented at the Mesoamerican Network Meeting, Riverside, CA.
1994   Cholula and Mixteca polychromes: Two Mixteca-Puebla regional sub-styles. In *Mixteca-Puebla: Discoveries and Research in Mesoamerican Art and Archaeology*, edited by H.B. Nicholson and E. Quiñones Keber, 79–100. Culver City, CA: Labyrinthos Press.

Lind, Michael, Catalina Barrientos, Chris Turner, Charles Caskey, Geoffrey McCafferty, Carmen Martinez, and Martha Orea
N.D.   Cholula polychrome. Unpublished manuscript from 1990 in possession of author.

Lister, Florence C., and Robert H. Lister
1978   The first Mexican maiolicas: Imported and locally produced. *Historical Archaeology* 12:1–24.
1982   *Sixteenth century Maiolica pottery in the Valley of Mexico*. Anthropological Papers of the University of Arizona, Number 39. Tucson, AZ: University of Arizona Press.

López A., Sergio, Zaid Lagunas R., and Carlos Serrano S.
1976   *Enterramientos humanos de la zona arqueológica de Cholula, Puebla*. Colección Científica 44, Departamento de Antropología Física, Instituto Nacional de Antropología e Historia, Mexico, DF.

López V., Pablo
1967   Reporte preliminár de la cerámica arqueológica. In *Cholula, Reporte Preliminár*, edited by M. Messmacher, 21–42. Mexico, DF: Editorial Nueva Antropología.

López de Gómara, Francisco
1964 [1552] *Cortés: The life of the conqueror by his secretary*. Translated and edited by L.B. Simpson. Berkeley: University of California Press.

MacEachern, S., D.J.W. Archer, and R.D. Garvin [eds.]
1989   *Household and communities: Proceedings of the twenty-first annual conference of the University of Calgary*. University of Calgary Archaeological Association, Calgary, Alberta, Canada.

MacNeish, Richard S., Fredrick A. Peterson, and Kent V. Flannery
1970   *The prehistory of the Tehuacan Valley, vol. 3: Ceramics*. Austin, TX: University of Texas Press.

Marquardt, William H.
1982 [1978]   Advances in archaeological seriation. In *Advances in archaeological method and theory: Selections for students from volumes 1 through 4*, edited by M.B. Schiffer, 416–464. New York: Academic Press.

Marquina, Ignacio
1951   *Arquitectura Prehispanica*. Memorias del Instituto Nacional de Antropología e Historia, No. 1, SEP-INAH, Mexico, DF.
1970a   Pirámide de Cholula. In *Proyecto Cholula*, edited by I. Marquina, 31–46. Serie Investigaciones 19. Instituto Nacional de Antropología e Historia, Mexico, DF.
1970b   *Proyecto Cholula*. Serie Investigaciones 19. Instituto Nacional de Antropología e Historia, Mexico, DF.
1975   Cholula, Puebla. In *Los pueblos y senorios teocráticos: El período de las ciudades urbanas, primera parte*, by E. Matos M. et al, 109–122. Departamento de Investigaciones Historicas, SEP-INAH, Mexico, DF.

McCafferty, Geoffrey G.
1984   A Middle Formative feature in San Andrés Cholula, Puebla. Report submitted to the Centro Regional de Puebla, Instituto Nacional de Antropología e Historia, Puebla, Mexico.
1986   The material culture of Early Postclassic Cholula and the "Mixteca-Puebla problem." Paper presented at the Annual Meeting of the Society for American Archaeology, New Orleans, LA.
1989   Ethnic boundaries and ehnic identity: Case studies from Postclassic Mexico. Master's thesis, Department of Anthropology, State University of New York at Binghamton, Binghamton, NY.
1992a   The material culture of Postclassic Cholula, Puebla: Contextual interpretations of the UA-1 domestic compounds. Ph.D. dissertation, Department of Anthropology, State University of New York at Binghamton, Binghamton, NY.
1992b   Book review of *Un entierro del clásico superior en Cholula, Puebla*, by Sergio Suárez C., and *Ultimos descubrimientos de entierros postclásicos en Cholula,*

Puebla, by Sergio Suárez C. *American Antiquity* 57(2):378–379.

1994 The Mixteca-Puebla stylistic tradition at Early Postclassic Cholula. In *Mixteca-Puebla: Discoveries and research in Mesoamerican art and archaeology*, edited by H.B. Nicholson and E. Quiñones Keber, 53–78. Culver City, CA: Labyrinthos Press.

1996a The ceramics and chronology of Cholula, Mexico. *Ancient Mesoamerica* 7(2):299–323.

1996b Reinterpreting the Great Pyramid of Cholula, Mexico. *Ancient Mesoamerica* 7(1):1–17.

1999 Reading the Fine Print about Quetzalcoatl at Cholula. Paper presented at the Annual Meeting of the Society for American Archaeology, Chicago, IL. In preparation for publication in *The Feathered Serpent as Political Currency during the Classic/Postclassic Transition,* edited by Rex Koontz and Geoffrey McCafferty. Under consideration for the Cotsen Institute of Archaeology, UCLA.

2000a The Cholula Massacre: Factional Histories and Archaeology of the Spanish Conquest. In *The Entangled Past: Integrating History and Archaeology* edited by Matthew Boyd, John C. Erwin, and Mitch Hendrickson, pp. 347-359. Proceedings of the 30th annual Chacmool Archaeological Conference, University of Calgary, Alberta, Canada.

2000b Tollan Cholollan and the Legacy of Legitimacy during the Classic/Postclassic Transition. In Mesoamerica's Classic Heritage: From Teotihuacan to the Aztecs, edited by D. Carrasco, L. Jones, and S. Sessions, pp. 341-367. University Press of Colorado, Boulder, CO.

2001 Mountain of Heaven, Mountain of Earth: The Great Pyramid of Cholula as Sacred Landscape. In Landscape and Power in Ancient Mesoamerica, edited by Rex Koontz, Kathryn Reese-Taylor, and Annabeth Headrick, pp. 279-316. Westview Press, Boulder, CO.

McCafferty, Geoffrey G., and Sergio Suárez C.

1995 The Classic/Postclassic transition at Cholula: Recent investigations at the Great Pyramid. Paper presented at the Annual Meeting of the Society for American Archaeology, Minneapolis, MN.

2001 Stamp-bottom bowls of Cholula, Mexico. *La Tinaja*

McCafferty, Geoffrey G., Sergio Suárez C., and Ruth Edelstein

N.D. Cholula and Teotihuacan in the Middle Classic period: Recent investigations at the Transito site (R-106). *Latin American Antiquity*, manuscript in revision.

McCafferty, Sharisse D., and Geoffrey G. McCafferty

1991 Spinning and Weaving as Female Gender Identity in Post-Classic Central Mexico. In *Textile Traditions of Mesoamerica and the Andes: An Anthology,* edited by M. Schevill, J.C. Berlo and E. Dwyer, pp. 19-44. Garland Publishing, New York, NY

1995 The feast of the water tamales as ritual performance at Postclassic Cholula. Paper presented at the Annual Meeting of the American Anthropological Association, Washington, DC.

2000 Textile production in pre-Columbian Cholula, Mexico. *Ancient Mesoamerica*, forthcoming.

Merlo J., Eduardo

1989 Los sitios arqueológicos explorados en Puebla. *Notas Mesoamericanas* 11:83–93. Universidad de las

Américas, Cholula, Puebla, Mexico.

Messmacher, Miguel

1967 Los patrones de asentamiento y la arquitectura en Cholula. In *Cholula, Reporte Preliminar*, edited by M. Messmacher, 6–17. Editorial Nueva Antropología, Mexico DF.

Miller, Daniel

1985 *Artefacts as categories: A study of ceramic variability in Central India.* Cambridge, UK: Cambridge University Press.

1987 *Material culture and mass consumption.* Oxford, UK: Basil Blackwell.

Motolinía, Fray Toribio de Benavente

1951 [1540] *History of the Indians of New Spain.* Translated by F.B. Steck. Washington DC: Academy of American Franciscan History.

Mountjoy, Joseph

1987 The collapse of the classic at Cholula as seen from Cerro Zapotecas. *Notas Mesoamericanas* 10:119–151. Universidad de las Américas, Cholula, Puebla, Mexico.

Mountjoy, Joseph, and David A. Peterson

1973 *Man and land in Prehispanic Cholula.* Vanderbilt University Publications in Anthropology, No. 4. Nashville, TN: Vanderbilt University.

Müller, Florencia

1970 La cerámica de Cholula. In *Proyecto Cholula*, edited by I. Marquina, 129–142. Serie Investigaciones 19. · Instituto Nacional de Antropología e Historia, Mexico DF.

1978 *La alfarería de Cholula.* Serie Arqueología, Instituto Nacional de Antropología e Historia, Mexico, DF.

1981 *Estudio de la cerámica Hispánica y moderna de Tlaxcala-Puebla.* Colección Científica, No. 103, Instituto Nacional de Antropología e Historia, Mexico, DF.

Nagao, Debra

1989 Public proclamation in the art of Cacaxtla and Xochicalco. In *Mesoamerica After the Decline of Teotihuacan, A.D. 700–900*, edited by R.A. Diehl and J.C. Berlo, 83–104. Washington, DC: Dumbarton Oaks.

Neff, Hector, Ronald Bishop, Edward B. Sisson, and Penny Sisson

1994 Regional sub-styles and provenience of Polychrome *Laca* with codex-style motifs. In *Mixteca-Puebla: Recent discoveries and research in Mesoamerican art and archaeology*, edited by H.B. Nicholson and E. Quiñones Keber. Culver City, CA: Labyrinthos Press.

Nicholson, Henry B.

1960 The Mixteca-Puebla concept in Mesoamerican archaeology: A re-examination. In *Men and cultures: Selected papers from the Fifth International Congress of Anthropological and Ethnological Sciences, Philadelphia, September 1-9, 1956*, edited by A.F.C. Wallace, 612–617. Philadelphia, PA: University of Pennsylvania.

1966 The problem of the provenience of the members of the "Codex Borgia group": A summary. In *Summa Anthropológica en homenaje a Roberto J. Weitlaner*, edited by A. Pompa y Pompa, 145–158. Mexico, DF: Instituto Nacional de Antropología e Historia.

1982 The Mixteca-Puebla concept revisited. In *The art and iconography of Late Post-Classic Central Mexico,* edited by E.H. Boone, 227–254. Washington, DC: Dumbarton Oaks.

1994   The Eagle Claw/Tied Double Maize Ear Motif: The Cholula Polychrome Ceramic Tradition and Some Members of the Codex Borgia Group. In *Mixteca-Puebla: Discoveries and Research in Mesoamerican Art and Archaeology,* edited by H.B. Nicholson and E. Quiñones Keber, pp. 101-116. Labyrinthos Press, Culver City, CA.

Nicholson, Henry B. and Eloise Quiñones Keber

1994   Introduction. In *Mixteca-Puebla: Discoveries and Research in Mesoamerican Art and Archaeology,* edited by H.B. Nicholson and E. Quiñones Keber, pp. vii-xv. Labyrinthos Press, Culver City, CA.

Niederberger, Christine

1976   *Zohapilco: Cinco milenios de ocupación humana en un sitio lacustre de la cuenca de Mexico.* Colección Científica, Arqueología, 30. Mexico DF: Instituto Nacional de Antropología e Historia.

Noguera, Eduardo

1937   *El altar de los craneos esculpidos de Cholula.* Mexico, DF: Talleres Gráficos de la Nación.

1941   La cerámica de Cholula y sus relaciones con otras culturas. *Revista Mexicana de Estudios Antropológicos* vol. 5, nos. 2–3. Mexico, DF.

1954   *La cerámica arqueológica de Cholula.* Mexico, DF: Editorial Guaranía.

1956   Un edificio preclásico en Cholula. *Estudios Antropológicos publicados en Homenaje al Dr. Manuel Gamio,* 213–24. Mexico, DF.

Nowotny, Karl A.

1961   Commentary to Codices Becker I/II. In *Codices Becker I/II* (compiled and with introduction by K.A. Nowotny). Graz, Austria: Akademishce Druck-u Verlaganstalt.

Olivera de V., Mercedes, and Cayetano Reyes

1969   Los Choloques y los Cholultecas: Apuntes sobre las relaciones étnicas en Cholula hasta el siglo XVI. *Anales del INAH,* Epoch 7, Vol. 1 (1967–1968):247–274. Mexico, DF.

Paddock, John

1987   Cholula en Mesoamérica. *Notas Mesoamericanas* 10:21–70. University of the Americas, Cholula, Puebla, Mexico.

Parsons, Jeffrey R., Elizabeth M. Brumfiel, and Mary Hodge

1996   Development Implications of Earlier Dates for Early Aztec in the Basin of Mexico. *Ancient Mesoamerica* 7(2):217-230

Parsons, Jeffrey R., Elizabeth M. Brumfiel, Mary H. Parsons, Virginia Popper, and Mary Taft

1982   *Late Prehispanic Chinampa agriculture on Lake Chalco Xochimilco, Mexico: Preliminary report.* Report submitted to the Instituto Nacional de Antropología e Historia, Mexico, DF.

Peterson, David A.

1972   *A Cholulteca trash pit and other excavations on the University of the Americas Campus.* Master's thesis, Department of Anthropology, University of the Americas, Cholula, Puebla, Mexico.

1987   The real Cholula. *Notas Mesoamericanas* 10:71–118.

Peterson, David A., and Z.D. Green

1987   The Spanish arrival and the massacre at Cholula. *Notas Mesoamericanas* 10:203–220.

Plog, Stephen

1985   Estimating vessel orifice diameters: Measurement methods and measurement errors. In *Decoding prehistoric ceramics,* edited by B.A. Nelson, 243-253. Carbondale, IL: Southern Illinois University Press.

Rattray, Evelyn C.

1981   Anaranjado delgado: Cerámica de comercio de Teotihuacan. In *Interacción cultural en México central,* edited by E. Rattray, J. Litvak King, and C. Diáz. Instituto de Investigaciones Antropológicas, Universidad Nacional Autonoma de México, Mexico DF.

1990   New findings on the origins of Thin Orange ceramics. *Ancient Mesoamerica* 1(2):181–195.

Reliford, William

1983   *Los Teteles: An early to middle urban site in the Valley of Puebla.* Master's thesis, Department of Anthropology, University of the Americas, Cholula, Puebla, Mexico.

Renfrew, Colin, and Eugene Sterud

1969   Close-proximity analysis: A rapid method for the ordering of archaeological materials. *American Antiquity* 34:265–277.

Ringle, Willliam M., Tomás Gallareta Negrón, and George Bey III

1998   The Return of Quetzalcoatl: Evidence for the spread of of a world religion during the Epiclassic period. *Ancient Mesoamerica* 9:183-232.

Robertson, Robin

1983   Functional analysis and social process in ceramics: The pottery from Cerros, Belize. In *Civilization in the Ancient Americas: Essays in honor of Gordon R. Willey,* edited by R.M. Leventhal and A.L. Kolata, 105–142. Albuquerque, NM: University of New Mexico Press and Cambridge, MA: Harvard University, Peabody Museum of Archaeology and Ethnology.

Robinson, W.S.

1951   A method for chronologically ordering archaeological deposits. *American Antiquity* 16:293–301.

Rojas, Gabriel de

1927 [1581]   Descripción de Cholula. *Revista Mexicana de Estudios Historicos,* 1 (6):158–170.

Sahagún, Bernadino de

1950–1982 [1547–1585]   *Florentine Codex: General history of the things of New Spain.* Translated by C.E. Dibble and A.J.D. Anderson. Salt Lake, City, UT: University of Utah Press and Santa Fe, NM: School of American Research.

Sanders, William T.

1989   The Epiclassic as a stage in Mesoamerican prehistory: An evaluation. In *Mesoamerica after the decline of Teotihuacan, A.D. 700–900,* edited by R.A. Diehl and J.C. Berlo, 211–218. Washington, DC: Dumbarton Oaks.

Sanders, William T., Jeffrey Parsons, and Robert Santley

1979   *The basin of Mexico: Ecological processes in the evolution of a civilization.* New York: Academic Press.

Santley, Robert S., and Kenneth G. Hirth, eds.
1993   *Prehispanic domestic units in Western Mesoamerica: Studies of the household, compound, and residence.* Boca Raton, FL: CRC Press.

Schiffer, Michael B.
1987   *Formation processes of the archaeological record.* Albuquerque, NM: University of New Mexico Press.

Séjourné, Laurette
1966   *Arqueología de Teotihuacan: La cerámica.* Mexico, DF: Fondo de Cultura Economica.
1970   *Arqueología del valle de Mexico: 1. Culhuacan.* Mexico, DF: Instituto Nacional de Antropología e Historia.
1983   *Arqueología e historia de valle de Mexico: De Xochimilco a Amecameca.* Mexico, DF: Siglo Veintiuno Editores.

Sheets, Payson
1991   What's up? A study of elevated contexts used for artifact curation at Cerén, El Salvador. Paper presented at the Annual Meeting of the American Anthropological Association, Chicago, IL.

Shennan, Stephen J.
1988   *Quantifying archaeology.* San Diego, CA: Academic Press.

Sisson, Edward B.
1973   *First annual report of the Coxcatlán Project.* Andover, MA: Robert S. Peabody Foundation for Archaeology.
1974   *Second annual report of the Coxcatlán Project.* Andover, MA: Robert S. Peabody Foundation for Archaeology.
1991/1992   Los dioses de Coxcatlán, Puebla. *Notas Mesoamericanas* 13:5–23.

Smith, Marion F.
1985   Toward an economic interpretation of ceramics: Relating vessel size and shape to use. In *Decoding prehistoric ceramics,* edited by B.A. Nelson, 254–309. Carbondale, IL: Southern Illinois University Press.

Smith, Mary Elizabeth
1973   *Picture writing from ancient Southern Mexico.* Norman, OK: University of Oklahoma Press.

Smith, Michael E.
1987a   The expansion of the Aztec empire: A case study in the correlation of diachronic archaeological and ethnohistorical Data. *American Antiquity* 52:37–54.
1987b   Household possessions and wealth in agrarian states: Implications for archaeology. *Journal of Anthropological Archaeology* 6:297–335.
1990   Long-distance trade under the Aztec empire. *Ancient Mesoamerica* 1(2):153–169.

Smith, Michael E., and Cynthia M. Heath-Smith
1980   Waves of influence in Postclassic Mesoamerica? A critique of the Mixteca-Puebla concept. *Anthropology* 4 (2):15–50.

Smith, Michael E., and Kenneth G. Hirth
1988   The development of cotton spinning technology in Postclassic Morelos, Mexico. *Journal of Field Archaeology* 15:349–358.

Smith, Robert E.
1958   The place of Fine Orange pottery in Mesoamerican archaeology. *American Antiquity* 24:151–160.

Smith, Robert E., Gordon R. Willey, and J.C. Gifford
1960   The type-variety concept as a basis for the analysis of Maya pottery. *American Antiquity* 25(3):330–340.

Solís, Felipe, and David Morales
1991   *Rescate de un rescate: Colección de objetos arqueológicos de el Volador, Ciudad de México.* Instituto Nacional de Antropología e Historia, Mexico, DF.

Spencer-Wood, Suzanne M.
1986   Introduction. In *Consumer choice in historical archaeology,* edited by S.M. Spencer-Wood, 1–24. New York: Plenum Press.

Spores, Ronald
1972   *An archaeological settlement survey of the Nochixtlán Valley, Oaxaca.* Nashville, TN: Vanderbilt University Publications in Anthropology, No. 1.

Stone, Doris
1982   Cultural radiations from the Central and Southern Highlands of Mexico into Costa Rica. In *Aspects of the Mixteca-Puebla Style and Mixtec and Central Mexican Culture in Southern Mesoamerica,* edited by D. Stone, 61–70. Occasional Paper 4, Middle American Research Institute. New Orleans, LA: Tulane University.

Suárez C., Sergio
1985   *Un entierro del clásico superior en Cholula, Puebla.* Cuaderno de Trabajo 6, Centro Regional de Puebla, Instituto Nacional de Antropología e Historia, Mexico, DF.
1989   *Ultimos descubrimientos de entierros postclásicos en Cholula, Puebla.* Cuaderno de Trabajo 7, Centro Regional de Puebla, Instituto Nacional de Antropología e Historia, Mexico, DF.
1994   El polícromo laca de Cholula, Puebla. In *Mixteca-Puebla: Discoveries and research in Mesoamerican art and archaeology,* edited by H.B. Nicholson and E. Quiñones Keber. Culver City, CA: Labyrinthos Press.
1995   La cerámica Lisa cholulteca. *Arqueología* 13-14:109-120.

Suárez C., Sergio, and Silvia Martínez A.
1993   *Monografía de Cholula, Puebla.* H. Ayuntamiento Municipal Constitucional de San Pedro Cholula, Puebla, Mexico.

Sullivan, Thelma
1982   Tlazolteotl-Ixcuina: The great spinner and weaver. In *The art and iconography of Late Post-Classic Central Mexico,* edited by E.H. Boone, 7–36. Washington, DC: Dumbarton Oaks.

Torquemada, Fray Juan de
1975–1983   *Monarquía Indiana,* 7 volumes (coordinated by M. Leon-Portilla). Instituto de Investigaciones Historicas, Universidad Nacional Autonoma de México, Mexico DF.

Turner, Chris
N.D.   UA-9. Manuscript on file in the Laboratorio de

Arqueología, University of the Americas. Cholula, Puebla, Mexico.

Tylor, Edward B.
1970 [1861]   *Anahuac: or Mexico and the Mexicans, ancient and modern*. New York: Bergman Publishers.

Uruñuela, Gabriela and Raúl Alvarez-Méndez
1989   Un caso de síndromo de Klippel-Feil en restas prehispánicas de Cholula, Puebla. *Revista Mexicana de Reumatología* 4(3):69-72.

Vaillant, George C.
1938   A correlation of archaeological and historical sequences in the Valley of Mexico. *American Anthropologist* 40:535–573.
1941   *Aztecs of Mexico: Origin, rise and fall of the Aztec Nation*. Garden City, NY: Doubleday.

Vega Sosa, Constanza
1975   *Forma y decoración en las vasijas de tradición Azteca*. Colleción Científica 23, Departamento de Monumentos Prehispanicos, SEP-INAH, Mexico, DF.

Weaver, Muriel Porter
1972   *The Aztecs, Mayas, and their predecessors: Archaeology of Mesoamerica*. New York: Seminar Press.
1981   *The Aztecs, Maya, and their predecessors: Archaeology of Mesoamerica* (second edition). New York: Academic Press.
1993   *The Aztecs, Maya, and Their Predecessors: Archaeology of Mesoamerica* (third edition). Academic Press, San Diego, CA.

Whalen, Michael E., and Jeffrey R. Parsons
1982   Appendix 1: Ceramic markers used for period designations. In *Prehispanic Settlement Patterns in the Southern Valley of Mexico*, by J.R. Parsons et al., Appendix I, 385–459. Ann Arbor, MI: Museum of Anthropology, University of Michigan, No. 14.

Whallon, Robert, Jr.
1968   Investigations of late prehistoric social organization in New York State. In *New Perspectives in Archeology*, edited by S.R. Binford and L.R. Binford, 223–244. Chicago: Aldine.

Wilk, Richard R., and Wendy Ashmore, eds.
1988   *Household and community in the Mesoamerican past*. Albuquerque, NM: University of New Mexico Press.

Wilk, Richard R., and William L. Rathje, eds.
1982   Archaeology of the household: Building a prehistory of domestic life. *American Behavioral Scientist* 25(6).

Winter, Marcus C.
1976   The archaeological household cluster in the valley of Oaxaca. In *The early Mesoamerican village*, edited by K.V. Flannery, 25–31. New York: Academic Press.

Wobst, Martin
1977   Stylistic behavior and information exchange. In *Papers for the Director: Research Essays in Honor of James B. Griffin*, edited by C.E. Cleland, 317–342. Anthropological Papers, No. 61. Ann Arbor, MI: Museum of Anthropology, University of Michigan.

Wolfman, Daniel
1968   Preliminary report on excavations at UA-1, July 1968. Report submitted to the Departamento de Monumentos Prehispanicos. Manuscript on file at the Department of Anthropology, University of the Americas, Cholula, Puebla, Mexico.
1990   Mesoamerican chronology and archaeomagnetic dating, A.D. 1–1200. In *Archaeomagnetic dating*, edited by J.L. Eighmy and R.S. Sternberg, 261–310. Tucson, AZ: University of Arizona Press.